Theorizing Identities and Social Action

Edited by

Margaret Wetherell
Open University, UK

First published 2009 by
PALGRAVE MACMILLAN

Palgrave Macmillan in the UK is an imprint of Macmillan Publishers Limited,
registered in England, company number 785998, of Houndmills, Basingstoke,
Hampshire RG21 6XS.

Palgrave Macmillan in the US is a division of St Martin's Press LLC,
175 Fifth Avenue, New York, NY 10010.

Palgrave Macmillan is the global academic imprint of the above companies
and has companies and representatives throughout the world.

Palgrave® and Macmillan® are registered trademarks in the United States,
the United Kingdom, Europe and other countries.

ISBN-13: 978–0–230–58088–6 hardback

This book is printed on paper suitable for recycling and made from fully
managed and sustained forest sources. Logging, pulping and manufacturing
processes are expected to conform to the environmental regulations of the
country of origin.

A catalogue record for this book is available from the British Library.

A catalog record for this book is available from the Library of Congress.

10   9   8   7   6   5   4   3   2   1
18 17 16 15 14 13 12 11 10 09

Printed and bound in Great Britain by
CPI Antony Rowe, Chippenham and Eastbourne

Contents

v

List of Figures

Series Editors' Preface

The concept of identity has had a long and chequered history in the social sciences – many chafe at its ambiguity and frustrating complexity – yet it remains the pivotal site for exploring the relations between social life and subjectivity. Who we are is always complicated – a matter of social classifications, shifting social categorisations and group memberships, and a matter, too, of the ways in which social and cultural materials are organised as psychology and taken on as personal projects. Identity draws attention to 'names' and 'looks'. It is lived out in grand narratives and performances which construct sometimes passionately invested 'imagined' routes and destinies as well as in the more mundane arenas of everyday interaction, inter-subjective relations and in social institutions. Identity guides and predicts social action. It highlights positions and intelligibility defining what is possible and liveable and what is unthinkable and excessively troubled.

We suggest, in short, that identity is one of the most interesting points at which the trajectories of post-colonial societies, globalisation and assumptions about 'liquid modernity' come into focus along with new formations of social class, gender relations and issues of inequality, rights and social justice. Identity is at the heart of some of the most intractable and troubling contemporary social problems – community conflict, racism, discrimination, xenophobia and marginalisation.

It is the key laboratory, too, for any social psychologist focused on the interface of personal lives and social lives.

Identity Studies in the Social Sciences brings together psychologists, sociologists, anthropologists, geographers, social policy researchers, education researchers and political scientists to address this territory. The interdisciplinary reach of the series is matched by the degree of theoretical diversity. The books reflect on and take inspiration from the many 'theory wars' in the social sciences which have used identity as their hinge and also develop new theory and critique for current times, including new ontologies and new politics to do justice to contemporary amalgams of practices and subjectivities. The series includes empirical work, scholarly debate and research reviews on the core social categories and the intersections of these including 'race', ethnicity, social class, gender, generation, disability, nationality and sexuality along with less easily nameable social and institutional categorisations and affiliations.

Identity Studies in the Social Sciences highlights the ways in which identities are formed, managed and mobilised in contexts and spaces such as schools, work-places, clinics, homes, communities and streets. We welcome you to this rich collection of accounts from the various front-lines of identity studies.

Margaret Wetherell, Valerie Hey
and Stephen Reicher

Acknowledgements

Genuinely collaborative work is becoming an unusual and fraught experience in academia, but this book and the ESRC Programme *Identities and Social Action* which funded the research were an exception and a delight. I am very grateful to all the researchers in the programme for their companionship, good will and stamina. Their achievements were remarkable and will persist. I want to particularly acknowledge those who authored the chapters in the two published collections for their willingness to revise and re-shape their chapters to find the themes and make the arguments.

Collectively, we owe an enormous debt to Kerry Carter, the Programme Administrator who put together this manuscript and managed the book projects. As we know, administrating academics is never easy and Kerry bit her lip, got on with it and did a superb job putting together the infrastructure for our activities. I am grateful for her skills and for all the great times during the six years we worked together. In the ESRC, I want to thank the managers assigned to the programme – Joy Todd and, then, Dr Chris Wyatt – for their support and hard work. *Identities and Social Action* was commissioned by the ESRC's Strategic Research Board. Prof. David McCrone was responsible for initiating this large investment in identities research, and Gabriel Channan, Prof. Satnam Virdee and Prof. John Solomos acted as the nominated Board members for the programme. I am extremely grateful to them and to the members of the Programme Advisory Committee (chaired by David McCrone) who mentored the work and advised me at all stages – Anjana Ahuja (*The Times*), Jabeer Butt (Deputy Chief Executive, Race Equality Foundation), Mark Carroll (formerly Department of Communities and Local Government), Prof. Paul Du Gay (Warwick University), Prof. Valerie Hey (Sussex University), Michelynn Lafleche (Director of the Runnymede Trust), Ben Page (Managing Director of Ipsos MORI Public Affairs), Prof. Stephen Reicher (St Andrews University), Prof. Steve Vertovec (COMPAS) and Claire Tyler (Chief Executive Relate).

Finally, I want to thank Philippa Grand, our Editor at Palgrave Macmillan, who has made the task easy and enjoyable, my colleagues at the Open University in the Psychology Department and in the Faculty of Social Sciences for their forbearance in the years I disappeared, my husband, Pete Williams, and my son, Sam Wetherell, for their unfailing good spirits, great meals and critical reading.

Margaret Wetherell
Open University
April 2009

List of Contributors

Charles Antaki is Professor of Language and Social Psychology in the Department of Social Sciences, Loughborough University.

Rupert Brown is Professor of Social Psychology at the University of Sussex.

Martin Bruder is a Postdoctoral Fellow at Cardiff University.

Dominic Bryan is Lecturer in Social Anthropology and Director of the Institute of Irish Studies, Queen's University Belfast.

Ed Cairns is Professor of Psychology at the University of Ulster.

Sean Connolly is Professor of Irish History at Queen's University Belfast.

Derek Edwards is Professor of Psychology in the Department of Social Sciences, Loughborough University.

Heather Elliott is a freelance researcher and writer.

Mick Finlay is Senior Lecturer in Social Psychology in the Department of Psychology at Surrey University.

Yasmin Gunaratnam is Lecturer in Sociology at Goldsmiths College, University of London.

Miles Hewstone is Professor of Social Psychology and Fellow of New College, University of Oxford.

Wendy Hollway is Professor in Psychology at the Open University.

Rosa Hossain is a Research Fellow at the University of Kent.

Joanne Hughes is Professor of Education at Queen's University Belfast.

Steve Jefferys is Director of the Working Lives Research Institute and Professor of European Employment Studies at London Metropolitan University.

Richard Jenkins is Professor of Sociology at the University of Sheffield.

Gareth A. Jones is Senior Lecturer in the Department of Geography and Environment at London School of Economics.

Erene Kaptani is a Research Fellow in the Sociology Department at the University of East London.

John Kirk is a Senior Research Fellow at the Working Lives Research Institute, London Metropolitan University.

Andrew Livingstone is a Research Fellow in the School of Psychology at Cardiff University.

Antony S. R. Manstead is Professor of Psychology at Cardiff University.

Jane Martin is Professor of Social History of Education at the Institute of Education, University of London.

Ann Phoenix is Professor and Co-Director of the Thomas Coram Research Unit, Institute of Education, University of London.

Adam Rutland is Professor of Developmental Psychology at the University of Kent.

Katharina Schmid is a Postdoctoral researcher at the University of Oxford.

Russell Spears is Professor of Psychology at Cardiff University.

Susan A. Speer is Senior Lecturer in Psychology at the University of Manchester.

Elizabeth Stokoe is Reader in Social Interaction in the Department of Social Sciences, Loughborough University.

Sarah Thomas de Benítez is a Consultant and Associate of the London School of Economics Centre for Analysis of Social Exclusion.

Christine Wall is a Senior Research Fellow at the Working Lives Research Institute, London Metropolitan University.

Chris Walton is Lecturer in Social Psychology at the Department of Psychology, Lancaster University.

Charles Watters is Director of the European Centre for the Study of Migration and Social Care, and Senior Lecturer in Mental Health at the University of Kent.

Margaret Wetherell is Professor of Social Psychology at the Open University and Director of the ESRC Identities and Social Action Programme.

Jane Wills is Professor of Geography and Director of The City Centre at Queen Mary, University of London.

Nira Yuval-Davis is Professor and Graduate Course Director in Gender, Sexualities and Ethnic Studies at the University of East London.

Introduction

The Identity/Action Relation

Margaret Wetherell

As the grandchild of a geologist I learned early to anticipate
the absolute mutability of hills and waterfalls and even islands.
When a hill slumps into the ocean I see order in it. When a 5.2
on the Richter scale wrenches the writing table in my own room
in my own particular Welbeck Street I keep on typing. A hill is a
transitional accommodation to stress, and ego may be a similar
accommodation. A waterfall is a self-correcting maladjustment
of stream to structure, and so, for all I know, is technique.

(Didion, 2006, p. 220)

... we conceptualise social identity as an understanding of one's
place within a categorical system of social relations along with
the proper and possible actions that flow from such a position.

(Reicher and Hopkins, 2001, p. 48)

This book explores the ways in which identity and social action articulate together. How are people mobilised, caught up and actively engaged
in social life? We examine the ways in which individuals are assembled, defined and positioned and how identities authorise, anticipate
and guide social action. In reflecting on these issues and trying to com-
prehend the puzzles they pose, we follow up a wide range of social
practices. These include the mundane, routine and habitual and those
which are singular, dramatic and life-changing – actions such as caring,
'passing', segregating, choosing, mixing, migrating, settling, travelling,
campaigning, performing, complaining, fighting, bonding, including
and excluding.

To a large extent the way researchers approach the identity/action
relation depends on the research questions in play. This is vividly

1

illustrated in the two extracts above. Joan Didion's geological metaphor, rather unexpectedly, compares identity (the ego) to a hill. In a few words she sketches in for her readers an image of self as the outcome of movement, a deformation taking shape as an accommodation to force and pressure. Self is figured here as an upsurging, a relentless, resistant but responsive creation. Identity may appear solid and finalised but her image suggests it is continually in process, and subject to sudden jolts, even though, more usually, change is imperceptible and glacial. Didion's standpoint here is historical. She is interested in how people get to be the way they are and how self emerges as a feature. From a social science perspective this translates into questions about identity formation. Several possibilities are left open. Identity could be formulated as something which is relatively fixed but which can be pulled and pushed into new shapes or, more radically, as entirely relational, a 'fold' in lines of force.

Reicher and Hopkins' standpoint is very different. Their scholarly as opposed to literary definition focuses on social identities rather than on personal biography, ego or character. Self and movement are again seen as conjoined but the interest here is predictive and future oriented. Their account suggests that social identities provide templates for action and organise what can and should happen next. But self-understanding is also defined through the social actions seen as possible and legitimate. In this way identity and social action specify, entail and enable each other. Reicher and Hopkins' perspective is cognitive in the sense that their definition focuses on current understandings. Identity is about actively making sense of one's circumstances and how one is placed. In contrast then to the questions Didion's metaphor raises, their focus is on what a sense of identity allows and encourages and what follows from it rather than how it is formed and how it got to be as it is.

Both these standpoints are exemplified in this collection. We are interested in personal identity, biography and trajectory and how people are made and change, and also we are interested in identity as a productive collective force. One of the central aims of the book is to highlight theory, and to encourage comparison and contrast between different accounts of the identity/action relation, highlighting the questions, methods and discoveries these accounts throw into relief. It is common-place in identity studies these days to stress mobility, complexity, entanglement and relationality. Scholars are now suspicious of stasis and the fixed traits and determining and unchanging essences, which were so crucial to the past history and etymology of 'identity'. Our interest in the identity/action relation is commensurate with these new directions. But the book is also the product of frustration because it is often not clear what is entailed when the traffic between identities and social action becomes the focus. What are the theoretical and methodological choices? What do current theoretical perspectives share and where do they differ?

To address the identity/action relation, the book draws on diverse disciplinary perspectives – those offered by geography, history, sociology and social psychology. The chapter authors review a rich range of intellectual resources to understand the social practices they analyse. The theories deployed range from Bourdieu's notion of 'habitus' to Winnicott's account of the formation of subjectivity; from Judith Butler's concept of performativity to Bakhtin's dialogical self; from conversation analysts and discursive psychologists' interest in mundane action and identity formulations to the focus on group relations found in social identity theory in social psychology and in other related approaches such as analyses of social capital and group contact. In introducing this work in this chapter, I will first reflect further on the theoretical perspectives discussed in this book and the points of commonality and difference between them, and then explain the organisation of the book.

Points of commonality and difference

The theoretical perspectives presented in this book differ markedly. What could be more different in some senses than, for instance, relational psychoanalysis, conversation analysis and social identity theory in experimental social psychology? But, as these theoretical perspectives become applied to identity and social action, as researchers bring these considerable theoretical and methodological apparatuses to bear on this relation, shared points of commonality emerge. Attention becomes drawn to the flow of social life and to participants' own perspectives and orientations. Perspectives built on binaries become less confident about usual dualisms and begin to recognise more indeterminate and open links between social phenomena.

In short, as attention switches to the *making of identity*, new ways of working come into view. The actor-network theorist Bruno Latour (2005) has clarified, recently and helpfully, what this emphasis entails. He argues (p. 28) that it involves a shift from attempts to define and describe social aggregates in abstract to an investigation of the ways in which people themselves work up, define and understand these aggregates. It is a move away from attempts to develop technical specifications and technical languages to concrete examinations of actual practice. The theoretical perspectives discussed in this book have each made this journey and for some such as conversation analysis it was always part of the original mandate.

Developing this further, Latour argues that our experience of society as participating members is of being multiply called upon, categorised, classified, registered, enrolled and enlisted, often in highly contradictory and antagonistic ways. The *process* of group making and re-making, and the endless work of forming and dismantling, claiming, reminding, identifying, re-establishing, rejecting and so on, is frequently what is most salient to the actual members of society and thus needs to become the main focus of research. Furthermore, when people are, willingly or unwillingly, captured, made solid and irremediably grouped, for longer or shorter periods, what they are most concerned about is not social scientists' specifications of social categories, social structures and social divisions. As participants, we are much interested in how these things immediately appear to us and how we, and those around us, make sense of, enlist and make capital out of the shame, embarrassments, delights and hindrances potent in how we are now placed.

If we re-frame this argument more thoroughly in terms of identity (c.f. Williams, 2000, chapters 6 and 7), then it is a case of recognising that participants in social life rarely can rest on their 'identity laurels'. In contrast, identity needs to be 'done' over and over. What 'it' is and who 'we' are escapes, is ineffable, and needs narrating, re-working, and must be continually brought 'to life' again and again. It is only in certain limited contexts such as autobiographies, *Hello* magazines and in immigration halls (important as these things are) that identities become finalised and accomplished once and for all time (and usually not even there). Responding to this insight, the history of identity studies has become the gradual unpicking of the original meaning and project of identity as 'self-sameness' (c.f. Wetherell, 2010) and the notion of identity as a fixed object. 'Staying the same' is, in fact, hard work and highly negotiable. Rightly then in recent years social scientists have become much more interested in how this is achieved. The authors in this book are interested in how people get tripped up and called upon, put together, identified and narrated in ways which prove motivating and saturated with emotion and which have consequences for what happens next in social life and in biographical trajectories.

If this, then, is the broad orientation shared by the theoretical approaches guiding the research described in this book, what are the differences? These differences and the choices they set up come most clearly into view if we think of theoretical perspectives as varying, first, in terms the 'substance' they accord to identity, second, in terms their reverence for mundane surfaces and willingness to generalise beyond the social world constructed by participants, and, finally, in terms of the openness and indeterminancy or determinacy ascribed to identity/action relations.

Substance

Accounts of identity practices and identity/action relations differ in the kinds of solidity, autonomous power and presence they accord identity. Recent work in the social sciences inspired by Deleuze, by the study of complexity and uncertainty, and by advanced Foucauldian and Lacanian logics (c.f. for some examples, Rose, 1996; Nobus and Quinn, 2005; Sorenson, 2005; Law and Mol, 2006; Blackman *et al.*, 2008; Frosh, 2010) represents the most mobile and effervescent end of the continuum. These approaches eschew the idea of identity, identity groundings and formations in favour of the study of sensuous activity, technologies of the self, the assembling of actor-networks and the 'reality' of incoherence as primary analytics. To illustrate these kinds of decentering moves, Lee and Brown pull out Lyotard's argument as an example:

> Lyotard makes a turn from the more or less stable possessive self to a more complex and mobile relational self. Decentering the subject involves a turn from an ontology of the individual, bounded subject to a more complex relational ontology. As Lyotard envisages it, this relational self is spatially complex, distributed across 'communication circuits'. It is the result of the disposition of messages. Crucially, on this view, the self has no ability to possess and can provide no harbour. With no boundary the subject can own nothing, not even itself. The humanistic characterisation of 'experience' and 'memory' as forms of property is put radically into question because what the subject seems to own, it is merely passing on.
>
> (2006, p. 259)

These accounts take the self as a site formed by or folded out of the crossing points of forces, movements and techniques. Here the focus is most dramatically, as in Judith Butler's (1990) early work on gender, on the practised reiteration of performances which construct appearances of solidity (see Chapters 1 and 3, for a discussion of Butler's work). The thing itself (gendered identity) arises from the repeated practice alone.

This take on 'substance' can be contrasted with accounts of the identity/action relation which similarly focus on what is made and on what changes but which are more confident that identity can be form of property, that the psychological and the social is a meaningful if porous boundary, and which posit a social psychological infrastructure which independently predisposes and organises social action and practice. In these accounts the organisation of identity and its social psychological infrastructure need not necessarily be conceptualised as innate or universally human – it could be seen as the outcome of past practice – but nonetheless self and identity have a presence in these accounts which mean that identity is never simply 'passed on' as Lyotard suggests.

Both relational psychoanalysis (see Chapter 1) and social identity theory in social psychology (see Chapter 12, for an account of social identity theory, and Chapter 8, for an example of an application of the theory in geography and politics) are approaches of this kind. They both suggest the self is organised so that certain templates for action are much more likely to occur than others. The mechanisms these two approaches propose, however, differ. Self-organisation occurs either through the force of unconscious identifications and the patterning of early relationships or, for social identity theory and other approaches in experimental social psychology such as analyses of intergroup contact and social capital (see Chapters 9 and 10), through the psychological concomitants of social categorisations and group memberships.

Here, for instance, is Livingstone *et al.*'s description of social identity theory:

> In the sense that we use the term, there are several aspects to the sociality of social identity. These follow from a basic definition of social identity as 'the individual's knowledge that he [or she] belongs to certain social groups together with some emotional and value significance to him [or her] of this group membership' (Tajfel, 1972: p. 32). As such, social (as opposed to personal) identity is the psychological basis of intergroup behaviour...acting in terms of one's membership of a social group entails acting in terms of a *different*, equally valid and meaningful aspect of one's self-concept.
>
> (Livingstone *et al.*, this book, Chapter 12, p. 238, emphasis in the original)

Like Reicher and Hopkins, in the definition noted earlier, Livingstone *et al.* go on to argue that social action and practice set the meaning of social identities – whether these are seen as privileged or disadvantaged, for instance, and set the meaning, frames and limits for comparisons with other groups to determine the value of an identity. Social norms, representations and conventional practices define the possibilities for legitimate group action (competition, discrimination, cooperation, etc.). In this way, social practices become embedded in self-concepts but this embedding, in interaction with the affordances of human psychology, conditions subsequent action.

In their work on practices of mothering and caring, Elliott *et al.* in Chapter 1 develop a rich theoretical framework which in fact combines Butler, Bourdieu and object relations theory. But here they explain the object relations strand in their thinking:

> From a psychoanalytic perspective, when a woman becomes a mother she can access dormant infantile experiences from when she was a baby, embodied experience that incorporates her own mother's handling. Through unconscious identification with this early mother, she can be attuned to her baby's needs without conscious knowledge. According to Winnicott, 'because she is devoted to her infant, [the mother] is able to make active adaptation. This presupposes (...) an understanding of the individual infant's way of life, which again arises out of *her capacity for identification* with her infant. This relationship between the mother and the infant starts before the infant is born' (1949: 189 our emphasis). The psychoanalytic concept of unconscious dynamics works on a relational, rather than individual, terrain.
>
> (Elliott *et al.*, this book, Chapter 1, pp. 24–25, emphasis in the original)

Again, as with social identity theory, the self is understood as formed relationally, in a sense, it is formed from past practice in this case the practices of child-rearing and family life. In both cases, despite the very significant differences in focus and analysis, identity, the sense of self and what is psychologically embedded are given substance and autonomous force.

Other perspectives on identity/action found in this book such as Bourdieu's classic notion of 'habitus' (see Chapter 2) and Bakhtin's notion of the dialogical and relational self (see Chapter 3) are vaguer and more equivocal on questions of identity substance. These approaches get by instead simply with notions of shared practical understandings which orient social action. For Bourdieu these practical understandings are more embodied, while Bakhtinian scholars focus on the discursive and on identity constructed from heteroglossic multi-voicedness.

Bakhtin's interest is, of course, primarily in language and literature, becoming later in the West a theory of the discursive self (Maybin, 2001). While, as Schatzki (2001) notes, Bourdieu rejects the psychological, arguing that habitus and what becomes written into the body through repeated practice is sufficient substance to explain the process of 'carrying forward' evident in social life and the ways in which past action constrains and sets the context for future action. As Jane Martin (this book, Chapter 2, p. 39) describes, ' "habitus" is a system of durable, transposable dispositions that predispose individuals to do certain things.' There is no need in Bourdieu's view to appeal to propositional knowledge, the cognitive, reasons and goals, self-concepts and subjectivities. Transposable dispositions are loosely specified but clearly these are not relational mobilities which fold to produce Lyotard's decentered self. But neither do they form a psychological infra-structure or accord much independent dynamism and energy to the self.

Mundane surfaces

As noted, one of the most invigorating aspects of focusing on the pairing of identity/action is the emphasis it throws on to everyday life and the meaning-making of the participants in the areas of social life being investigated. Because action is seen as 'practiced' rather than instinctual, automatic or entirely reactive, people's own standpoints, their interpretations, their conclusions and their past histories are privileged over macro-structural determinations. The theoretical perspectives presented in this book, while sharing this broad interest, differ, however, in the kinds of attention they pay to everyday life, in how interesting they find it, and in the methodological priority given to the close description of people's activities.

At one extreme lies conversation analysis and discursive psychology (see Chapters 5, 6 and 7) where researchers aim to focus entirely on participants' orientations and activities and indeed mandate against going beyond these (c.f. Schegloff, 1997, for perhaps the best-known expression of this stricture). Conversation analysts argue that the world has already been interpreted and put together by the participants. The task of the researcher is to show how they do it and the patterns in their activities. Schegloff, for instance, argues as a consequence that it is hubris on the part of critical scholars to think we know better or can see more clearly. This work, as Part II of this book illustrates, takes the mundane surfaces of everyday life very seriously indeed, examining small slices from domains of everyday activity to demonstrate the patterned ways in which participants accomplish social life. These researchers like to collect examples of naturally occurring interaction in consequential settings and argue that only in these kinds of data can the doing of identity actually be found, in contrast, for example, to other qualitative methods which simply generate talk *about* identity. Stokoe and Edwards explain:

> As a data-gathering source . . . interviews are advantageous as they enable researchers to collect guaranteed 'content' about their research questions. However, as has been argued elsewhere, accounts elicited in interviews comprise post-hoc reflections on participants' own or others' identity memberships, rather than how they are occasioned within, and for, the practices of everyday life. As Sacks (1992: 27) observed, researchers end up 'studying the categories Members use, to be sure, except at this point they are not investigating their categories by attempting to find them in the activities in which they're employed'.
>
> (this book, Chapter 5, p. 98)

What is found, however, on the mundane surface can be truly startling as the micro-power of identity practices comes into view. This work demonstrates forms of empowering and disempowering which can have a profound impact on who people can be and on what happens next but which would be near impossible to notice or recognise as they rapidly pass in interaction and impossible also to articulate in an in-depth interview (see Chapters 5, 6 and 7 for examples). Once drawn to scholarly and practitioner attention, however, vaguely apparent 'problematic patterns with no names' become discussable and institutional practices can change. This work pays particular attention to participants' own categorisation schemes and thus the usual litany of social identities based on gender, race, class, nationality and so on is broadened to include local schemes, for example, parent, slag, nasty person, bully, in Stokoe and Edwards' work on neighbourhood mediation.

Other approaches to identity/action similarly focus on everyday activities, people's accounts and words but would strongly contest that reflections on identity in interviews are off the mark and to one side of actual social action. Many would argue that the study of people's biographical narratives, for example, through the gathering of oral histories (see Chapter 2) or through intensive ethnographic case studies (see Chapters 4, 8 and 11), reveals the patterning and trajectory in individual lives and reveals, too, the memorialising practices and meaning-making resources that would be carried through into new contexts (c.f. Lawler, 2007, for a lucid account of the connections between, narrative, memory, practice and identity). Similarly those interested in the ways in which identities are valued and the types of cultural capital they accrue (see Chapters 8, 9 and 10) would similarly argue that interviews allow access to enormously consequential information about knowledge and evaluative practices and identity hierarchies.

With the exception of a possible ally in Erving Goffman, conversation analysts and discursive psychologists are alone in their reluctance to deploy academic, critical and theoretical machineries of representation to cast further insight on social life (Goffman's notion of performance is discussed further in Chapter 3). Goffman (1959), for instance, famously once said about his own work on the presentation of self in everyday life that although social theorists might argue that ordinary people are sleeping-walking social dopes, mystified by ideology and unable to perceive their real conditions of existence, he preferred himself not to cast judgement but instead to sneak in and study the way people snore. For theorists of identity practices such as Bourdieu and Butler and for researchers examining integration, intergroup conflict and political campaign-making using social identity and contact theory and analyses of social capital and invented traditions (see Chapters 8, 9, 10 and 11), the mundane surface may be beguiling but it will never be enough to watch the people snore without attempting to explain why certain versions of the world come to dominate, where power lies and why some kinds of identity practices are so difficult and troubled, and others so untroubled.

Indeterminancy

Theories which focus on identity/action usually discover a kind of openness and indeterminancy to social life. There is constraint to be sure in the sense that past social practice and forms of action set the scene for future practice, and events typically unfold along the tram-lines of existing possibilities. But most analyses of identity and social action typically come to endorse the 'could be otherwise' nature of social life and expect that events might at any point jump the tracks being laid down. We have already noted Bourdieu's term 'dispositions' which holds in play both provisionality and ordering. But here again, there is room for different emphases. These no doubt are predictable from the positions and differences I have already presented and so my discussion will be brief.

Several of the researchers brought together in this book favour quantitative methods (see Chapters 9, 10 and 12) – these of course typically work probabilistically even if the aim is high levels of certainty. But in experimental social psychology, for example, the goal is to detect causal relations and causal patterning, manipulating core variables, and excluding or holding constant others, to highlight ordered relationships. To the extent, however, this work looks to the social shaping of self-concepts, motivations, and perceptions of legitimacy and expected practice it is also open to social change. As noted earlier, Reicher and Hopkins (2001) argue that the kinds of comparisons group members engage upon with other groups and the ways in which they positively distinguish their groups from others will vary historically, culturally and across different scenes of collective action. This variability gives an openness to social identity theory, for example, which makes it reasonable to claim it as a theory of identity practices despite its continuing ambitious focus on cause and effect relations (see Chapter 12).

In effect, this and similar work such as the strands of psychosocial work discussed in Chapter 1 often relies on a process/content distinction. The content of people's identifications, the social and cultural resources which define identities and their consequences are malleable, provisional and ultimately indeterminate, but underlying identity/action relations are processes which are seen as more determinate, predictable and enduring. For object relations theory in psychosocial studies, as we have seen, processes are marked out rather differently but there is the same sense that phenomena like projection, identification, repression and so on are seen as fixed mechanisms which provisional senses of identity will be built around (c.f. Wetherell, 2003, for a comparison of discourse and psychoanalytic theories in this respect).

Obviously, for other theorists of identity/action indeterminacy and negotiability extend in every direction. Here the particular detail of each case becomes much more salient. This specificity can be in conflict with generalisation and knowledge accumulation. The case by case emphasis can render the grounds for extending arguments to other contexts unclear and weak. For some, the concept of social practice itself sometimes provides the only stability. Other theories find robust repetitions (e.g. the patterns detected by conversation analysts and performativity theorists, see Part II and Chapter 3) but are not sufficiently entranced by these to take them as a norm or a scientific ideal. Variations, the highly context specific, and twists and turns in manifestations are equally to be expected and equally of interest depending on the research questions and the focus set.

Organisation of the book

These, then, are the kinds of theoretical perspectives and choices which the collection of research examples in this book illustrates. The chapters in this collection, along with those in our companion volume (*Identity in the 21st Century: New Trends in Changing Times* also published by Palgrave), are based on the sustained period of intensive collective work which took place within the UK Economic and Social Research Council Programme on Identities and Social Action (see www.identities.org.uk). The 25 research projects which composed the programme worked with over 12,000 participants (see Appendix A for a list of the 12 projects informing this particular book). The authors' conclusions about identity/action configurations are thus empirically rich and authoritative as a consequence. They derive from research adopting an extensive range of methods including quantitative surveys, 'street' ethnography, in-depth qualitative interviews, psychoanalytically informed longitudinal observation, participatory theatre techniques, oral history, studies of talk-in-interaction and archival research. Research in the United Kingdom predominates, with one chapter reporting from Puebla, Mexico, while investigative sites in the United Kingdom range from Northern Ireland to Wales and across a range of communities in England.

The book is divided into three parts. We look first at the identity/ action relation as it is played out in individual lives and within the domain of personal biography. Then, in Part II, attention switches to the domain of talk-in-interaction in institutional settings and, finally, Part III takes up on identity/action relations in group, neighbourhood, community, city and national contexts.

Part I, *Biographies and Personal Trajectories*, consists of four chapters, each concerned with change, transition and movement in individual lives and how identity is configured and re-configured as a consequence. Heather Elliott, Yasmin Gunaratnam, Wendy Hollway and Ann Phoenix take as their topic in Chapter 1 the transition to first-time motherhood. They demonstrate how the identity change which occurs when becoming a mother for the first time is not just a matter of performativity (repeating the new until it becomes an accustomed identity practice) but is also profoundly psychosocial involving layers of identification and investment in dialogue with the performances of previous generations. Chapter 2 by Jane Martin with John Kirk, Christine Wall and Steve Jefferys develops the generational theme further. These authors explore generations of teacher activists and investigate how a radical 'habitus' in Bourdieu's sense develops. Through case studies of particular teacher/activists, they show how individuals become engaged and mobilised in different historical periods. The mobilities considered in the third chapter from Nira Yuval-Davis and Erene Kaptani are those associated with migration. They explore through participatory theatre techniques the ways in which members of refugee communities develop and perform new narratives of belonging. This chapter explores the meaning of performance, and its implications for understanding the relations between identity and action from a number of different theoretical perspectives adding to Butler's work which was a resource for earlier chapters, Goffman's ideas and Bakhtin's emphases on the dialogical self. Finally in Part I, Gareth A. Jones and Sarah Thomas de Benítez examine migration in a less conventional sense – the travelling and movement of Mexican 'street youth', demonstrating the ways in which their identities become fixed and unfixed but remain always provisional, blurred and open to further change.

Part II, *Interactions and Institutions*, consists of three chapters using conversation analysis and discursive psychology to illuminate identity/ action relations in three different institutional settings. Elizabeth Stokoe and Derek Edwards in Chapter 5 examine the social actions of disputing and mediating and the identity categories emergent in these. Their data consists of a rich set of tape-recorded phone-calls to neighbourhood mediation centres and recorded interviews conducted by police with suspects in neighbourhood crime. In Chapter 6, Susan Speer focuses on interaction between transsexual patients and psychiatrists in an NHS Gender Identity Clinic. This is an illuminating account of the details of 'passing' as a woman which rethinks what is at stake in gender performance. Finally in Part II, Charles Antaki, Mick Finlay and Chris Walton present some of the data from their investigations in residential homes for people with learning disabilities. They focus on the everyday act of 'choosing' and show how the organisation of this activity constructs identities and presents staff with some major dilemmas as duties to empower residents conflict with other imperatives. Overall, these three chapters beautifully illustrate what fine-grain analysis can add to the study of identity practices and clearly demonstrate how interactions make identities and make institutions.

Part III, *Communities, Cities and Nations*, examines the identity practices at stake in relations between groups in neighbourhoods and communities, scaled up in political campaigns, in the scenes and rituals of urban public life and in contests over national belonging. The practices investigated here are those of mobilising, including, excluding, belonging, bonding, settling, segregating and mixing and the family of theoretical resources drawn upon range from social identity theory and other perspectives (such as contact theory) in social psychology to analyses of social capital and 'invented traditions'. In Chapter 8, Jane Wills presents a powerful analysis of political mobilisation and how campaigns such as the London Citizens living wage campaign work by 'enlarging' identity, creating super-ordinate identities, but also skilfully managing difference and diversity. Chapter 9 from Katharina Schmid, Miles Hewstone, Joanne Hughes, Richard Jenkins and Ed Cairns compares segregated (predominantly Protestant and predominantly Catholic) and mixed (Protestant and Catholic) neighbourhoods in Belfast in light of ideas about the role of contact between groups in breaking down hostility. Their work shows that mixing allows (and is sustained by) more complex patterns of identification. Their work disconfirms recent social capital analyses presented by Robert Putnam which suggest that community diversity decreases cohesion, and thus has crucial implications for policy. Chapter 10 from Charles Watters, Rosa Hossain, Rupert Brown and Adam Rutland then similarly explores issues of contact and social capital in this case to understand the identity/action relationships involved in settling and integrating. Their focus is on first and subsequent generation migrant children and again against current orthodoxy the findings suggest the importance of ethnic diversity for positive identity/action outcomes. In Chapter 11, Dominic Bryan and Sean Connolly switch attention back to city life and the longer historical story. Their chapter focuses on public rituals and use of public space in Belfast and demonstrates how these enable and reflect civic identities in play. Finally, in Part III, Andrew Livingstone, Russell Spears, Antony Manstead and Martin Bruder extend the discussion out to national identity and examine identity/action relations in Wales. Their chapter presents an incisive demonstration of social identity theory in social psychology and the light it casts on identity practices.

Conclusion

The research described in the chapters in this collection thoroughly embeds the study of identity in social life. Every chapter begins with action and investigates what subsequently happens to identity. This is a very different standpoint from traditional sociological and social psychological concerns with mapping types, traits, stereotypes, categories and groups. In this short introduction I have been able to contrast a wide range of intriguing perspectives on the identity/action relation.

I have compared those which posit identity and action as separate sub-
stances and analytic frames to those which see identity and action as
simply different facets of the same productive flow of social life. I have
compared accounts of identity which conceive of the self as a site or
meeting place for different, perhaps antagonistic, patterns of relation-
alities with accounts which understand identity and its psychology as
more substantial and determining. Debate will continue, of course, but
we hope the book will stimulate some new thought about these most
basic questions concerning the identity/action relation.

References

Blackman, L., Cromby, J., Hook, D., Papadopoulos, D. and Walkerdine, V. (2008)
Creating Subjectivities. *Subjectivity: International Journal of Critical Psychology*
22, 1–27.
Butler, J. (1990) *Gender Trouble: Feminism and the Subversion of Identity*. New York:
Routledge.
Didion, J. (2006) *The Year of Magical Thinking*. London: Harper Perennial.
Frosh, S. (2010) Psychoanalytic Perspectives on Identity: From Ego to Ethics. In
M. Wetherell and C. T. Mohanty (eds.) *The Sage Handbook of Identities*. London:
Sage.
Goffman, E. (1959) *The Presentation of Self in Everyday Life*. London: Allen Lane.
Latour, B. (2005) *Reassembling the Social*. Oxford: Oxford University Press.
Law, J. and Mol, A. (eds.) (2006) *Complexities*. Durham, NC: Duke University
Press.
Lawler, S. (2007) *Identity: Sociological Perspectives*. Cambridge: Polity.
Lee, N. and Brown, S. (2006) The Disposal of Fear: Childhood, Trauma, and Com-
plexity. In J. Law and A. Mol (eds.) *Complexities*. Durham, NC: Duke University
Press.
Maybin, J. (2001) Language, Struggle and Voice: The Bakhtin/Voloshinov Writ-
ings. In M. Wetherell, S. Taylor and S. J. Yates (eds.) *Discourse Theory and Practice:
A Reader*. London: Sage.
Nobus, D. and Quinn, M. (2005) *Knowing Nothing, Staying Stupid*. London:
Routledge.
Reicher, S. and Hopkins, N. (2001) *Self and Nation*. London: Sage.
Rose, N. (1996) Identity, Genealogy, History. In S. Hall and P. Du Gay (eds.)
Questions of Cultural Identity. London: Sage.
Sacks, H. (1992) *Lectures on Conversation* (Vols. I and II, edited by G. Jefferson).
Oxford, UK: Basil Blackwell.
Schatzki, T. (2001) Practice Theory. In T. Schatzki, K. Knorr-Cetina and E. von
Savigny (eds.) *The Practice Turn in Contemporay Theory*. London: Routledge.
Schegloff, E. A. (1997) Whose text? Whose context? *Discourse and Society* 8,
165–87.
Sorenson, B. M. (2005) Immaculate Defecation: Gilles Deleuze and Félix Guattari
in Organization Theory. *The Sociological Review* 53(1), 120–33.
Wetherell, M. (2003) Paranoia, Ambivalence and Discursive Practices: Concepts
of Position and Positioning in Psychoanalysis and Discursive Psychology. In

R. Harre and F. Moghaddam (eds.) *The Self and Others: Positioning Individuals and Groups in Personal, Political and Cultural Contexts*. New York: Praeger/Greenwood Publishers.

Wetherell, M. (2010) The Field of Identity Studies. In M. Wetherell and C. T. Mohanty (eds.) *The Sage Handbook of Identities*. London: Sage.

Williams, R. (2000) *Making Identity Matter*. Durham: Sociology Press.

Part I

Biographies and Personal Trajectories

1
Practices, Identification and Identity Change in the Transition to Motherhood

Heather Elliott, Yasmin Gunaratnam, Wendy Hollway and Ann Phoenix

Identity transformation is of major concern in the social sciences (Brooks and Wee, 2008), but there is currently little agreement about the processes through which it occurs. This chapter illustrates the ways in which processes of identity change can be theoretically accounted for by analysing the ways in which Silma (a pseudonym), a first-time mother of Bangladeshi parentage, engages in practices that demonstrate to herself and others that she can successfully 'do' motherhood. The chapter can therefore serve to illuminate, and contribute to understanding the role of practices in identity transformation more generally. In summary, using vignettes from one case, we aim to provide a psychosocial account of the identity transitions involved in becoming a mother, highlighting how practices, of many different kinds, are vehicles for identifications, investments in motherhood and identity change.

When women become mothers, they face the challenges associated with having primary responsibility for caring for a dependent and vulnerable infant. They do so in contexts laden with historical and cultural meanings within which they have to find ways of making sense of their unique experiences of becoming mothers. This simultaneity of the historical–cultural determination of what it means to be a mother and the unique first-timeness of the experience mean that new motherhood identities should not be understood simply as pre-given and externally produced, but as developed and creatively made by mothers themselves out of the social, material and psychic resources available in their external settings, their relationships, their life histories and current experiences. In this chapter, therefore, we adopt a psychosocial approach to the puzzle of how mothers craft motherhood as both cultural and personal by giving equal analytic weight to social and psychological processes in the transition to motherhood.

Silma is one of our sample of first-time mothers living in Tower Hamlets, a borough in the East End of London. Through vignettes and interview extracts from her case, we aim to provide a psychosocial account of the identity transitions involved in becoming a mother, highlighting common themes in our sample concerning how practices, of many different kinds, are vehicles for identifications, investments in motherhood and identity change. She was interviewed three times: a week after her daughter Abeedah's birth, then six months later and finally a few weeks after Abeedah's first birthday. Our research questions reflected several theoretical frameworks that can inform an understanding of identity processes: we wanted to know about women's experiences of becoming mothers, how dimensions of social difference such as ethnicity, religion, culture, age and class impacted on their changing identities and how they were positioned and positioned themselves in expert discourses that were made available through health and social services and the media.

The first interview focused on the story and meanings of the pregnancy as well as the birth, while the second was about events, changes and experiences since birth and the mothers' evolving identities as babies became more able to control their bodies and interact with people and objects. The final interview focused on changes for the mothers, babies and their social networks since the second interview. At each interview the questions were designed to elicit 'experience-near' accounts of specific life events in the sequence and wording of the interviewee as unimpeded as possible by the structure of the interview agenda.

There is a preference, in social science, for studying a sufficient number of cases to allow analysis of cross-case patterns. The use of vignettes from a single case thus runs the risk of dismissal as idiosyncratic and not generalisable. Our paradigm for making more general conclusions is not based on statistical generalisability, or on a cross-case comparative methodology. Our approach is one of extrapolating general principles from a single case in three ways: by the sustained testing of theoretical concepts against the data, by inductively analysing narrative themes produced by a particular mother and interviewer and by contextualising these in the available literature and in what other mothers in similar and different circumstances say. The limits to generalisability are sought in theory, in other empirical studies, and by carefully situating the meaning and relevance of our evidence in its particular social and interactional contexts (Lieblich *et al.*, 1998). Careful attention to setting requires, and allows, us to locate the meaning of data within the wider case, without isolating data fragments from their context.

Since 'identity' is not transparent to the person experiencing a transition, this has implications for method, as does our emphasis on relationality in theorising identity (Hollway, 2008, 2009). We wanted to avoid eliciting accounts that drew on generalising discourses about identity and motherhood and we avoided reference to 'identity' both in recruitment and in data production. The methods used in this study[1] aimed to allow the expression of multiplicity, complexity and contradiction and to allow access to experiences including the unsaid and the unsayable as well as what is spoken (Frosh, 2002). We therefore used an evolving form of the Free Association Narrative Interview method, designed to elicit accounts expressed in participants' own words and follow up their trains of thought in any way that came to mind (i.e. free associations, Hollway and Jefferson, 2000).

Our theoretical focus here is upon practices, performativity and identifications. The overarching concepts that contribute to this exploration are broadly as follows. We examine how identity can be produced and claimed through repeated everyday embodied routines and unconscious practices (Bourdieu, 1977, 1990) and how the transition to motherhood is a period when new routines of childcare have to be established and some other routine practices are likely to be disrupted and questioned.

We highlight how everyday mothering practices are identity practices that are always in process, rather than achieved (de Marneffe, 2006; Baraitser, 2006a, 2006b). Early motherhood is a time when identity can get noticed and worked upon by mothers and those around them, uncovering the iteration of gendered and cultural norms that are brought to life and reconfigured through routinised discursive and material performances (Butler, 1990). These accounts of practice can be rendered psychosocial by addressing the ways that this new mother's internal world (fashioned from a life history of prior experiences) and her external world (the social and material features that structure her current experiences) play mutual parts in how she responds to the demands of being a mother.

Silma in context

The population of Tower Hamlets is ethnically mixed. Fifty-one percent is white, from a variety of ethnic groups, with Bangladeshi people constituting the largest ethnic group (at 33% on the 2001 Census, in comparison with 0.5% in England and Wales). Most are Muslim by religious background (with 36% of the Tower Hamlets population enumerated as Muslim, ONS, 2001). Many Bangladeshi young people are British born, as are some of their parents. A growing number of young professionals, largely white, live in the newly developed areas close to the City, the financial district of London (Dench and Gavron, 2006).

The area is unique in terms of its physical and socio-economic geography. It is ranked in the top 5 most deprived local authorities in England in terms of its residents. It includes the office district of Canary Wharf and therefore receives large numbers of relatively affluent incomers daily. At a neighbourhood scale it is a complex mosaic of small pockets of recently developed affluence in close proximity to areas of high deprivation. Pressure on land for development is high so the urban landscape is dynamic.

(InstantAtlas, 2006)

Bangladeshi populations in the United Kingdom are characterised by high levels of ill health, low educational achievement, unemployment and poverty (Salway *et al.*, 2007). The Government's Equalities Review (Equalities Review Panel, 2007) has identified Bangladeshi and Pakistani women as socially and economically disadvantaged, with especially low rates of employment, qualifications and work experience:

The majority of inactive Pakistani and Bangladeshi women say they do not want to work because they are looking after the family and home. ... There is evidence that the reasons for Pakistani and Bangladeshi women's employment penalty arises from a belief that good motherhood involves staying at home and providing their own childcare.

(Equalities Review Panel, 2007, pp. 100–101)

The report also highlighted the 'penalties' faced by mothers of young children in these groups 'in terms of limited career progression, large pay gaps and discrimination' (op cit., p. 9). Silma's mother was diagnosed with cancer, three months after Silma's baby was born. She was one of the three Bangladeshi grandmothers in our sample who were seriously ill or who had died before their grandchild was born (this was the case for only one of our non-Bangladeshi interviewees). As we shall see, this had implications for Silma's mothering career. Whilst recognising this wider context, we do not wish to deploy Silma's ethno-religious identity in culturalist or racialising ways which essentialise, ignore a plurality of positioning and obscure agency and possibilities for transformation (Phillips, 2007). Rather, we aim to highlight the specificity of the circumstances in which mothers mother and the variety of individual experiences *within* social and cultural practices as women come to inhabit motherhood identities.

Silma became a mother in Tower Hamlets during a period of government investment in early years services (the borough was home to six Sure Start programmes, developed to improve the life chances of young children and families) and concern about local maternity services (Tower Hamlets PCT and Barts and the London NHS Trust, 2007). Tower Hamlets had been targeted in the terrorist attacks of July 2005 and the impact was still reverberating through the borough when Abeedah was born the following year. A focus group discussion conducted with some Bangladeshi mothers in Tower Hamlets alongside the research project found that many valued the multiculturalism of the borough and the numbers and visibility of other Bangladeshis and/or Muslims. For some Bangladeshi mothers the 'comfort' of Tower Hamlets was also related to concerns about hostility towards Muslims following the terrorist attacks in London (Gunaratnam and Elliott, 2007). Silma talked of being 'comfortable' in Tower Hamlets and much of her day-to-day life since becoming a mother was conducted locally. Her preference for staying local was shared by many of the mothers in our sample, particularly the Bangladeshi and white working-class mothers, reflecting the significance of the domestic sphere and proximity to extended families during their babies' first year.

Silma, one of nine Bangladeshi mothers in our study, is one of seven siblings. She gave birth to Abeedah at 24 years of age. She was, therefore, younger than the national average age of first-time mothers (27 years at the time), as were most of our group of mothers. Like the rest of the Bangladeshi women in our sample, she was already married when she became pregnant (only two of the other ten mothers were). She was one of five women living with their husbands' families of origin when her child was born (having done so since she married a year previously), and one of three still living with her in-laws a year later. At the time of our interviews Silma was living with her husband and Abeedah in her mother-in-law's council house, which was also home to her brother-in-law's family. She was one of ten working-class women in our sample (an assessment based on her occupation and her qualification for local authority accommodation). She had worked in a department store before she became pregnant but resigned when she experienced severe morning sickness and, in common with nearly two-thirds of our sample (11 of 19), was not employed a year after giving birth.

Negotiating and embodying conflictual performative practices

Drawing upon the work of Bourdieu, we theorise practice as an improvised bodily art-form and know-how, deriving not only from conscious aims and goals but also from how 'the body thinks for us'. In Silma's case our concern with practices includes an engagement with the ways in which Silma holds Abeedah, communicates with her, changes her nappy and feeds her, how she moves around and occupies the spaces of her shared home and how she dresses. Such 'practical sense' is defined by Bourdieu, as the capacity to 'habilement' (skilfully, expertly, adroitly) resolve the small challenges of everyday life, with regard to what is appropriate in a given time and place (our translation). So while practice may feel like 'second nature' (1990: 56) and be characterised by 'what goes without saying' (1990: 92), it is also produced by, expressive of and attuned to the cultural, the social and the realistic ('appropriate'). While appearing to be 'natural', Bourdieu's work suggests that taken-for-granted practices have to be worked out, learned and routinised. For new mothers, the process of routinisation of childcare tasks is often anxiety provoking and, initially, requires planning and thought until they become practised.

Bourdieu's work on practice raises questions about where first-time practices come from, such as those involved in new mothering. For instance, Silma was initially nervous about her lack of experience and knowledge of mothering and relied on the expertise available in hospital and from women in her family. Yet, Bourdieu's notion of practice also suggests how the unconscious – which for Bourdieu is 'never anything other than the forgetting of history' (1990: 56) – can produce a sort of incorporated learning from individual experience that makes practices feel like second nature.

From a psychoanalytic perspective, when a woman becomes a mother she can access dormant infantile experiences from when she was a baby, embodied experience that incorporates her own mother's handling. Through unconscious identification with this early mother, she can be attuned to her baby's needs without conscious knowledge. According to Winnicott, because she is devoted to her infant, [the mother] is able to make active adaptation. This presupposes (...) an understanding of the individual infant's way of life, which again arises out of *her capacity for identification* with her infant. This relationship between the mother and the infant starts before the infant is born.

(1949: 189 our emphasis)

The psychoanalytic concept of unconscious dynamics thus works on a relational, rather than individual, terrain.

In their debate about the psychological work involved in the transformation of women into mothers, Baraitser (2006a, 2006b) and De Marneffe (2006) draw on Butler's notions of performativity to highlight how new mothers mimic practices already saturated with meaning, re-working them until they make them their own:

> In taking on motherhood, we don, like a wig, an array of sedimented ideas about who we are without having the slightest notion – yet – of who we ourselves are as mothers. We 'mime' motherhood, we act the part, and the part requires the adoption of certain roles – caretaker, diaper changer, breastfeeder, walker-of -the-floors at night – which are saturated with ideological and historical meanings about mothering, womanhood, nurturing, self-sacrifice, and so on... a new mother's life is narrowed to a repetitive round of care-giving tasks and a constricted universe of preoccupations. But it is what she does with those conditions, in their specificity and in the new, creative relation with her child, that gives rise to her individual experience of mothering.
>
> (de Marneffe, 2006: 248)

De Marneffe's depiction aptly fits Silma's account of the initial strangeness of her new mothering identity as well as the process by which she starts to make it her own. Silma describes her return home from hospital with her daughter thus.

> When I was coming out the car, yeah, they were all at the door. (...) And then um (.) (softer) then I was thinking, 'What shall I do?' I was a bit nervous. Then I had to make her milk, and then I fed her, changed her nappy, changed her clothes and put her to sleep. (louder) And then I used to like look at the clock every time, it was like (softer) three hours (louder) every three hours. But then she's drinking little by little bit, so it's like every two to two and a half hours actually.

In de Marneffe's sense, she 'acts the part' of a mother (and is seen to 'act the part' by her extended family, all gathered at the door), for example by following the professional advice given to her in the hospital. However, her repetitive performance (conveyed by the repeated 'and then') of feeding her baby gives her confidence that she is expert enough to improvise and to depart from the guidance. When the first interview takes place, five days after she has brought Abeedah home, she has already reworked and personalised her feeding practices in what de Marneffe suggests is a 'creative relation' with her daughter:

> Because I'm there with her 24/7 and feeding her, changing her nappy, even when she's asleep I get the milk ready for it to be um at least a little hot to warm. Um and I find now, her nappy changing, I just do it quickly before she starts struggling like this, I know her nappy changing time, and I keep on like looking at her, even if she sleep (...) She does it bit by bit, and when I open her nappy she just wees (...). So I'm waiting for her to wee at the same time as well. (...) She gives me a signal.

Winnicott observed how, for the early weeks of the new infant's life, most mothers enter a preoccupied state of heightened sensitivity, lasting a few weeks, for which he coined the term 'primary maternal preoccupation' (1956). The mother emerges 'as the infant releases her' (1956: 302). This state is one in which identifications with the infant and intense love dominate over usual preoccupations. Silma illustrates the intensity of early mothering as she carries out the same tasks over and over again, day in day out ('I'm there with her 24/7'). For some mothers this 'narrowing' of life (de Marneffe, 2006: 248) is claustrophobic (Baraitser, 2006a), but Silma stresses how she becomes a mother as the everyday tasks of motherhood become part of her practice and she forges a unique connection with her baby through this work. In coming to know her baby intimately, she knows herself to be a mother. In this sense, identifications with infants can provide the attentive attunement necessary to meet the needs of a new baby who cannot yet communicate verbally. This process can also potentially be facilitated by mothers' conscious identifications with their own mothers since this provides them with ideas for how to perform the practices of motherhood. In Silma's case, the fact that she has a much younger sister means that she has seen her own mother's mothering practices at close quarters and has also helped to care for her sister. Her conscious and unconscious identifications meant that she had an internalised relationship to draw on or mimic as she began learning to 'do' motherhood through her own mothering practices.

Trying to understand how the world is brought to life and activated by what Silma does as a mother brings us to the idea of practice as performative of identity. Feminist scholarship on performativity (stimulated by Butler, 1990, 1993, 1997) has emphasised how identity can be made and unmade through the repetition of practices and discourses. This conceptual framework is psychosocial in that 'the script survives the particular actors who make use of it, but [which] requires individual actors in order to be actualised and reproduced as reality once again' (Butler, 1997: 409). A recognition of practice as performativity in Silma's case means that we are interested in the particular configurations of identity 'scripts' in her life – as culture, gender, faith, generation and class – and how her unique biography affects and is affected by the choices she makes in whether and how she enacts these scripts. For example, clothes can be taken as a literal performance of identity (Puwar, 2004), yet they can also represent a playing with, a dipping into and a miming of identifications, orientated to the demands of varying and changing social settings rather than being consistent over time. Here we can grasp the playfulness, temporality and multiplicity of some performed practices.

In reflecting on features of her current changes, Silma described her old self as 'so wild', out with friends all the time, staying out late. Now, she says, 'I've gone a bit mature, more understanding, like a more motherly type'. She is 'around family more'. 'Strangely', she says, this has affected her clothes-wise, having been a 'jeans maniac', she now feels less comfortable in them and refers to shalwar kameez as 'normal clothes' and 'the ones I really like' (she received four sets as birthday gifts). That she finds this change 'strange' suggests that it is either not something that she has consciously chosen but that she has discovered in her changed preferences or that she sees it as sufficiently discontinuous with her previous preferences to require marking for the interviewer. Silma's reported new preference can be read as marking a new set of identifications, one that also includes spending more time at home and socialising with her aunts rather than her younger sisters and friends. Using clothes to symbolise her changing status as closer to the women in her mother's generation than her sisters' is a way for Silma to stake a claim to a motherhood identity and to vacate some aspects of more youthful identifications. Yet Silma mentions that she sometimes wears jeans when she goes out and also that she goes out to meet her friends in Pizza Hut and McDonalds. The new embodied practice of wearing shalwar kameez thus seems to be a domestic 'performance', where Silma chooses to follow a cultural 'script' in ways that facilitate her inclusion by her aunts and contribute to the way she occupies the motherhood identity she has long desired.

This analysis suggests that Silma's performative dress practices are instrumental and consciously chosen. However, it is also likely that such practices are underpinned by unconscious identifications with the maternal generation in her family (her aunts and her own mother) as well as with idealised, abstract versions of mothers that, for her, require the donning of new clothes. Nonetheless, she does not relinquish her embodied youthful style completely and 'does' young, fashionable style when she goes out with peers. She also continues her enthusiasm for performing youthful style through her daughter's clothes. Here we can see a multiplicity to identity and identifications.

The recognition of multiplicity in identifications implies conflict, since it raises questions of if and how a person achieves coherence or integration (Hollway, 2009). The idea of unconscious dynamic conflict as the psychic motor for action is common to all psychoanalytic theories and was used by Erikson (1959) to theorise identity transition through the life course, not as smooth, but accomplished through ordinary conflicts among the multiplicity of elements that jostle to make up an identity at a given time. These elements do not 'belong' to the self in any fixed way; rather the psychological boundaries of identity are seen as more or less porous, so that there is a continual interchange between internal and social worlds: 'We are constructed of dynamic, internalised relationships between self and object. In turn we externalise our inner worlds onto our outside relationships, which turn again to influence our inner organisation throughout our development as children and adults' (Scharff, 1992: xviii).

In this (object relations) perspective, 'objects' importantly include others and parts of others. The processes of introjection (which involves internalising other people's characteristics or words and making them a part of the self) and projection (in which thoughts and emotions – often the threatening or unwanted ones – are attributed to others) are fundamental forms of transaction between bodies and objects in their environments (Hinshelwood, 1995). We say bodies advisedly here, because these dynamics, not being accessible to conscious awareness, are experienced in sensual emotional ways. We use the concept of identification in this way, meaning not the conscious identifications that people claim (as when Silma tells the interviewer 'I've gone a bit more mature, more understanding, like a more motherly type'), but the unconscious ways in which parts of others are taken into the self and parts of the self imaginatively put into others. For example, in the early days Silma says that breast feeding 'is (laughs) really nice, I'm like "oh my little one's having something from me" (hmm) I feel really nice, I don't know (laughs) about anybody, but I feel really nice when she has my breast milk'. She explains that breast feeding helps Abeedah to put on weight because 'she was like me, tiny'. Identifications with the baby can take any available form and Silma's attachment to being 'tiny' provides one such vehicle. Here the quality of tinyness is being extended from herself into Abeedah while she is also giving her something tangible of herself, namely her breast milk.

A further example illustrates Silma's new identification with her mother as she talks about her feelings straight after Abeedah's birth. She says 'to be a mother, it's a totally different feeling (mm), you know how your mother brought you up and gave birth to you, and the love between – the bond between the baby and the mother, it's a really special feeling'. Here, she seamlessly moves between her own new feelings of being a mother to her baby and a position as her mother's baby. It demonstrates how new mothers are simultaneously 'self-as-mother', 'self-as-child' and therefore, according to Gous (2005), 'mother-of-self-as-child'. Their identifications are multiply intersubjective in character because identification with their babies necessarily puts new mothers in pivotal positions in the middle of three generations since they have been babies of their own mothers (c.f. Mooney *et al.*, 2002). This access to simultaneous identifications with their mothers and with their babies affords a powerful transmission of maternal identity practices from one generation to the next in a way that does not have to be consciously learned to have effects (Faimberg, 2005).

Attention to unconscious intersubjective processes gives added dynamism and depth to the unconsciousness and automaticity inherent in Bourdieu's (1990) concept of habitus that is central to his notion of practice. For Bourdieu, *habitus* – variously described as principles, dispositions, schemes and embodied history – generates and organises practice (1990: 53). As Nirmal Puwar observes,

> The world (described by Bourdieu as objective structures and social fields) lives in our habitus (incorporated structures), not as a simple imprint that determines us, but rather as something we activate through our practices, however unconscious and automatic this social action may be.
>
> (2004: 110)

In Silma's account of a visit to her aunts with her younger sister, we can see something of the interplay between the social and the subjective elements of practice in the ways that generational difference is made salient by Silma. In this scene there is a conflict between new and old parts of Silma's identity as her identifications shift between her, her aunts and her younger sister. She explains that previously she would never stay around in the room listening to the aunts, but that now 'it's quite interesting how they talk'. Her new interest in her aunts is reciprocated. Her aunts now formally invite her, the new mother, to their homes rather than expecting her to drop in informally, as she had before her daughter was born and as her younger sister still does. Being recognised as a mother by others in her family is an important part of her mothering identity. In this situation, her young sister gives her 'dirty looks' and, according to Silma, says,

> 'Oh my God, you're talking like Mum...you're not my Mum. You used to be like this. You used to be worse than me' (laughs). But now...because I've changed, and I don't want my little sister to be in that state...she goes 'oh what about when you used to stay out late, did anyone hurt you?' And I was like, 'Yeah that was *me*' (laughs).

In the accusation 'you're talking like my Mum', Silma's sister recognises Silma's new identifications with her mother's generation. At the same time she acknowledges what Silma has rejected as part of this move, namely the part that 'used to be worse than me', staying out late. Silma, having wanted to be a mother for a long time, is likely to have fantasies of what mothers should be like, that come from her long experience of experiencing her mother and aunts 'doing motherhood'. These may well inform her new interest in her aunts. Given that these changes are recent, the fact that Silma evaluates her old self with an apparently surprised 'Yeah that was me', followed by a laugh, indicates how marked she perceives her identity change to be.

This is a good example of the joint action of practices, relational positioning and dynamic identifications in Silma's identity transition. She starts by noticing her different treatment by the women of her mother's generation. It is not just their new positioning of her (for instance, the formal invitations they now extend to her), but her own preferred practices that have changed: she likes to stay around with these aunts listening to 'how they talk', something she did not do before she had a baby. The contrast between her new identity as a mother and her old one is experienced through her relational positioning, here exemplified in how she experiences her young teenage sister giving her dirty looks for seeking out the aunts' company and for 'talking like Mum'. Now Silma identifies as a mother rather than a daughter when she worries about her little sister doing what, until recently, she used to do. Silma recognises her inconsistency but puts it down to being 'because I've changed'.

Silma's changed preferences, for her aunts' company in her dress and her protectiveness of her sister, indicate that the transition to motherhood is consequential and significant in her life at this time. However, the insistent quality of her claims to motherhood may become more relaxed as she repeatedly experiences people taking her maternal identity for granted and it becomes embedded (and embodied). We should also recognise that her claims are produced in an interview setting that explicitly is framed as finding out about how she experiences new motherhood. Our interviews with Silma over a year show changes in her consumption of clothes and demonstrate the cultural syncretism and evolution of her dress style. We cannot predict whether Silma will continue to prefer to wear shalwar kameez in the future; whether she will dress differently when she is meeting up with friends in Pizza Hut or McDonald's, or what she will wear if she returns to employment. In other words, our thinking about the performativity of practice needs to accommodate situatedness, temporality and the intersectionality and multiplicity of identifications in time and space. The multiplicity of identities and contexts in which Silma is positioned (like all the mothers in our sample) produces ordinary, mundane conflicts that make changes to identity positions somewhat disjunctive.

Claiming a motherhood identity

Identity claims are likely to be enhanced by the public demonstration that rarer, higher status, mothering practices have been accomplished. The example below demonstrates how Silma was able to surprise her family (and herself) by claiming recognition for the performance of a valued cultural skill.

When Abeedah was six months old, the interviewer (Heather) asked Silma about ceremonies associated with Abeedah's birth (a question that we asked all the mothers). First, Silma described how her mother and mother-in-law gave Abeedah her first haircut: her hair was shaved off and weighed before being buried, and the equivalent weight of the hair, in money, was donated to charity. The interviewer is curious about the cultural origin and meaning of the tradition, but Silma is vague and moves the conversation away from the search for cultural meaning, to a longer narrative about how she has since shaved Abeedah's hair twice. We join the interview at the interviewer's fourth attempt to identify the cultural significance of the practices in Silma's account:

> *Heather:* And why is the hair buried then, what is the thinking behind that?
>
> *Silma:* I (.) don't know the exact story behind it. (Heather: Hmm) Um, but all I know is ever since (inaudible) like every baby who is born we just (.)
>
> *Heather:* It's just tradition?
>
> *Silma:* Yeah, yeah and I've never come round to asking anyone why, what's the reason behind? It's just the once, the birth hair, that's it yeah.
>
> *Heather:* And how have you –
>
> *Silma:* I mean I love bathing her and then cutting her hair. (Heather: Do you?) I cut her hair two days ago by myself. (Heather: Uh huh.) And I bathed her, so that was a good experience. That's the second time I've cut her hair on my own. (Heather: Uh huh.) Yeah (laughs)
>
> *Heather:* And tell me about how that was.
>
> *Silma:* The first time I thought 'OK then, can I do it?' Nobody was home, they were all out shopping and I said 'OK then' And, um she'd been scratching her head for quite a few days, and I thought maybe it's because of feeling hot, or because her hair was irritating her. (Heather: Uh huh.) And I said 'OK then. I've got (an actual baby blade) so let me just try' (laughs) And I just put her on my lap, just wrapped a cloth . . . and I was talking to her and I just started shaving it off slowly. And then I got the bath ready and I bathed her. And everyone (laughs) came home and it was like 'Oh my god, did you?' And I said 'Yeah I managed quite well'. (Heather: Yeah.) Um, she wasn't fidgeting or anything, so that was quite good, yeah (laughs).
>
> *Heather:* Yeah, and the bath-
>
> *Silma:* My mum was surprised, my mum was like, 'you didn't? How did you do that?' I was like 'I just did it for myself'. I phoned her after I did it, I was like, 'Mum' I said 'guess what? I've just cut Abeedah's hair'. My mum was like. 'How? Did you make any scratches on her head?' I said 'No I didn't'. 'Did you cut her head?' I said 'No I didn't' (laughs).

This interview interaction and Silma's narratives of Abeedah's head shaves are 'intensely located' (Wetherell and Edley, 1998: 170), situated in multiple and interrelated contexts. Silma shows herself and her family how she is becoming a mother through the activity of shaving Abeedah's hair (without scratches or cuts). This is suggested in the phrase 'I just did it for myself' where one might expect 'by myself' or 'for Abeedah'. At the discursive level, how Silma gives meaning to these practices, as well as how she resists other meanings, can be understood as a part of her ongoing identity work in becoming a mother.

This account was produced within an interview interaction, between two mothers of different ethnicities, ages and classes, as well as in a wider social environment where researchers have commented on a 'climate of fear and suspicion' amongst Muslim research participants towards the intentions of researchers, in a sustained period of state surveillance and heightened research interest following concerns about Islamic fundamentalism and terrorism (Sanghera and Thapar-Bjorkert, 2008: 552). In order to understand better the role of practice in identity change, we need to take account of how all these different contexts might frame Silma's interview narratives, while also investigating how the meaning of the practice of shaving Abeedah's hair is produced and 'moves' throughout the interview interaction. We can do some of this by examining areas of contestation in the above extract. It is notable how the interviewer's questions repeatedly interpellate or 'call' (Althusser, 1971) Silma to position herself in relation to cultural identifications. In resisting these calls, she demonstrates that there are other, familial and maternal, identifications at play. So while Silma closes down the conversation on cultural meaning, it is the interviewer, in the above exchange, who tries unsuccessfully to move the conversation on from hair cutting to bathing. The interviewer's own experience of motherhood is too removed from Silma's for her to grasp immediately the intricacies of negotiations over the distribution of care within an extended family or to put together memories of the fragile jerkiness of a new baby's head with Silma's evident pride in her accomplishment of the shaving. This is a revelatory moment in which Silma draws upon a narrative of transformation to showcase a temporary settlement of new identifications achieved in the practice of competently shaving Abeedah's head. Her identity work is produced through a narrative that organises time (Bakhtin, 1981; Ricoeur, 1984), and uses it to mark and display her identity transitions within a biographical chronology and context.

Silma's account here is full of the tensions experienced in her performance of a new identity. She expresses these tensions in different voices and positions that contest each other and clamour for attention in the reported speech of her in-laws and of her mother's surprise at her competence. This dramatised moment of identity transition is achieved through talk about a practice redolent with cultural history and normalised in contemporary repetition. Silma also uses her narrative to enact and signify a move away from her previous biographical positioning as the 'weak one' in her family of origin to a stronger, more independent and adult positioning. (This change is supported by evidence elsewhere in Silma's interview data.)

Silma's shaving of her baby's head takes place on a rare day when she is alone in the house and so able to attempt a more autonomous version of motherhood than the one her family apparently expects from her, subverting their expectations and positioning of her. The space and impetus for trying out a new practice is also created by her mother's debilitating illness, which requires Silma to be 'strong' (and assume caring responsibilities for her mother), disrupts her expectations of what her own mother would do for Abeedah and so cuts short the apprenticeship in motherhood Silma had expected. It is not surprising then that Silma reports that she repeated the shaving of Abeedah's head, performatively making the practice part of her own repertoire of skills, and also that she insists on telling the interviewer of her success.

Conclusions

Silma's mothering practices derive from a range of social sources, including health practitioners and her own mother. However, they are also produced from unconscious processes of identification with both her mother and baby and from her desire to position herself within her imagined notions of what constitutes the motherhood identity in which she has long been invested. Silma works at becoming a mother by learning and repeating the practices necessary to mothering: those that are routinised and quotidian, such as feeding and bathing; those that are ritualised and culturally specific, such as shaving her baby's head and some (e.g., dress codes) that serve to mark her changed generational positioning. Such practices constitute the 'doing' of motherhood and involve a moving away from identifications with non-mothers and towards identifications with experienced mothers.

Silma's case illustrates the ordinary dynamic conflicts entailed in becoming a mother. These can be enacted and worked on through relationships with people. For example, Silma's claiming of new-found maturity involves ordinary conflict in that it is resisted and resented by her younger sister, but welcomed and encouraged by her mother and aunts. At the same time, conflicts can be enacted in relation to objects. Our example here was how Silma seems to be trying out the renunciation of youthful dress styles, at least when she is at home. At the same time, she is able to retain and project these desires through the ways in which she dresses her daughter. We exemplified how such positioning and enactment works through unconscious as well as conscious identifications. These conflicts and contradictions provide an insight into the way that identities are continually in process as points of temporary attachment, rather than being fixed and completed (Hall, 1996). In so much as our analysis suggests the irregular, bumpy and unpredictable movements involved in the transition to new motherhood identities, it also suggests that new motherhood identities are not simply pre-given and activated, but are dynamically and creatively made and remade.

Note

1. Interviews were supplemented with detailed reflexive field notes (Elliott, 2007) and six participants were recruited to a year-long weekly psychoanalytically informed observation. A special issue of the journal 'Infant Observation', edited by Cathy Urwin who led the observation study, presents this side of the research and the six cases of becoming a mother that resulted (Urwin, 2007). An afterword compares the interview and observation methods (Hollway, 2007).

References

Althusser, L. (1971) *Lenin and Philosophy*. London: New Left Books.
Bakhtin, M. M. (1981) *The Dialogic Imagination: Four Essays*. (ed.), M. Holquist. (Trans.), C. Emerson and M. Holquist. Austin and London: University of Texas Press.
Baraitser, L. (2006a) Oi' Mother Keep Ye' Hair On! Impossible Transformations of Maternal Subjectivity. *Studies in Gender and Sexuality* 7(3), 217–38.
Baraitser, L. (2006b) Reply to Commentaries. *Studies in Gender and Sexuality* 7(3), 249–57.
Bourdieu, P. (1977) *Outline of a Theory of Practice*. Cambridge: Cambridge University Press.
Bourdieu, P. (1990) *The Logic of Practice*. Cambridge: Polity Press.
Brooks, A. and Wee, L. (2008) Reflexivity and the Transformation of Gender Identity: Reviewing the Potential for Change in a Cosmopolitan City. *Sociology* 42(3), 503–21.
Butler, J. (1990) *Gender Trouble: Feminism and the Subversion of Identity*. London: Routledge.

Butler, J. (1993) *Bodies That Matter: On the Discursive Limits of Sex*. London: Routledge.

Butler, J. (1997) Performative Acts and Gender Constitution: An Essay in Phenomenology and Feminist Theory. In K. Conboy, N. Medina, and S. Stanbury (eds.), *Writing on the Body: Female Embodiment and Feminist Theory*. New York: Columbia University Press.

De Marneffe, D. (2006) Commentary on Baraitser: 'Oi' Mother Keep Ye' Hair On! Impossible Transformations of Maternal Subjectivity. *Studies in Gender and Sexuality* 7(3), 217–38.

Dench, G. and Gavron, K. (2006) *The New East End*. London: Profile Books.

Elliott, H. (2007) *Writing Psychosocial Field Notes*. Paper presented at the ESRC Identities and Social Action Psychosocial Research Group Meeting.

Equalities Review Panel (2007) *Fairness and Freedom: The Final Report of the Equalities Review*. Wetherby, West Yorks: Communities and Local Government Publications.

Erikson, E. (1980/1959) *Identity and the Life Cycle*. New York and London: Norton.

Faimberg, H. (2005) *The Telescoping of Generations*. London: Routledge.

Frosh, S. (2002) *After Words: The Personal in Gender, Culture and Psychotherapy*. London: Palgrave.

Gous, A. M. (2005) *The Ghosts in the Nursery: The Maternal Representation of a Woman Who Killed Her Baby*. University of Pretoria PhD thesis.

Gunaratnam, Y. and Elliott, H. (2007) *Report of a Tower Hamlets Focus Group with Bangladeshi Mothers*. Available from Open University Psychology Department.

Hall, S. (1996) Introduction: Who Needs Identity? In S. Hall and P. du Gay (eds.), *Questions of Cultural Identity*. London: Sage.

Hinshelwood, R. D. (1995) The Social Relocation of Personal Identity as Shown by Psychoanalytic Observations of Splitting, Projection and Introjection. *Philosophy, Psychiatry, Psychology* 2, 185–204.

Hollway, W. (2007) Afterword. *Infant Observation* 10(3), 231–6.

Hollway, W. (2008) The Importance of Relational Thinking in the Practice of Psycho-Social Research: Ontology, Epistemology, Methodology and Ethics. In S. Clarke, P. Hoggett, and H. Hahn (eds.), *Object Relations and Social Relations*. London: Karnac.

Hollway, W. (2009) Relationality: The Inter-Subjective Foundations of Identity. In M. Wetherell and C. T. Mohanty (eds.), *Sage Handbook of Identities*. London: Sage.

Hollway, W. and Jefferson, T. (2000) *Doing Qualitative Research Differently: Free Association, Narrative and the Interview Method*. London: Sage.

InstantAtlas (2006) *London Borough of Tower Hamlets: Project*: THIS Borough. http://www.instantatlas.com/downloads/cs_ip_lbth.pdf [Accessed 26 May 2006].

Lieblich, A., Tuval-Mashiach, R. and Zilber, T. (1998) *Narrative Research: Reading, Analysis and Interpretation*. Thousand Oaks CA: Sage.

Mooney, A., Statham, J. and Simon, A. (2002) *The Pivot Generation: Informal Care and Work after Fifty*. Bristol: The Policy Press.

Office of National Statistics (2001) *Census 2001 – Ethnicity and Religion in England and Wales*. http://www.statistics.gov.uk/census2001/profiles/commentaries/ethnicity.asp [Accessed 26 May 2008].

Phillips, A. (2007) *Multiculturalism without Culture*. Princeton and Oxford: Princeton University Press.

Puwar, N. (2004) *Space Invaders: Race, Gender, and Bodies out of Place*. Oxford: Berg.

Ricoeur, P. (1984) *Time and Narrative,* Volume 1. Chicago: University of Chicago Press.

Salway, S., Platt, L., Chowbey, P., Harriss, K. and Bayliss. E. (2007) *Long-Term Ill Health, Poverty and Ethnicity.* London: Joseph Rowntree Foundation.

Sanghera, G. and Thapar-Bjorkert, S. (2008) Methodological Dilemmas: Gatekeepers and Positionality in Bradford. *Ethnic and Racial Studies* 31(3), 543–62.

Scharff, D. E. (1992) *Refinding the Object and Reclaiming the Self.* Northvale, New Jersey: Jason Aronson.

Tower Hamlets PCT and Barts and The London NHS Trust (2007) *Review of Maternity Services Models of Care.* Tower Hamlets PCT and Barts and The London NHS Trust.

Urwin, C. (2007) Doing Infant Observation Differently? Researching the Formation of Mothering Identities in an Inner London Borough. *Infant Observation* 10(3), 239–52.

Wetherell, M. and Edley, N. (1998) Gender Practices: Steps in the Analysis of Men and Masculinities. In K. Henwood, C. Griffin, and A. Phoenix (eds.), *Standpoints and Differences: Essays in the Practice of Feminist Psychology.* London: Sage.

Winnicott, D. W. (1949) Mind and Its Relation to the Psyche-Soma. In D. Winnicott (1958) *Through Paediatrics to Psychoanalysis.* London: Hogarth.

Winnicott, D. W. (1956) Primary Maternal Preoccupation. In D. Winnicott (1958) *Through Paediatrics to Psychoanalysis.* London: Hogarth.

2
Biography, Education and Civic Action: Teaching Generations and Social Change

Jane Martin with John Kirk, Christine Wall and Steve Jefferys

In this chapter, we draw on the cultural representation and imagining of four successive and distinctive teaching generations to explore the identity generators of civic action, using a language of politics emerging out of a discourse heavily influenced by a critique of unbridled free-market capitalism. Given that previous research have shown that teachers acted as resources for social movements of various kinds including the early labour movement and 'first wave' feminism (Martin, 2007), we perceived this occupation to be a particularly appropriate lens through which to obtain some insights into questions of motivation, activist 'careers' and the lifestyle correlates of activism. Writing with the intellectual tools of Pierre Bourdieu in mind, we attempt to bring theory and research into dialogue by way of an empirical mapping of lives in educational settings in a range of historical moments. In developing this agenda, we offer a synthesis of our findings with regard to teachers' civic engagement, acting within education, within their teacher associations and within their communities. Our purpose is to use teachers' biographies to illuminate the identity/social action relation with particular attention to questions of time, space and place.

Generally, the Western world presents the time of history as teleological. Following Kristeva's (1986) conception of 'Women's Time', we advocate a deconstructive approach, using generations in terms of tiers that are not only linear, but co-exist in time and space. Therefore, we view time as multiple and socially constructed. In his classic essay on generations, defined and used as shared birth year, Karl Mannheim (1997) tried to capture overlapping temporalities of simultaneous action. To illustrate how different historical periods have mutually agreed-upon, basic perceptions of the universe, he emphasised an original and distinctive consciousness reflecting the codes of an established generational culture. This is analogous to Raymond Williams's (1961) concept of 'structure of feeling' as articulated in *The Long Revolution*, which he had defined as being 'the culture of a period'. As there are several generations alive at once, the understanding is that members of any one generation can only participate in a temporally limited section of the historical-social process. From the point of view of Bourdieu's (1999) theory of social practice, the individuals profiled here are similarly located in terms of their common experience of a specific 'field' of action constituted by their shared participation in schooling processes. Drawn together with the concept of the 'habitus' and most centrally 'capital', Bourdieu understands the social world as made up of different but overlapping fields of power which function according to their own tacit logic or set of rules which may explain specific forms of reproduction by successive generations through historical time. Primarily we use his suggestions relating to the 'habitus' to elucidate the interweaving of civic action and teacher identity, making sense of the slippery status of ways of seeing and being within the world.

Learned more by experience than by teaching, 'habitus' is social practice linked to, for example, linguistic competence, lifestyle, politics and prestige, combined with particular habitual acquisitions, attitudes and tastes. A structured and structuring structure, 'habitus' is a system of durable, transposable dispositions that predispose individuals to do certain things. Given the cross-generational design of our project, it makes good sense for us to theorise our research findings in respect of teachers' activism in terms of 'habitus'. Thus, we refer to what Nick Crossley (2003) describes as a theory of 'radical habitus' which generates protest and critique. Within such a view, biography is used to reconstruct the acquisition of a 'radical habitus' historically to the extent that it inscribes the individual with a repertoire of practices, with a history, that facilitate or otherwise the taste for contention. We decided to approach the structure of telling through a series of shifts, of micro-histories, slicing up teachers' stories and narratives into extracts and grouping them chronologically in order to relate them to history and to context. The first task was to particularise biographical texts from teachers beyond our reach then – at the second stage – to set them alongside the embedded, lived memories of work and non-work using life-history material from the larger project.

Focusing particularly on teacher–state relations within the United Kingdom, we map the contours of the stories/policy dialectic with the help of the work of Gerald Grace. He identifies four broad phases intended to be indicative of policy trends as opposed to a precise historical chronology. Thus, Grace (1987) depicts the opening decades of the twentieth century as characterised by a politics of confrontation when elementary school teachers experienced government education policy as class cultural condescension, which they bitterly resented. The second timeline Grace identifies is that of the inter-war years. During this period, some organised teachers celebrated the construction of empowering identities as trusted professionals. On the other hand, we shall see that some teachers remained more critical of the conditions surrounding teachers' work in state schools. Nonetheless, by the outbreak of the Second World War state teachers in Britain seemed to have attained to respectable white collar/white blouse security as one of the accepted lesser professions associated with what Grace calls an *ethic of legitimated professionalism*. The third phase of teacher–state relations is 1940 to the mid-1970s. Then, under the influence of war, new political and intellectual groupings forged a new settlement in favour of welfare philanthropism. It gave expression to central tenets around planning, state intervention and universal forms of social provision that began to assert education's importance.

If we consider Grace's final period from the late 1970s/early 1980s we can see how, with reformist 'welfare' solutions widely questioned, teachers saw the breaking of this social democratic and professional consensus and the return of a politics of confrontation in terms of the trajectory of government policy. Among other things, the arrival of the market heralded the growth of subject specialisation, pedagogic and control-oriented accountability, all of which limited teachers' claim to professional autonomy. Since the election of a New Labour government in 1997, there has been some softening of 'rhetoric' tempered by continuities regarding a culture of 'naming and blaming teachers' for declining standards. Increased levels of public spending have accompanied further years of mandated reform, and promotion of change implementation by external interest groups (including government agencies and corporate bodies) as opposed to educator groups.

What does this mean, then, for the link between the construction of the 'teacher' occupational identity and social action across the broad sweep of historical time considered here? What can we identify with regard to teachers' long-standing mandate to act as agents of democracy and social change? Since there was no continuous system of educational provision until the 1944 Education Act, which stipulated both the abolition of tuition fees at all state-maintained schools and the distinction between 'elementary' and 'higher' schooling, our first two teaching generations are represented by elementary and primary teachers. Using Grace's periodisation outlined above, we look at the durable effects of participation in protest at the individual level. Dr Robert Jones, moving on to Charles and Florence Key in the second phase of teacher–state relations, represents our first generational tier. These three teachers were prominent in the development of London education. Our second cohort consists of a married couple who became primary teachers in the 1950s and 1960s, respectively. In our third teaching generation, the testimony of another married couple teaching in the same secondary school illustrates that the impact of the past continues in the present. Two men who started their working lives in the first decade of the twenty-first century follow this. Historically and politically, a male secondary school teacher who self identifies as a working-class organic intellectual takes us full circle.

Teaching to change: From confrontation to consensus and back?

A lifelong elementary teacher, Dr Jones was a member of the Fabian Society. Having attended a local board school in Liverpool he began his working life as a pupil teacher in the mid-1880s, following which he took college training at Cheltenham to prepare for the Teachers' Certificate. From 1889 to 1894, he taught at an elementary school in Liverpool when he took a post in London and subsequently spent the remainder of his teaching career in the metropolis. University Extension provided access to enhanced personal education and Robert obtained a First Class degree in Economics and went on to gain a doctorate in 1912 when head teacher at Hague Street elementary school in Bethnal Green. His professional expectations raised and headships in Hackney and, finally, at Monnow Road in Bermondsey followed, in 1916.

Dating back to the systematisation of compulsory elementary schooling from the 1870s, Monnow became the most prestigious board school in the London borough of Bermondsey. In a place of abject poverty, its location in a not-too-bad street facilitated its development into a Higher Grade School, one of those set up by the London School Board in order to provide post-elementary schooling for some of their pupils. As a school 'type', these institutions disappeared in the 1900s following the issue of new regulations imposing strict requirements and limitations on their work. Under the School Board's successor, the London County Council (education authority for the capital from

1904), Monnow became a selective central elementary school to which pupils gained access via an examination. As a group, central schools offered an extended schooling for working-class children whose families could contemplate the costs but would be very unlikely to be able to afford secondary school expenses, and they were particularly strong in London (David, 1980; King, 1990). Monnow had an arty culture, with its own school song that Robert wrote, built around the idea of a peculiar 'Englishness'. The topography was plain, all heroic metaphors and celebrations of past glory within a literary framework symbolised by Shakespeare's Globe Theatre and intended to give expression to particular visions of collective identity. He also pioneered school journeys and exchange visits with Eton College, the world-famous independent school for boys, near Windsor. In the spring of 1928, Monnow was the first English school of any type to broadcast on the Continent, from the Hall of the Reformation in Geneva, the site of the first assembly of the League of Nations.

Robert probably agreed with fellow Fabian H.G. Wells when he wrote, 'the Socialist movement *is* teaching, and the most important people in the world from the Socialist's point of view are those who teach' (Wells, 1909, p. 265). Written in terms resonant of Ruth Lister's (1997) notion of 'citizenship agency', this requires the conscious belief that one can act. Clearly, a doer, Robert went on to acquire a professional identity beyond his immediate locality as the author of numerous textbooks, Fabian tracts and press articles. In so doing, he exposed the divisions within the educational system as resting primarily upon non-educational grounds. In January 1929, the *Bermondsey Labour Magazine*, the journal of the Bermondsey Independent Labour Party, published an affectionate valedictory under the title 'Some Good Friends of Bermondsey'. 'Lucky are the boys who have had the chance of training under a great man, a great teacher, and a great organiser like Dr. Jones. His presence at Monnow is a tremendous asset to our borough'.

Historically, the socialist press defined interests in schooling in terms of political citizenship and democratic participation. An important factor in the local context of specific events was the social welfare initiatives of the Wesleyan Methodist Bermondsey Settlement House. Class bridging projects in the slums, late-Victorian settlement houses provided sites where elite men and women experimented with unconventional ideas about politics and class relations, which extended notions of learning as lifelong, intended to empower learners and enhance an individual's capacity to engage with others in community affairs as a means of addressing social problems. This practical creed gave tangible expression to the political theories of the Idealists, which saw the role of the school as the focus of a sense of community and citizenship around the pivotal figure of the teacher as the educator of the citizen-to-be.

Monnow pupils visited the settlement and settlers distributed school prizes, while Monnow girls sent Christmas gifts to those with disabilities in the neighbourhood. Inevitably, the first generation of settlers proffered differing analyses of poverty, but some spearheaded a 'radical habitus' that grew out of their ability to connect with the structural defects of capitalism underpinning the grimy particularities of life in the dockside neighbourhoods of south London.

The evidence in the school magazine, *The Monnow*, dating from 1909, suggests that the satisfaction Robert Jones derived from teaching had a lot to do with this notion of educational activism. Committed to progressive social and political change, he championed the creation of Monnow as a 'University of Bermondsey'. In the summer of 1919, Robert waxed rhapsodic.

> In every little thing you do that you think worthy of a Monnovian – in all such things as these, no less than in your actual lessons (indeed far more) you build up our Monnow, brick by brick, into a University of Bermondsey that shall send out boys and girls fit to be citizens of no mean city.
>
> (*The Monnow*, July 1919, p. 60)

Here is the reflexive voice of an activist from our first teaching generation. Robert sustained his 'belief in the game' (*illusio*), creating a context for testing out innovative solutions to urban poverty and debates about the moral vocation of citizenship. Grasping the politics and philosophy of Idealism, his way of living had community at its centre, organised around a common good located in the sphere of voluntary action and education. On his retirement in 1932, the media described Monnow as the 'school that boys did not wish to leave' (*The Star*, 20 May 1932). Across the river, another teaching couple shared his preferred vision of the future society. Although younger than he, they also belonged to the second generation of apostles touched by the 'religion of socialism', a term in common currency in the 1880s and 1890s.

Florence Key (née Adams) was a native of Wapping, London, and the daughter of a licensed victualler. During the First World War, she became an assistant teacher in the girls' department at Dempsey Street Elementary School, Stepney, where she met her future husband and political partner, Charles Key. Born in rural Buckinghamshire, Charles witnessed extreme and grinding poverty after the death of his father before he was six years old. To make ends meet his mother worked as a char and took in lodgers, one of whom became Charles's patron, providing the financial support that enabled him to move to London and start his working life as a pupil teacher. The London School Board was one of the leading authorities in the development of teacher education and Charles attended the Mile End Pupil Teacher Centre in Stepney, followed by college training at Borough Road from 1903 to 1905. Unlike his wife, Charles's career trajectory led on to headship.

Looking back, Charles recalled stirrings of political consciousness in debating contests for pupil teachers organised by volunteer workers at Toynbee Hall settlement house, in Whitechapel. In 1905/6, he joined the Independent Labour Party and appeared on public platforms in the Limehouse district of London shortly after. Charles was one of 39 Labour candidates swept to power on Poplar borough council in November 1919. Two years later he was deputy mayor and at the centre of the Poplar Rates Rebellion of 1921 when 30 Labour councillors were sent to prison for their refusal to collect Poplar's poor rate. Charles did not go to jail but was prominent in the campaign to secure the release of those who did, writing the pamphlet *Guilty and Proud of It* (1922) to explain their actions. This was socialism in action. Emulating Dick Whittington, Charles was thrice Mayor of Poplar (1924, 1928, and 1933) and subsequently moved from the local into the national political field, following his friend and mentor, George Lansbury, as MP for Poplar, Bow and Bromley (in 1940).

Although Florence was part of a popular movement that spanned labour and suffrage organisations, she chose to commit herself to feminism rather than socialism. Before the First World War, she joined the Women's Freedom League that began as a breakaway from the Women's Social and Political Union, the prime mover of suffrage militancy. Later she became a pioneer member of the National Union of Women Teachers (NUWT) that began as an Equal Pay League (in 1904) formed within the largest teaching union, the National Union of Teachers (NUT). In 1909, the League changed its name to the National Federation of Women Teachers. Support grew and in 1919, the London section joined with the Women Teachers' Franchise Union to split from the NUT. Women teachers who turned to the new organisation united in demonstrations and deputations, lobbying and public statements, seeing their struggle as an intrinsic part of the wider women's movement for full political, social and economic parity with men. The NUWT published its own journal (the *Woman Teacher*) and communicated its ideas through a column in a general educational journal, *The Schoolmistress*, which claimed to have the largest circulation of all educational magazines among women teachers.

Therefore, self-defined feminist teachers fought for equality, claiming the three elements of citizenship identified by T.H. Marshall (1952) – the civil, the political and the social. From the vantage point of the networking and notions of political identity sustained in the *Woman Teacher*, the union itself was an education in citizenship. For example, significant campaigns were undertaken to enable women to vote and to hold political office on the same terms as men, to give them access to higher education and to equal pay and conditions in the workplace. At root, learning and teaching provided a sounding board for civic engagement. On 25 October 1925 Florence Key wrote that 'The greatest work of a teacher lies, not in the impartment of instruction, but in the training of the individuality of the child and in helping it to express itself as a happy and useful member of the community.' The language of citizenship she employs suggests that for her, citizenship is a relationship, a web of practices and duties binding individuals together as a blueprint for a future good society. It also reveals the enduring political importance of conscience. Carried forward from the Edwardian era, its appeal meshed and intermeshed with constructions of 'active citizenship' associated with the Idealist philosopher T.H. Green, who argued that education should develop the ideal to be good in each individual. Constituted through ideas of positive social action, Julia Parker (1998, p. 15) maintains that this required that all be free to develop those qualities of mind and character 'which might contribute to the common wealth'.

Florence became union president in 1932. Her conference speeches on the question of equal pay illustrate the identity/action relation, providing evidence of a 'radical habitus' informing practice. In 1929, for example, Florence 'pointed out that the dilution of women's labour by the employment of unqualified women as teachers increased the proportion of women teachers to men and thus artificially strengthened the argument of supply and demand' (*Woman Teacher*, 15 February 1929, p. 134). She demolished popular perceptions that the head of a mixed school must be a man in feminist terms and confidently asserted the need for the educated woman to have both a career and a fulfilling personal life. Far from married women workers being a danger to the community, in her eyes 'the real menace lay ... in that section which led luxurious lives on unearned incomes' (*Woman Teacher*, 23 September 1932, p. 302). Nevertheless, many of her comments indicate reluctance to contemplate the adoption of 'voluntary spinsterhood' and a tendency to defend the institution of marriage, suggesting the question had almost become 'should a woman marry? Not should a married woman work?' She firmly identified with working wives and mothers saying, 'It was a question of freedom but we did not want freedom only for spinsters, for we demanded the rights of every woman to go forward on her own feet with equal opportunities' (*Woman Teacher*, 10 January 1930).

Media representations show that the teacher role was crucial in relation to identity claims. They reflect also the relative value of this teaching couple's capitals to achieve legitimacy and standing in the political field. On the one hand, a *Star* reporter said of Charles, 'if I am asked where this new type of London statesman and leader had got it all from, I can only say that for many years he was a London schoolmaster'. On the other, the *Woman Teacher* (22 January 1932) quotes a journalist on the *East London Advertiser* reaffirming local pride in the achievements of Florence Key, defining her in opposition to what was called the 'school marm' stereotype with her 'high spirits and joyous disposition'. The articulation of class-consciousness, educational achievement and professional identity suggest that a particular white working-class gendered 'habitus' was of benefit to Charles in following the path from pupil teacher to professional politician. For Florence, the NUWT offered a chance to invent a self. Unable to halt its decline and with their immediate political aims achieved, in 1961 the survivors disbanded the union that had been their personal mission.

Post-1945: Teachers, citizenship and the state

In this section, we move out of the archive into living history, by examining the oral testimony. The study involved a main sample of 40 teachers with a geographical split between the north-west of England and the south-east. They all volunteered to take part and represented a broad spectrum of professional and biographical profiles in terms of age, experience, personal history, levels of the promotional structure and domestic arrangements. We use a structure of generational tiers – retired, mid-career and new entrants to the occupation – to locate the teachers' stories and illuminate the society/individual dialectic.

Since we were interested in the way teachers act politically within education, acting within their teacher associations, we asked each one about union membership. By the 1950s, the membership of the NUT largely consisted of primary and secondary modern teachers, the majority certificated but with a growing number of graduates though it was still losing male members to the more militant and aggressive National Association of Schoolmasters (NAS). Two decades on, the Professional Association of Teachers seceded from the NUT following the affiliation to the Trades Union Congress in 1970 and the period of teacher militancy between 1968 and 1974. For the project teachers, contextual factors such as the union coloration of a particular school site influenced choices made. Besides the NUT, we found 'organised teachers' as a category restricted to the NAS, the National Association of Schoolmasters/Union of Women Teachers (NAS/UWT) and the head-teachers associations.

What angered retired primary school teachers the most, when remembering a life in education, were the new contracts and conditions of service imposed by the Thatcher government re-elected in 1987. Contrasts were drawn between the autonomous professionals of their generation and teachers practice in the twenty-first century. Individually and collectively, they set great store by respect and one reason for the respect afforded past teachers in the context of the locality was their giving of their time voluntarily to look after school clubs, organise sports and school trips. There was a pervasive sense of frustration at a narrowing of the contexts in which teachers worked, re-defining their professional location, influencing relations between home, school and community, teachers and civic engagement.

Retired primary school teacher Susan explained her decision to join the NUT in the 1950s in ways that suggested she found the NUWT problematic, saying she was 'not too keen on the NUWT at all'. The only child of working-class parents who were intent upon securing the best opportunities that they could for her, they were proud of her achievement in becoming a teacher. At the end of her interview, however, she recalled alternative early ambitions. She hankered after being a librarian but assumed her parents could not afford the four-year university course that this required. Questions of gender recurred in her account, 'for a girl it was often teaching or bank work and I didn't want to go into a bank'. Susan taught in the rural mining communities that she had known all her life, stated that she had been on strike once and attended conference as a delegate's wife. She chose to use gender scripts to explain her lack of career progression. 'I made the decision that I would stay as a classroom teacher because I wanted to be able to encourage my own children, have time for my own children and my husband.' She linked her social action discursively to involvement in out-of-school activities like school trips.

Susan met her husband, Roy, at a social organised by the NUT. His mother and uncle were both teachers and his sister also went into teaching. Unlike Susan, Roy *was* a career teacher and went on to a primary school headship. Despite having been an elected official within the NUT, he subsequently felt pushed out by antipathy towards head teachers and joined the National Association of Head Teachers (NAHT) in the 1970s. For him, the notion of a community school was a central aspect of the context within which teachers work though he did not think it mattered whether they opted to live 'in' or 'out' of the immediate locality. In his account, the links with 'community' were through school sports. Saturday mornings were devoted to 'football teams and whatnot', weekday evenings to school cricket. He was at pains to emphasise that he saw this as 'the only way of doing the job'. We see here the old iconographies of teacher identity, with the virtues of care, dedication and self-investment, which he believed in. The role of teacher involved developing a rapport with parents as well as children. He explained,

> you've got to educate the children, but at the same time you've got bear in mind that the parents have a role in this and if you can talk to parents as if they're human beings on your level, then you get on far better and your results are far better with the children.

He thought the policy changes of the late-1980s had deprofessionalised teachers, making them 'slaves to the system'. The metaphor powerfully reflects a sense of disempowerment among teachers.

Those who started teaching in the 1980s and beyond accepted new governmental guidelines and new national objectives and curriculum. However, these teachers' narratives and actions suggested that in defining their own occupational identities they sought to reappropriate the discourse of what Ivor Goodson (2003, p. 126) calls practical and reflexive professionalism. By which he means a body of knowledge 'concerned with the intricate definition and character of occupational action, in this case the practice and profession of teaching'. A major plank of the rhetoric builds on the standards agenda pushed for by central governments but in reworking a commitment to active *care* for students, they related it to a belief in social practice and moral purpose. In this sense, it connects with broader social agendas of equity and emancipation. This was particularly evident in the narratives of teachers in ethnically diverse inner-city schools. Take, for instance, the work-life histories of a teaching couple working in the same urban secondary school in the north-west.

Alison defined her social background as middle class. She grew up in an affluent suburb, attended local Roman Catholic schools with university (where she met her future husband) and teacher training thereafter. Her first teaching post was in an inner-city area characterised by various levels of social deprivation including a strong gang culture. At this stage in her career narrative, teaching was part of her very identity:

I defined myself, my life by I was a teacher in an inner city school, the children liked me, and I was seen as successful. I defined myself through that. I got quite a lot of criticism from that, from my family, who thought I was working too hard, that type of thing and then you know, they were proud of me, my husband was proud of me, of what I was achieving.

Alison went on to work in a single-sex (boys) school before rejoining her previous head teacher in her current school, of which she was Deputy Head. Looking back, she recalled that her family always saw her as a 'mother-earth type character' and her testimony strongly pointed up religious influences underpinning the decision to teach. 'I mean I am quite a spiritual person and I think that this is what I was always meant to do ... providing some stability for these children and the community.'

'Alisons' definition of a good teacher was 'someone that cares' and she found a mentor in a previous colleague who had been appointed head teacher of her present school before she rejoined him as a member of staff. It is telling that she describes him as 'like some angel', wanting to 'make a difference for children in this area'. In her blueprint for educational change, she sought to promote a vision of education that was community-based, lifelong and directed towards social equality. As she put it, 'I'd like to see school, what we call a full service extended school with doctors' surgeries and health clinics, dentists, child care, even a shop on site.'

Her husband, Tony, was a mature entrant to teaching. He did not come from a traditional working-class background but he, too, felt propelled to work in urban schools. In common with Alison, this came down to a sense of duty, a notion of commitment. More than that, he talked about the special quality of teacher–pupil relations in a school where many of the children were from single parent households and he played the role of a father figure in their lives. The job of teaching is a central part of his identity practices and he describes himself as becoming 'evangelical' in social situations, waxing lyrical about the difference that his school was making. He described the influence of teacher trade unions as 'a necessary evil' on a par with school inspections! Tony had been involved in school sport but in keeping with a leitmotif of contemporary politics was now acting as the schools' enterprise co-ordinator. A 'pet project' of the then Chancellor Gordon Brown, enterprise education was a policy initiative directed towards the creation of a new generation of 'moral entrepreneurs'. For Tony, it meant teaching financial literacy alongside relevant and appropriate school trips and competitions. Opting to work in a poor area, then, is an act of engagement for this teaching couple, and this implies – as the reference to 'evangelical' suggests – a notion of vocation as 'mission'.

Making connections: Civic idealism, identity projects and social action

Testimonies from contemporary teachers indicate a form of civic idealism found in a complex 'radical habitus' bound up with certain basic concepts such as community and respect underpinning a notion of the educator as potential change agent. Ways of thinking repeated often enough to assume a habitual form that resonates with Williams's (1961) notion of a 'structure of feeling' across time as it is lived by different teaching generations. In this case, a notion of a radical tradition in state education addressed to a range of problems, as exemplified in such emphasis upon the moral vocation of citizenship organised around a notion of the common good. This becomes evident in narratives that force us to think about the interplay between the 'habitus' and examples of reflexivity.

Max, a young male primary school teacher in his mid-20s, revealed how he had quickly become disillusioned with the ideology of the market, with input replaced by output as the key evaluative rule of education. 'It's becoming a lot more; I don't know…it feels more like a business. It feels more like it's some sort of company and you're reaching your quota and you're reaching your target rather than a school.' Contrary to the dominant performance indicators in the opening decade of the twenty-first century, he believed teaching to be an intuitive act and placed great emphasis on the school as an organic entity. Inseparable from his twentieth century past, reflecting on his own experience of primary education enabled him to compare the current system with a time when the schooling pedagogic process placed more emphasis on the child. Politicised reflexivity, a feature that Bourdieu under-valued, is an extension of his teaching practice. All of which makes it possible to speak of a 'radical habitus' and demonstrate its complexity.

In the inner city working-class area in which Max worked, where for some children their home lives were not supportive of education, he was clear that his role as a teacher was to create a positive impact on the lives of children through creating a safe environment for learning. As part of this commitment to the children in this poor neighbourhood, he also taught at a Saturday school funded by the educational charity Support and Help in Education. SHINE was set up in 1999 in order to assist underachieving pupils in disadvantaged metropolitan areas by extending the school week through running small classes for pupils focussing on enriching the curriculum and raising the expectations of these children. Maxs' participation in this scheme, in the context of his self-description as a teacher highly critical of the effect of the present school regime on childrens' experience of education, demonstrates the 'radical habitus' in action. This action describes a resistance to the rhetoric of 'blame' attached to teachers and an unquestioning allegiance to private philanthropy, while at the same time acknowledging the importance of his trade union as a necessary defender of his employment rights.

This type of commitment is evident in the testimony of Joseph, too, a black teacher starting out in the profession. The emergence of a 'radical habitus' with regard to teaching can be seen as a product of his own schooling experience. This experience is in key senses formative and informs his actions later in life when he decides to become a teacher. He talks about 'not being taken seriously' by some teachers when he was a pupil, and this he recognises as racially coded behaviour. He felt he was viewed as able to attain 'a certain level and not beyond that', pre-judged and thus prevented, potentially, from fulfilling his ambitions. His role now as a teacher he defines as 'making a difference', his response to 'not being taken seriously', during his own school days. He says, towards the end of the interview, that he will 'stick to this kind of [inner-city] school which is where I think I will make the most of a difference. Yeah, I think I prefer this sort of school I suppose; yeah.' Adding:

> I suppose at the end of the day if I could touch just one person, say from a situation, a school setting like this where half the pupils think they won't achieve anything, if I could make one person realise that they have got all the chances within them to excel and compete with the best of the pupils in the very good schools, I think that would be a job well done for me I suppose.

This is the type of civic idealism referred to above. However, Joseph does not romanticise his role, or the children that he works with.

Fundamental to his pedagogy and practice is a clear-eyed understanding of the difficult contexts in which they both operate.

Teacher identity and social action is bound up with other dimensions such as ethnicity, but also class. The emergence of a 'radical habitus' turns on such co-ordinates to inform practice. Thus, Dave, Head of Department in a school in the north-west, speaks of his own working-class background as constitutive of his current identity and practice as a teacher. 'I don't think that does leave you, because it's not just about where you come from, it's about how you see the world around you and the connections that you make, you know.' With Dave we almost come full circle in the discussion, his view of education, as we see below, echoing that of Florence Key. Speaking of his work, he says,

> I was treated as an individual at school which has helped me see the individuals in front of me rather than you're all just a middle set or a top set, it helps me to dispel my expectations or stereotypes or prejudgements... [And] I ran a lot of football teams and drama stuff at the last place, too, and I know that football kept guys in school... but they stayed in school, and for some, that's a victory, for others, like Rob, you know, he got his apprenticeship from British Rail and became an engineer, it's what you need to get the kid so they'll be safe enough as a young adult to not make the mistakes, you've got to cherish them and you've got to hold onto them, you know, sometimes that's all you can do but you know that each day they'll get one day older and one day wiser.

There is a deep commitment here, one derived through professional development, but powerfully informed by a structure of feeling with deeper roots in the social interactions of community, class and culture, and one that defines, too, a 'radical habitus' that shapes social action. In conjunction with other factors, the 'habitus' can play a potential explanatory role in relation to the 'fit' between a rejection of materialist values, the taste for contention and pursuing occupations which allow radical pedagogues to pursue their values and projects by means of working with disadvantaged groups.

Conclusion: Philanthropic projects and organic intellectuals

Our reading of these teachers' narratives suggests that we need to balance questions of structure-agency in building a theory of social identity and social action visualised in respect of time and futurity. Teachers are not timeless role incumbents and the nature and organisation of active citizenship builds on historically contingent foundations. To return to the political vocabulary with which we started, much of this idealism is still present and it is important to note the past/present relation under-pinning contemporary teachers' over-representation within the ranks of what are termed new social movements (Crossley, 2003). In common with other studies, our research suggests that teacher activism is not confined to a narrowly political domain and our subjects sought out teaching because it allowed them to pursue their values and projects by means other than protest. At the level of the individual biography, the formation of a 'radical habitus' turns on questions of identity and community, as well as markers of social difference. It also stems from the family and the higher education system as agencies of political socialisation.

As we detect from Bourdieu, the 'habitus' derived from culture and upbringing acts as a classifying mechanism for making sense of the world. Andrew Sayer (2005), discussing the moral significance of class, flags up ethical considerations in his argument by placing a sharper emphasis on conscious reflection – a feature that Bourdieu under-valued. This is where morality places a crucial mediating role in our discussion of historical approaches to teachers' identity formation, reproduction and change. The argument of this chapter is that both past and present teachers talked about 'making a difference'. Reflection on the profes-sional and generational 'habitus' suggests the continuance of an ethics of care with the teacher–pupil relationship as the epitome of what is involved in caring about the world as a moral stance. It is in this con-fluence that an inchoate but deeply principled belief in the potential of the educator as change agent came, alongside a view of teaching on a par with a religious vocation. Historically, the caring and nurturing that characterise acts of teaching means that teachers were and are involved in a variety of philanthropic projects and we argue that the sense of civic idealism was essentially part of this context. Twenty-first century teach-ers' might express themselves in terms of the entrepreneurial culture and may no longer share the vocabulary and presuppositions of moral citizenship articulated by the Idealist philosophers but in this sense the post-Second World War arrangements of welfare philanthropism live on.

Set against the backdrop of the historical phases sketched at the start, the narratives support the broad sweep of the view fostered. As far as Grace's arguments are concerned, our discussion involves a new phase after the counter-reformation of the 1980s, which marked the effective abandonment of the system established in 1944. This is to represent a shift under the Blair administrations of 1997–2008 as an attempt to construct a new educational consensus from a New Labour government preaching social inclusion and missionary morality. In these years, the emphasis was on tightening up delivery on targets, tests and league tables. Workforce remodelling, a consequence of the new workload agreement, was something different from before (DfES, 2003). The price of social partnership was greater flexibility and less demarcation – no longer was it necessary to obtain Qualified Teacher Status to teach in state schools in England. All pose a challenge to both the security and the identity of teachers with new conceptions of professionalism as far as working conditions and pay, the curriculum and assessment, are concerned.

It is remarkable that the aims of education, which many of our teachers brought forward, sought to unify moral and material means and ends. They identified three things, which a school had to do. They were training for a working life, training for an inner life and training for a communal life as a citizen. In these senses, the value of education and training for self-fulfilment as well as for social and economic advance was appreciated. This thinking may embrace a broad ethical egalitarianism, critical of the capitalist society in its social and moral effects, but we are only speaking of nine of our 40 project teachers' here. Of these nine, in only a very few cases was it addressed to the collective advance of working-class communities though we found contemporary teachers who had organic links with other agencies – community activists, the labour movement, the women's movement and could learn from and with them. We do not wish to commit an act of symbolic violence in our meaning making, but it would seem reasonable to posit that wittingly, or unwittingly, some project teachers still subscribed to the notion of the cultural elevation of the masses.

Of those who did *not*, Dave positioned himself as an organic intellectual. In the Gramscian sense, this involves something akin to 'acting for and with' pupils, rather than 'acting upon' them, as the cultural elevation model suggests. He resolutely opposed the elitist orthodoxy that monopolised the means of learning, preserving discussions of content and control that tended to perpetuate the structural class-based division. For Dave, like Robert Jones and Florence Key before him, this notion of social action was part of his very identity and practice.

Acknowledgements

We would like to acknowledge Dr Tim Strangleman who discussed some of these ideas with us at project meetings.

References

Bourdieu, P. (1999) *Practical Reason*. Cambridge: Polity.

Charlie Key of Poplar, *The Star*. 4 January 1941, press cuttings Tower Hamlets Local History Library.

Crossley, N. (2003) From Reproduction to Transformation: Social Movement, Field and the Radical Habitus. *Theory, Culture and Society*. 20 (6): 43.

David, M. (1980) *The State, the Family and Education*. London: Routledge and Kegan Paul.

Department for Education & Skills (2003) *Raising Standards and Tackling Workload: A National Agreement*. London: HMSO.

East London Advertiser. 2 January 1932, press cuttings Tower Hamlets Local History Library.

Goodson, I. (2003) *Professional Knowledge, Professional Lives*. Buckingham: Open University Press.

Grace, G. (1987) Teachers and the State in Britain: A Changing Relation. In M. Lawn and G. Grace (eds.) *Teachers: The Culture and Politics of Work*. Lewes: Falmer.

Jones, R. (1919) Monnow at Work: The University of Bermondsey. *The Monnow*. July, p. 60.

Key, C. (1922) *Guilty and Proud of It!* London: Poplar.

Key, F.E. (1925) Teachers and Politics. *Woman Teacher*. 25 October, p. 37.

Key, F.E. (1932) From the President. *Woman Teacher*. 7 October, p. 5.

King, S. (1990) Technical and Vocational Education for Girls. A Study of the Central Schools of London, 1918–1939. In P. Summerfield and E. Evans (eds.) *Technical Education and the State Since 1950*. Manchester: Manchester University Press.

Kristeva, J. (1986) Women's Time. In T. Moi (ed.) *The Kristeva Reader*. Oxford: Basil Blackwell.

Lister, R. (1997) *Citizenship: Feminist Perspectives*. Basingstoke: Macmillan.

Mannheim, K. (1997) The Problem of Generations. In M. Hardy (ed.) *Studying Ageing and Social Change*. London: Sage.

Marshall, T.H. (1952) *Citizenship and Social Class*. Cambridge: Cambridge University Press.

Martin, J. (2007) Thinking Education Histories Differently: Biographical Approaches to Class Politics and Women's Movements in London, 1900s to 1960s. *History of Education*. 36 (4–5): 515–34.

Parker, J. (1998) *Citizenship, Work and Welfare*. Basingstoke: Macmillan.

Sayer, A. (2005) *The Moral Significance of Class*. London: Routledge.

Wells, H.G. (1909) *New Worlds for Old*. London: Macmillan.

Williams, R. (1961) *The Long Revolution*. London: Chatto and Windus.

3
Performing Identities: Participatory Theatre among Refugees

Nira Yuval-Davis and Erene Kaptani

The aim of this chapter is to explore processes of identity constructions and transformations in the participatory theatre space and the
links between these and social action. After a short description of the
research project, the chapter sums up our main approach to the notions
of identity and identity construction via a critical examination of previous theorizations of identity, especially those who used theatrical
metaphors in their work. Drawing mainly on Goffman (1959), Butler
(1990,1993), Bakhtin (1981, 1984) as well as Boal (1979, 1995, 2004),
we focus especially on the relationships between self and non-self in
identity constructions, narratives and practices. The last section of the
chapter explores and illustrates the relationships between these processes and different kinds of social action, inside and outside the theatre
space.

Our research project aimed at exploring, with the use of participatory
theatre techniques, how identities are constructed, communicated to
others, contested and authorized and how these are linked to particular
forms of social action, in this case of refugees' settlement in London and
integration into British life.

The research involved working with four refugee community organizations in East London – Kosovan (mainly youth group), Kurdish
(mainly theatre group), Somali (women's only) and an ethnically mixed
group of students of advice work. Two Playback performances and five
Forum Theatre workshops took place with each group. In addition,
post-theatre individual interviews were carried out with a selection of
members of the different groups.

The methodologies used in this project were Playback Theatre (Fox,
1986), where the audience tell stories based on their own experiences
that are then 'played back' to them by actors on stage and Forum Theatre

(Boal, 1979), where personal stories of conflict and oppression are acted out by the participants themselves who, by stepping in and replacing the protagonist, test out strategies for action. The Forum Theatre scene is the final product of several rehearsals and performance training, such as image work and character building, with the participants who become the performers. The semi-structured individual interviews explored further the choices taken and the suggestions made by participants during the theatre sessions, and more generally, their views on their lives in London.

The overall theoretical–methodological perspective of the research has been that all knowledge – and imagination – are situated (Stoetzler and Yuval-Davis, 2002) and that all analysis has to be intersectional and deconstructive. Intersectional (Brah and Phoenix, 2004; Crenshaw, 1989; Yuval-Davis, 2006a), as although each social category has its own discursive ontological basis, in concrete terms they are constituted and constructed by each other (e.g. there is no such category as 'refugees' as a concrete social category – they all differ from each other in terms of their gender, class, ethnicity, stage in the life cycle, sexuality, location, etc. as well as being unified, at least formally, by a common legal status and often by a common public discourse). This intersectional perspective aims at undermining essentialist and reified constructions of subjects.

Thus, while 'Refugees' as well as 'Muslims' tend to be constructed in the media and in the popular imagination in fixed, reified and stereotypical ways, our research was able to illustrate how false and problematic such constructions are. Although in three out of the four groups we worked with, the organizations were created around common ethnic origin (Kosovan, Kurdish and Somali), they have all challenged, through their narratives and performances as theatre participants, any homogenized construction of 'ethnicity', 'religious affiliation' and 'refugee' migratory status. They have all had very different histories of migration, as well as different social, economic and political locations as refugees in Britain. Moreover, they are all 'Muslims' but in very different ways from each other, as well as from their homogenized stereotypical media constructions (Crawley, 2005; Marfleet, 2007; Silverman and Yuval-Davis, 1999). Islam, in different versions, was sometimes very marginal to their lives as well as to their conceptions of self, while for others it constituted major cultural and ethnic performative focus of their lives. Yet for others it played an important role but only as a marker of boundary between them and other groupings of people in their country of origin as well as in Britain. We found similar trajectories also in the fourth group we worked with, a mixed group of students from refugee and migrant origins studying for a diploma in advice work. Overall, as the discourse analysis of the participants' narratives show, the research participants avoided using homogenized constructions of identities except when they referred to their experiences of encounters with the general public and especially with agents of the state.

Theorizing identity performances

Adopting such an epistemological approach to identities research so as to avoid essentialist analytical models and dichotomies of either macro-level structuralism or post-modern subjectivities as informers of identity formations has been stressed by sociologists for quite some time (Cohen, 1992; Gilroy, 1993; Hall, 1996).

Identity is a contested concept, used in multiple ways in different academic disciplines as well as in everyday discourse. Some, like Brubaker and Cooper (2000) and Anthias (2002), have even argued that as identity is being used in several, very different, ways, it is best to dispense with its use altogether. In our research we have retained the notion of identity but were careful to specify its boundaries. We have based our approach on Yuval-Davis's previous work (2006b), in which she locates identity on a different analytical level from other components of belonging – social location on the one hand and normative values on the other hand. These three analytical levels tend to collapse into each other in the discourse of identity politics, which is a particular discourse of the politics of belonging (that needs to be differentiated sharply from that of belonging).[1]

Identities may be conceived of as narratives, stories that people tell to themselves and others about who they are, who they are not and who/how they would like to be (Cavarero, 2000; Ricoeur, 1991). The related question of what they should do in relation to the latter is a major link between identity and social action – the subject matter of this chapter.

Identity narratives can be verbal, but can also be constructed as specific forms of practices (Fortier, 2000). Not all of them are about belonging to particular groupings and collectivities – they can be, for instance, about individual attributes, body images, vocational aspirations or sexual prowess. However, even such stories often relate, directly or indirectly, to self and/or others' perceptions of what being a member in such a grouping or collectivity (ethnic, racial, national, cultural, religious) might mean. These narratives of identities are more or less stable in different social contexts, more or less coherent, authorized and/or contested by self and others, depending on specific situational factors.

As mentioned above, there are many different theoretical approaches to the issue of identity. We have chosen to focus on three in particular that not only play central roles in debates on identity, but also use theatre and drama as a central metaphor in their theorizations and thus have affected our own approach to the subject.

Erving Goffman in his book *Presentation of Self in Everyday Life* (1959) analysed the interaction between what he called personality and society as theatrical 'impression management', involving teams of performers, front and back stage, role development and various techniques to protect the 'show' from possible disruptions. Goffman, however, in the preface to his book, also pointed out the difference between theatre and the so-called 'real life', as in the latter, there is no differentiation, unlike in the theatre, between the other players and the performance audience.

In the participatory theatre techniques which we use in our research project, the division between 'life' and 'stage', 'participants' and 'audience' is equally much more blurred and shifting than in traditional theatre, as one becomes the other or moves from one status to another. As we shall see later on, part of the project of participatory theatre, especially Forum, is to go beyond Goffman's framework and to use theatre techniques in order to achieve the deconstruction and transformation of such 'impression management' which defines the identity roles the refugees – and other 'disempowered' people – encounter in 'real life'. At the same time, as there is no imported script for the characters in participatory theatre, the relationships and interactions among the participants cannot be dismissed as having nothing real or actual happening to them during theatre sessions and the theatrical narratives can be interpreted as contingent identity narratives.

The presence or absence of the 'script' is crucial and relate to the question to what extent one can equate between a dramatic role – or even an everyday life role in the sociological Parsonian (1951) meaning – and an identity. In other words, are identities ascribed or an outcome of people's autonomous constructions?

In order to answer this question, we turned to the 'performativity' approach to identity, as developed by Judith Butler (1990). In Butler's approach the difference between theatre and life is much less clear than even in Goffman. Although she argues (1993) that the stage space is more easily regulated than the social space outside it, she conceives identities – presumably on and off stage – as performed within given discourses. For her 'performativity' is not 'the act by which a subject brings into being what she/he names, but, rather, as that reiterative power of discourse to produce the phenomena that it regulates and constrains' (1993: 2), and to which the subject is hailed and interpellated. However, the discourse is not just a given, but has a history – it 'accumulates the force of authority through the repetition or citation of a prior, authoritative set of practices' (ibid.: 227).

If the performative assumes a subject constitution within the authoritative and normative discourse, performance – again presumably on and off stage – can also be used as an act of resistance. Unlike in *Gender Trouble* (1990), Butler suggests in *Bodies that Matter* (1993) that performance, such as an act of 'drag', can be subversive, as 'it reflects on the imitative structure by which hegemonic gender is itself produced and disputes heterosexuality's claim on naturalness and originality' (ibid.: 125). As we shall see, participatory theatre techniques developed other techniques to challenge and subvert authoritative power relations.

However, one of the weaknesses of the Butlerian approach to identity construction is its lack of relationality. As Williams (2000: 78) points out, Butler, following Foucault (1986: 180), theorizes identity and subject production more as a grammatical entity than a speaking entity: 'The "I" is thus a citation of the place of the "I" in speech, where that place has a certain priority and anonymity with respect to the life it animates' (1993: 226). In this sense, the authoritative discourse plays a similar role to a pre-given text of a theatre play. Participatory and improvisation theatre, by contrast, avoids pre-given narratives and encourages more spontaneous ones that are emerging from the relations, time and space of the present, thus allowing space to interrogate performative discourses in its performances.

Furthermore, the Butlerian approach does not really enquire from where the performative – or subversive – identity narrative comes from. In our different theatre techniques used in this research, such as those of character building, the dramatic 'I' is actively constructed by the group through the participants asking relevant questions of the player, facilitating the creation of a 'shield/mask' for the 'I' as a character, which makes contestation of normative gender or other power discourses easier.

To understand these processes of character building as well as more generally the ways identity narratives are constructed, we have turned to Bakhtin (1981, 1984) who emphasizes another aspect of theatre practice, that is dialogue, as the constitutive element of identity construction. To use his words:

> to be means to be for the other and through him, for oneself. Man has no internal sovereign territory, he is always on the boundary; looking within himself he looks in the eyes of the other or through the eyes of the other. I cannot do without the other; I cannot become myself without the other; I must find myself in the other; finding the other in me in mutual reflection and perception.
>
> (1984: 311–12; see also Williams, 2000: 90)

Or – to use the words of one of our research participants about the Playback narratives and enactments:

> I liked the stories coming back to the audience. You don't know what is your part in the story but if somebody else's doing it for you then you can see(clearer) what is your part in it.
>
> (SBI1)

The dialogical construction of identity, then, is both reflective and constitutive. It is not individual or collective, but an 'in-between' state of 'becoming' in which processes of identity construction, authorization and contestation take place. It is important to emphasize, however, that dialogical processes, by themselves, are not an alternative to viewing identity constructions as informed by power relations but just the opposite – analysing the processes via which identity narratives are constructed in the communal context is vital in order to understand the ways that intersectional power relations operate within the group. Unlike Frosh and Baraitser (2003), who, following Levinas (1985) and Benjamin (1998), call for a recognition of the other as an ethical act, we consider recognition as a double-edged act, in which rejection as well as acceptance is possible, within the boundaries of 'us' as well as that of 'them', involving contestations as well as authorizations of identity constructions. It is from this perspective (sometimes called 'transversal' and is considered an alternative perspective to that of identity politics, Yuval-Davis, 2006c) that one should examine the dyad of me/us-them that the dialogical approach constructs as an alternative to a divisive dyad of me/others. In such a transversal dialogical epistemology, there is recognition that from each positioning the world is seen differently, and thus any knowledge based on just one positioning is 'unfinished' (to differentiate from 'invalid') and thus there is a need of a dialogue between people of differential positionings. Transversal politics recognize and respect differences but views them as encompassed by, rather than replaced, notions of equality. Transversal politics differentiates – both conceptually and politically – between positioning, identity and values and does not assume a fixed relationship between them. People with similar positioning and/or identity can have very different social and political values. The boundaries of transversal dialogue are those of common values rather than of common positionings or identifications.[2]

Identity and social action in participatory theatre

Until now we focused on the ways dramatic metaphors of theatre, performance and dialogue have been useful in our explorations of processes of identity constructions using the methodology of participatory theatre.

If identities are narratives (performative and/or dialogical) about self, constructing more or less coherent sense of 'personal order' (Wetherell, 2003) which can be individual or collective, they are necessarily closely related to narratives of personal and collective memories that provide cognitive, emotive and imaginative endorsement to these narratives as a way of 'making sense' to self and the world. These modes of 'making sense' may vary greatly not only between the ways individuals and different others construct them from their situated gazes (Stoetzler and Yuval-Davis, 2002) but also in the ways the same individual might view her/himself in different temporal and spatial positionings. However, central planks of these constructions of self are biographical and as such are closely related to social events and social actions.

As Boal (2004: 39), following Brecht (1965), stated, theatre provides an excellent space in which identities and social action are intimately related:

> Theatre is a conflict, struggle, movement, transformation, not simply the exhibition of states of mind. It is a verb, not an adjective. To act is to produce an action, and every action produces a reaction-conflict.

The question is what kind of actions, by whom and for what kind of purpose.

When discussing the history of Forum Theatre that he founded, Augusto Boal (1995) tells the story of how he and his revolutionary theatre group used to perform theatre plays on social and political oppression at the end of which they called the audience to go and fight for the revolution. They did this until one day, Virgilio, a Brazilian farmer, approached him after the performance and called him and the group to join with him and his comrades in carrying out the armed struggle. Boal had to admit that neither he nor his fellow actors had the knowledge, means or intention to fight themselves – they saw their role purely as agitators, inspiring people to fight. Virgilio told him how disappointed he felt that while they encouraged the peasants to sacrifice their lives for the struggle, they themselves could go any time back to their comfortable homes and turned his back to him.

Boal never forgot Virgilio. This was just the first step in his development of Forum Theatre in which he gradually asked the audience more what forms of social actions and interventions would be suitable in their particular situations. Eventually his performances culminated with the members of the audience actually coming to the stage, showing in their own words and actions, what kinds of alternative strategies they thought might be effective in particular moments.

In Playback Theatre the members of the audience do not make interventions in the dramatic scenes. Rather, the actual telling of their own narratives before the other members of the audience and members of the theatre team becomes part of the social action that is taking place in the theatre space, as well as the inspiration of the actors who improvise 'playing back' these narratives.

The fact that in either participatory theatre technique there is no direct link or call for particular social action outside the theatre does not mean, of course, that there might not be a link between identity narrations within the theatre space and outside social action, either actual or desirable. Boal (2004) claims that this kind of theatre is a rehearsal for real life, but as we observed, 'real life' was also very much what was taking place within the participatory theatre sessions themselves, which included a wide range of social processes, especially in the groups which long pre-existed our theatre sessions. The active embodied engagement in different identity constructions that the dramatic performance elicited is another arena of social action that takes place within the theatre space.

In our participatory theatre sessions we observed not only how participants identified with each others' stories; not only how, sometimes, especially around processes of new character building, they had the space of dissent from common performative identity constructions, but also how they were able to go beyond all these through their newly acquired identity/roles as performers and just imagine themselves as youngsters, as Londoners, as having different gender and ethnic backgrounds. These particular imaginations, identities and actions mobilized by the identity of the 'actor-citizen', in what makes participatory theatre a transformative action tool.

One of the most important elements in this is the relationship between the particular resources (economic, social, cultural, political) that such biographies have provided the individual and the groupings in their pursuit of particular identity-related social actions. One of the most known developmental theorist of identities, Erich Erikson (1968: 314) once said (quoted by Phoenix and Rattansi, 2005):

> I must register a certain impatience with the faddish equation, never suggested by me, of the term identity with the question 'Who am I?' the pertinent question, if it can be put into first person at all, would be 'What do I want to make of myself and what do I have to work with?

In other words, Erickson emphasizes the dynamic, ever changing, process of identity construction and the ways it relates (but is not reducible to), on the one hand, to one's normative value system, and, on the other hand, to one's social location, positioning on various grids of social, political and economic power, which would provide a certain range of resources and leverages, within which one continuously position oneself and act (Yuval-Davis, 2006b). The social actions people were involved in as part of/against/apart from social collectivities to which they and/or others consider they belong to determine to a great extent who they and others think they are. They also determine what/where/how they want to get on with their life projects and what social, political, economic and cultural resources they have to mobilize to support them in these endeavours. Moreover, narrating identity constructions which are continuously being authorized and/or contested by individual and collective 'us' and/or 'the other' is in itself part of ongoing dialogical social actions.

The me/others and me/us dyads constitute two very different approaches to the construction of identity and have very different implications regarding the relationships between individual and collective identities, as well as between identity and social action. We found in our research evidence of processes of identity constructions that followed both pathways. The first was usually confined to constructions of reified, racialized identities and to situations in which the refugees were confronted by official discourse related to who they were and how they should behave. The second, much more contested, shifting and multiple, related to group processes of power dynamics and constructions of collective identities. Both of these processes involved different forms of social actions within the theatre space, which related both to the social relationships of the different people within that space, as well as to various replications of (and preparations to) social actions outside it.

Identity processes and social action within and outside the theatre space – some illustrative examples

The narratives collected in the research provide us with an embodied, illustrative and dialogical knowledge (Kaptani and Yuval-Davis, 2008).

This can be seen not only in the specific narratives which are told, listened to, played and responded to in various legitimizing or contesting ways, but also in the accumulative nature of the separate narratives, that often built on each other, directly, in opposition or just by association. The dialogical and non-linear accumulative production of identity narratives in playback illustrates what we argued above about the shifted boundaries of the 'us' and 'them'. Especially when the expectations of the 'me' to belong to 'us' are not materialized thus the 'us' becomes 'them'. The stories came from the differentially situated members of the mixed group which started by one participant's experience of being in a Turkish restaurant in Hackney (she herself did not come from Turkey) and feeling the ambivalence of multicultural Britain as both home and not-home. This triggered another story by a participant from Turkey, who shared with us the experience of, feeling lonely and newly arrived from Turkey, seeing a Turkish restaurant and entering it, he expected to finally find 'home away from home', only to encounter a waiter who was completely indifferent and rejected any pre-ordained emotional bonds to which their common ethnicity might commit. Another story of belonging followed in which a Kurdish woman told us how she could feel confident and 'at home' in particular places in London and with particular groups of friends and fellow students, but when she stepped away from these sheltered spaces she felt she was looked at as a 'foreigner' and could not be understood and accepted. Following this, the 'Playback' process of individual story telling led to a whole debate among the group members about language, belonging and exclusion, and it was performed as a medley by the creative team at the end of the session.

If in Playback the accumulative narratives were distinguishably individual even though linked to each other, during the Forum Theatre sessions they culminated in a collective embodied narrative. The image work exercises, in which people 'sculpt' images using their bodies and/or objects, provided a graphic illustration of how dialogical contexts can be penetrated by differential inputs and power relations and construct the 'us' from the separate 'me's'. For example, in the Kosovo group we asked the participants to construct an image of 'power' in a space which contained only a table, few chairs and a small plastic bottle. Each member of the group constructed an image of power by placing the chairs in her/his chosen configurations. After all the members of the group had made several individual attempts, they were asked to compose one image collectively without talking to each other. For a while the different members of the group were constructing their own images, dismantling those of others and reconstructing different images by taking turns. Gradually, however, the actions of the different members started to complement each other's more until they all agreed on one common image: The chairs were put up in hierarchical positions, a young male, who held a dominant position in the group (and who had consistently dismantled others' constructions of the image which did not include him on top), was standing on top of them holding the bottle, and the rest of the group members were posing in different subservient positions directed to him.

There were also pressures towards group conformity in the Kurdish group and the establishment of boundaries of what acceptably can be expressed in the theatre space and what is not acceptable. One of the male group leaders, reflecting in his interview on a 'deviant' story of one of the participants who described her family's sufferings as a result of her father being sent to fight in the homeland for many years, asked, 'which is the most important – the life of a family here or the struggle of millions of people in the "homeland"?' (FSI). An echo of a similar 'internalised' censorship was heard in the story of a woman who, through Playback, told us about her depression. She said that to see her story publicly acted out, made it permissible for her to acknowledge it and not to negate it as something that 'I was not allowed to feel because I should feel lucky to be in the UK. You see, the important thing has always been the struggle back "home" and not the struggle of my life here' (MBI).

In this way, the theatre provided space for appropriation and transformation of collective norms and provided possibilities for longer term social change, while at the same time it continued to reflect some of the wider intersectional social context in which the participants lived and related to each other.

The importance of the 'safe' theatre space when dealing with outside power dynamics can be seen clearly in cases of role reversal in which the participants replayed roles similar to those in which in 'real life' they felt completely disempowered. For example, a Somali refugee played the role of a mother who was called to the head-teacher's office to explain why her daughter did not attend classes at school. The daughter had been bullied and beaten up severely at school so her mother allowed her to stay at home that week. The mother, with an obvious lack of confidence, fear of being reprimanded and very limited English, tried to explain the situation but to no avail, while the head-teacher demanded that she fill in an accident form. This, of course, she could not do. In the Forum Theatre scene the participants' interventions managed to compel the head-teacher to telephone an interpreter to help explain the situation, but it was still not good enough. The head-teacher demanded that the interpreter come to the school in person to help fill in the form, which of course she was not able to at a moment's notice. This was the last straw for the mother. In this atmosphere of distrust she lost her temper and in the context of the theatre shouted at the head-teacher, in her own language, 'you do not believe me or the interpreter – you treat me like an animal!' As the participant actor reflected later on:

> I felt quite powerful [vis-à-vis] this person, [who was] sitting and thinking that they [she] are, you know, they can do everything and I could talk to her like I wanted to talk and get rid of my feelings, which was good really.
>
> (SV1)

One of the refugees in the mixed group transformed her attitude to the 'other', this time other migrants and refugees like herself, by being encouraged to actively intervene in one of the scenes. Although she came to the United Kingdom originally as a refugee, she has been working as an advice worker and she said that for the last ten years was used to being listened to by people, as she was always instructing and advising them. This is what had happened in the first sessions of the Forum Theatre in which she was always only instructing the other members of the group what to do instead of taking action herself by embodying the 'oppressed'. She realized that she did not have the confidence outside this role of an official adviser to take on an action herself, and that she had stopped actively listening to others except when she was asked to solve a specific problem for her clients. Through Forum Theatre she realized that she had to build up her confidence, share more and listen to other people's experiences, backgrounds and views. The best way for her to undertake this transformation was to act by taking on the characters of different people. She said,

> I was used to run away, make excuses or disappear as I did not like to intervene because of my lack of confidence but through Forum I learnt that it was beneficial to actively intervene and listen to other people's point of views, experiences and learn from their actions. I realised that some other people in the group who are not refugees also feel like me and that I'm not on my own.
>
> (MZI)

Social relations outside the theatre space affected – and were affected by – the actions within the theatre space. These could enhance existing power relations, but they often also facilitated new modes of resistance and challenge. Moreover, the theatre space offered a space for discussion and debate around issues and identity performative norms that often were not allowed to emerge elsewhere, in the community context outside the theatre space and shed light to formations of 'community' and 'refugee' as not be a homogenous 'us'.

For example, in one of our groups, while we were developing the characters for a family scene, debates started on what it entails to be a young woman in London. A male participant stated that girls can only become emancipated by attending community centres and leading a meaningful existence by following collective values. A young female participant argued back, stating that community centres are strict and do not reflect the needs and way of life of her generation. Another example relates to the participants' opinions and interventions on a domestic conflict scene in the mixed group. The debate took place among the participants regarding a scene where a wife who wanted to study and find work (and was offered help to do so via the Sure Start programme) argued her case with her husband who had his doubts about her being able to look after the children and the household while working. Participants' interventions and opinions varied and brought up conflictual expectations and aspects of the participants' identities in the group, based both on their differential social locations and on their differential normative value systems. Some of the male participants wanted the woman to wait till her husband gave her the permission to talk about her issues, while some of the women were confrontational and adopted a feminist activist approach, arguing that they were not going to cook and serve their husbands any more until they showed them more respect. Other women's interventions were based on cultural and gendered prescriptions such as 'men are like babies', and on reasoning, arguing that, 'human beings have [possess] reason, so the couple will be able to negotiate'. The most impact came from an intervention by a woman who told the 'husband': 'I'm not going to cook and serve you food anymore – eat me if you like, as you are treating me like food, you swallow me and spit me.' (MF1)

In addition to different roles and interventions from different participants in the groups, changes started to occur within one 'self'. For example, a Kosovan boy, used to revel in a 'stiff upper-lip' masculinity and held positions of power in the group, found himself, after several sessions, sharing with the group his vulnerability and pain when he was caught, as a child interpreter, between the wrath of his father and the aggressive commands of the social worker. Even when the incident was more widely known and shared among the group members, as in the case of the Somali woman whose house was burnt by racist youngsters in the neighbourhood, the theatre scene gave a new poignancy to her story. As one of the participants of the group stated: 'I heard about it but I could not picture it, visualise it, until they done it. To see things as they happened. When you hear it, it is more distant. Our emotions are not connected to it than when you see it' (SBI1).

The theatre medium was particularly useful for the participants to reproduce and expose some of the oppressive social and governmental practices directed at them and other members of their communities.

The lack of interpreting and the complicity of the state towards using young family members instead of professionals was one of the main themes in the Kosovo group. After stories told in Playback and enacted by the participants themselves later in Forum, the solutions found were either those of young people needing to speak up and negotiate with their parents the difficulty they experience in attempting to mediate between them and the statutory agents, and/or the need for the community centre to provide an interpreter scheme. The person whose scene it was found the courage to tell his 'Dad' in the theatre space what he had never told his father: 'Dad, you know what; get a translator next time because I'm not coming.' (LP1).

Indeed, what took place within the participatory theatre workshops provided the space for these solutions to emerge and materialize even beyond the actual workshops, as the Kosovo group has indeed created a scheme for helping families with interpreting!!

In the Somali Group the participants found that, having the chance to both perform themselves, as Somali refugees, and as the 'other': Home Office officials and Head-teachers made them realize that their lack of understanding procedures and their associated anxiety about can create misunderstandings and intensify conflicts. They reflected at the end of the sessions that better mediatory systems have to be put in place and the Centre is working towards that, especially at schools.

Even when no practical solution could be found, the participants were able to explore the connections between issues on the domestic front and more general state policies. For example, in the domestic conflict scene, the participants pointed out how policies, such as Sure Start, that are aimed at support and integration of women refugees can be divisive when no suitable support is being given to the husbands and when state policies are top-down and not case-sensitive. As one participant said,

> They (the couple) have to see among themselves what is good for themselves rather somebody imposing them. One organisation is working with her that way while the other organisation is not helping him and rejecting him. It seems, the system without realising it is causing the friction.
>
> (SF3)

Not all of the scenes in every group could be successfully 'forumized' – that is become a basis for more efficient and successful strategies of coping with such practices in real life, as sometimes the participants could not find suitable levers to prevent their sense of disempowerment and fear. However, even in such cases, sharing through enacting the situation, and trying to find ways of combating it, created a shared sense of 'us' against 'them'. Furthermore, they achieved a sense of empowerment through the solidarity and humour shared among them, even if no better ways were found to empower the participants for future social actions.

Such was what came to be known as 'the Communication House scene'. The 'Communication House' is where asylum seekers in London have to report, not knowing whether after the interviews they will be allowed to stay in the United Kingdom, be detained or deported. The tool of drama was very powerful here, allowing the participants to replicate the physical sense of complete disempowerment, being stripped of any possible contact with a supportive outside world. They were stripped of any personal items, they were guarded by police, they were not allowed to have an advocate or interpreter and they could be detained or deported any time without warning. In that scene, the participants could not find a way to empower or assert themselves – they ended up trying to resolve their situation by attempting to apply either threats of aggression or self-humiliating flattery, mockery or even bribery. They were always defeated. Through scenes like the above we could 'view' and 'look at' state policies and how the asylum seekers themselves experience them.

While in the 'Communication House' all refugees are constructed in one performative identity narrative of 'the other', in most everyday situations which confront the refugees, their differential social locations, identifications and normative value systems provide them with different tools to deal and act with whatever and whoever confront them. We would like to end this section of the chapter by recounting the differential ways in which members of the different refugee communities with whom we worked dealt with a similar situation, that is that of a parent and the sick child. This theme arose during Playback sessions in all groups, and can illustrate the differential social and cultural capital that the different refugees could mobilize and act with, in civil society as well as in encounters with state agents.

The first story was that of the Kosovan mother whose baby suffered from a mysterious illness that the hospital could not explain, even though they brought an interpreter. Being of a European origin, she decided to ask the doctors for the Latin name of the illness, and able to contact her relatives in the 'homeland' by phone, could get their help in contacting local doctors and finding out that her baby suffered from jaundice. Another example was that of the Kurdish refugee, a film actor, who was able to mobilize his professional resources and use them creatively, after his child, who suffered from seizures but always recovered before the ambulance came, meaning that the doctors could not find anything wrong with him. Once he videoed such a fit, they diagnosed epilepsy and could prescribe the right drugs.

The Somali woman, however, was the one most deprived of such helpful resources. When her child was found to suffer from unexplained bruises, nobody believed her that this is an inherited medical condition and both her children were taken away. Only after she contacted the Somali women's community centre could she mobilize a public and legal campaign in support of her case. This is but one example of how community organizations can provide empowering resources for racialized, marginalized and excluded members of civil society.

Conclusion

In this chapter we examined some of the ways participatory theatre techniques can help us to understand processes of identity construction, communication, authorization and contestation, as well as the relationships between these and social action. Of particular importance was the examination of the relationship between individual and collective identities, the construction of me/us as well as us/them and the permeation of power relationships in dialogical 'us' constructions as well as in us/them social spaces. Moreover, we also demonstrated that although all identities are relational, not all identity constructions need to be related to the 'I' space and that participatory theatre helps us to understand the complexity and plurality of identity constructions as well as processes of identity appropriation and transformation. Importantly, however, the identity performances involved other characters apart form the self, both those with whom the participants experienced a conflictual or oppressive relationship – real or imaginary – and those of the other characters included in the scene building. By taking on different roles, the participants were constructing temporal and varied identities and at the same time were able to transfer, adjust or transform cultural, social and ideological positions from one role to another. Nevertheless it is important to emphasize that, as in the case of all characterizations, the embodiment of the roles by people who are differentially socially located in terms of gender, ethnicity, stage in the life cycle, class and so on affect profoundly the ways they are imagined and enacted, hence the importance of the intersectional perspective when analysing identities and social action.

Working with participatory theatre techniques also provided us with an excellent tool to examine the relationships between identity and social action and the ways performance can dislocate and challenge performative identity constructions as well as provide a range of strategies for empowering social actions.

Notes

1. While a sense of belonging is personal, the politics of belonging are specific political projects aimed at constructing belonging in particular ways to particular collectivity/ies which are, at the same time, being constructed themselves by these projects in very specific ways and within particular boundaries.
2. Please see also Yuval-Davis (1994) and Cockburn and Hunter (1999).

References

Anthias, F. (2002) Beyond Feminism and Multiculturalism: Locating Difference and the Politics of Location. *Women's Studies International Forum* 25(3), 275–86.

Bakhtin, M. (1981) *The Dialogical Imagination*. Austin: The University of Texas Press.

Bakhtin, M. (1984) *Problems of Dostoevsky's Poetics*. Manchester: University of Manchester Press.

Benjamin, J. (1998) *Shadow of the Other: Intersubjectivity and Gender in Psychoanalysis*. New York: Routledge.

Boal, A. (1979) *Theatre of the Oppressed*. London: Pluto Press.

Boal, A. (1995) *Rainbow of Desire*. London: Routledge.

Boal, A. (2004) *Games for Actors and Non Actors*. London: Routledge.

Brah, A. and Phoenix, A. (2004) 'Ain't I a Woman'? Revisiting Intersectionality. *Journal of International Women's Studies* 5(3), 75–86.

Brecht, B. (1965) *The MessingKauf Dialogues*. London: Methuen.

Brubaker, R. and Cooper, F. (2000) Beyond Identity. *Theory and Society* August, 29, 1–47.

Butler, J. (1990) *Gender Trouble: Feminism and the Subversion of Identity*. New York: Routledge.

Butler, J. (1993) *Bodies that Matter*. New York: Routledge.

Cavarero, A. (2000) *Relating Narratives: Storytelling and Selfhood*. London: Routledge.

Cockburn, C. and Hunter, L. (1999) Transversal Politics. Special Issue of *Soundings* 12 (summer).

Cohen, P. (1992) Hidden Narratives in Theories of Racism. In J. Donald and A. Rattansi (eds.) *'Race', Culture and Difference*. London: Sage.

Crawley, H. (2005) *Evidence on Attitudes to Asylum and Immigration: What We Know, Don't Know and Need to Know*. Centre on Migration, Policy and Society Working Chapter No. 23, Oxford University. *www.icar.org.uk/pdf/micioo04*.

Crenshaw, K. (1989) *Demarginalizing the Intersection of Race and Sex*. Chicago: University of Chicago Press.

Erikson, E.H. (1968) *Identity: Youth and Crisis*. New York: Norton.

Fortier, A. (2000) *Migrant Belongings: Memory, Space, Identities*. Oxford: Berg.

Foucault, M. (1986) What Is an Author? In P. Rabinow (ed.) *The Foucault Reader*. Harmondsworth: Penguin.

Fox, J. (1986) *Acts of Service – Spontaneity, Commitment, Tradition in the Non Scripted Theatre*. USA: Tusitala Publishing.

Gilroy, P. (1993) *The Black Atlantic. Modernity and Double Consciousness*. London: Verso.

Frosh, S. and Baraitser, L. (2003) Thinking, Recognition and Otherness. *Psychoanalytic Review* 90(6), 771–89.

Goffman, E. (1959) *The Presentation of Self in Everyday Life*. London: Allen Lane.

Hall, S. (1996) Who Needs Identity? In S. Hall and P. du Gay (eds.) *Questions of Cultural Identity*. London: Sage.

Kaptani, E. and Yuval-Davis, N. (2008) Participatory Theatre as a Research Methodology. *Sociolological Research On Line* 13(5), September.

Levinas, E. (1985) *Ethics and Infinity*. Pittsburgh, PA: Duquesne University Press.

Marflett, P. (2007) *Love Immigrant Labour, Hate Migrants: Refugees in a Global Era*. Basingstoke: Palgrave.

Phoenix, A. and Rattansi, A. (2005) Proliferating Theories: Self and Identity in Post-Eriksonian Context: A Rejoinder to Berzonsky, Kroger, Levine, Phinney, Schachter and Weigert and Gecas. *Identity* 5(2), 205–25.

Ricoeur, P. (1991) Life in Quest of Narrative. Narrative Identity. In D. Wood (ed.) *On Paul Ricoeur: Narrative and Interpretation*. London: Routledge.

Silverman, M. and Yuval-Davis, N. (1999) Jews, Arabs and the Theorization of Racism in Britain and France. In A. Brah, M. Hickman and M. Mac (eds.) *Thinking Identities: Ethnicity, Racism and Culture*. Basingstoke: Macmillan.

Stoetzler, M. and Yuval-Davis, N. (2002) Standpoint Theory, Situated Knowledge – and the Situated Imagination. *Feminist Theory* 3(3), 315–34.

Wetherell, M. (2003) Paranoia, Ambivalence and Discursive Practices: Concepts of Position and Positioning in Psychoanalysis and Discursive Psychology. In R. Harre and F. Moghaddam (eds.) *The Self and Others: Positioning Individuals and Groups in Personal, Political and Cultural Contexts*. New York: Praeger/Greenwood Publishers.

Williams, R. (2000) *Making Identity Matter: Identity, Society and Social Interaction*. Durham: Sociology Press.

Yuval-Davis, N. (1994) Women, Ethnicity and Empowerment. *Feminism and Psychology* 4(1), 179–97.

Yuval-Davis, N. (2006a) Intersectionality and Feminist Politics. *European Journal of Women's Studies* 13(3), 193–209.

Yuval-Davis, N. (2006b) Belonging and the Politics of Belonging. *Patterns of Prejudice* 40(3), 197–214.

Yuval-Davis, N. (2006c) Human/Women's Rights and Feminist Transversal Politics. In M. Marx Ferree and A.M. Tripp (eds.) *Transnational Feminisms: Women's Global Activism and Human Rights*. New York: New York University Press.

4
Tales of Two or Many Worlds? When 'Street' Kids Go Global

Gareth A. Jones and Sarah Thomas de Benítez[1]

As their spatialised nomenclature suggests, street children or youth are expected to be located in, or their lives related to, a specific geographical locale. In the minds of most casual observers, and even many 'informed' ones, young people will frequently be described as 'always there', be it at a market, bus depot or road junction. These young people may be working, and perhaps sleeping too in public spaces – or they may be seen to do little more than 'hang out' – whatever, there is a perception that their lives are devoid of opportunities for change and the sense is one of permanence.[2] Having 'run away', young people on the street seem to become a fixture of particular locales, though simultaneously marked as 'out of place' within them (Ennew and Swart-Kruger, 2003). At the same time, it is understood that young people on the street move around and use migration as part of their survival strategies, to avoid police, vigilantes and social workers, and are often 'moved on' as part of clean-up campaigns (Scheper-Hughes and Hoffman, 1998). But despite earlier migration histories, the perception is that movement has served to get people to this point where daily lives display enormous imagination to create a presence, but little hope of getting out (Gigengack, 1999; Beazley, 2002; Young, 2003; Van Blerk, 2005). Departures from the street are often described by those left behind as short term, suffixed with the comment 'they will be back'.

Indeed, it is often the researcher that has a sense of being mobile. Our research with young people whose lives revolve around the streets involved frequent extended meetings over a number of years.[3] During this time, after a period of absence from meeting one group at the market an almost ritualistic conversation would open with questions about how far *we* had come. In the case of Gareth and Sarah, our willingness to travel distances to see them was a constant source of amusement and bemusement for the participants. Questions would check how long it took to fly to Mexico from 'England', as well as the cost, the need for a passport, whether one could take alternative routes or even swim. Conversations of course would often involve the query as to whether we might be able to take one of them with us. Twenty-one-year-old Ramon, for example, every inch tough looking and streetwise insisted that he could come to England and work in the university. He knew, he said, that he had left school at primary level, and admitted to being illiterate, but he could learn. After all, he pointed out, 'there is nothing here for me, washing windscreens, doing the same thing every day. For how long?'. Much as it might have been intriguing to introduce Ramon into the rarefied atmosphere of a UK university we all knew that his request was part of an everyday tactic for searching out possibilities of change however far fetched. Even for Elsa, coming less than halfway across the city from her home, there would be occasional comments about what her neighbourhood was like and whether they could visit. Our participants knew full well that we could arrive and depart at will, and they expected us to do so. This was an observation born of experience. They had had so many encounters with government and NGO outreach workers, church groups, even a camera crew from Spain, all of whom sought to empathise and befriend, almost all of whom left. Our return therefore was important, a sign of some commitment and honesty on our part, but underscoring the apparent immobility on theirs.[4]

The exception to this immobility or fixity is the possibility of deterioration and possibly death. Street children and youth are seen to be 'wasting away', through drugs or lack of food, of succumbing to disease or infection, to be maimed, to present learning difficulties or non-normative 'social behaviours'. Their identities are assumed to form in the breach – through the lack or loss – and despite their 'difference' street children are assumed to be the same. Our research questions the ascription of identities as fixed, singular and ultimately determined, and drawing on Butler's (1993) ideas of performativity we have questioned how identity labels are acquired, and embrace the artifice by 'acting out' a set of presumed actions and emotions (Herrera et al., 2009). Yet in trying to imagine identities as open-ended we are uncomfortable with the deployment of euphemistic or metaphorical labels for identities as 'fractured', 'fragmented', 'splintered', 'schizophrenic', or referring back with hindsight to our original research proposal, as 'multiple'. In conducting ethnographic fieldwork with young people who *do* undertake prolonged drug use, present learning difficulties and display suicidal ideation, these terms jar with our ethical sensibility (see Jones et al., 2007). The process of ethnography has allowed us to maintain a sense of indeterminacy in our research by exploring the 'something else' in accounts of daily life, the 'subjective, wilful, and complexly and compellingly human' (Hannerz, 1969: 14), that allow people to 'get by' and resist the impositions of others. We have considered whether alternative notions such as 'blurred' or 'unresolved' identities are an improvement, avoiding a steer to deteriorations or break ups/downs, or simply represent beguiling possibilities.

Such terms are, of course, only hints as to the fluidity of identities. In this chapter we want to suggest that street children and youths' lives reflect a complex relationship between identities 'recognised' as fixed and fluid subject positions, between mobility and stasis, as being cast as 'out of place' and embedded in relations to family, nation, as well as work, and religion. Specifically, we ground the chapter in the life histories of two young people, Esteban and Jiménez, whose early lives as children involved extended periods living and working on the streets in Mexico but who subsequently migrated to the United States and Spain. We position their narratives and biographies in the context of writings on mobilities and 'subaltern cosmopolitanism'. We want to consider the experiences of Esteban and Jiménez in terms of their migration, their physical movement, and how they deployed and represented a series of mobilities. Here we mean that their spatial movement has been embedded in social as well as economic life and relations, and in turn their identities have been reflected in and affected by their movements. We draw from their narratives, however, that they both in different ways display a shift over time from 'reluctant' to 'harnessed' mobility.

Mobilities, transnational identities and failed globalisers

The perception of young people on the streets as static is in contrast with the prevailing sense of (hyper)-mobility and fluidity that pervades accounts of contemporary modernity. Ideas of movement, especially over significant distances and across borders, have shifted in short time from a linear conceptualisation of sending–transmitting–receiving, of step-wise moves and possible returns, to concepts of networks, webs, threads and rhizomes (Hannam et al., 2006). Shifts to more multi-locational, diasporic, transnational or post-global arrangements have brought increasing awareness of the complicated associations conjured up by categories such as family, community, ethnicity and nationhood (Castles, 2002; Chamberlain and Leydesdorff, 2004; Glick Schiller et al., 1992). An earlier complacency that identity categories were relatively stable was in any case being challenged. Indeed, the metaphorical 'character' for this new mobile age of unfixed identities was according to Bauman (1995: 91) the 'stroller, the vagabond, the tourist and the player' or for Gupta and Ferguson (1992) the figure of the nomad. The unsettling suggestion was that in a world inhabited by mobile 'strangers', that identities were being disrupted and reformed accentuating what were already considered to be identities in flux. As Vertovec (2001) notes, transnationalism and identity sit awkwardly with one another; transnational networks operate among people who feel a common identity, often based on a place of origin, while many contemporary migrants negotiate their identities, often with great difficulty, within social worlds that span many places (e.g., Menjívar, 2002). Identity attachments achieved 'away' moreover might depend on direct nostalgia for 'home' (Parkin, 1999), while the very notion of 'home' has changed radically (Golbert, 2001). Although Bauman argues that the 'stranger' still holds the memory of having been somewhere else, emotively suggesting that '[s]he still smells of other places', the cultural effects of (hyper)-mobility were deemed to hold new promise for identity and sociality (D'Andrea, 2006), transgressing cultural distances in a spontaneous multicultural 'conviviality' (Gilroy, 2008) or shared cosmopolitanism (Hannerz, 1996).

One concern of course was of privileging 'a' cosmopolitan mobility (Ahmed, 1999; Gidwani, 2006). Poorer people were rarely described as mobiles or cosmopolitans – lacking the purchasing power to buy into the consumption patterns, hook into cyber frontiers, their lifestyles enclaved by illegalities, linguistic limits or host intolerance, their movements might be massive but their identities a little too 'sticky'. Transnational lives might be understood as forms of resistance to exclusion and oppression 'at home', using global networks and localised linkages open up livelihood opportunities (Kothari, 2008), but it was not clear if mobility within a global economy demanding 3-D labour (dirty, demanding, dangerous) and where states have erected barriers to citizenship really did 'trip up' exclusion and empower, or were the means for continued oppression (Benhabib, 1999). To avoid an elision of mobilities and cosmopolitans with wealth, education and taste, and thereby representing the 'others' as parochial and eschewing new identity possibilities, a number of writers argued that case for 'subaltern cosmopolitans' (Gidwani, 2006; Jeffrey and McFarlane, 2008; Kothari, 2008). This work suggests that there is nothing essentially progressive about cosmopolitanism. Working out how to live in different cultural settings, create economic and social contacts, and deal with ideas of home and belonging from positions of apparent 'outsiderness' is vital if we are to appreciate what is happening with global mobilities. From the standpoint of Esteban and Jiménez this endeavour is suggestive of some valuable questions. How do young people attributed with no great sense of 'home' – as 'street children' – understand their experiences of movement? How has mobility affected sociability, given that street life may have involved relating to a group and mobility as an individual stranger? What does 'transnational community' mean, if anything, to young people who in some sense ran away from 'home' or family networks? How has the experience of moving lead them to appraise their life before – in societies they might feel let them down, their life in the 'new home' or what awaits them on return? How and what do we understand of these people, now regarded as 'former' street children – what have they now become?

Our research considers mobility of young people from Mexico. With over 20 million people of Mexican origin residing abroad, few countries have been more challenged to reconcile their identities to ideas of migrancy, transnationalism or 'Diaspora'. Government concern for the implications to 'Mexicanidad' has resulted in instructions to consuls and cultural groups to support national days, festivals, film and food fairs to reinvigorate an idea of Mexican citizenship (Levitt and de la Dehesa, 2003). Most of the 'Tijuaneros' – the vernacular term for Mexicans making their way 'north' – expect to cross the border illegally (see Martínez, 2002; Quinones, 2007), an endeavour that in 2005 the Mexican Ministry of Foreign Relations appeared to endorse with the free distribution of 1.5 million copies of 'The Mexican Immigrant' handbook providing details on how to cross a border increasingly 'hardened' with bespoke surveillance equipment, the use of biometric measures and secondment of military personnel (Amoore, 2006; Chavez, 2008). The handbook was just more evidence to nativist lobbies in the USA such as the Federation for American Immigration Reform that 'mobile Mexicans' would undermine 'white' identities and 'Balkanise' the nation state through a 'clash of civilisations'. For would-be 'subaltern cosmopolitans' without visas and having to avoid enthusiastic vigilante groups from the infamous Neighbourhood Ranch Watch and the Minute Men, the only recourse was the 'killing deserts' in what Rosas (2006) terms a process of 'managed violence'. For most Mexicans then mobility is far from and 'hyper'; those successful earn the opportunity to experience what Gómez-Pena (1996) has called 'Othercide', or The Killing of Otherness.

A second concern with the mobile cosmopolitan, subaltern or not, is how we consider age. On the one hand, we might highlight young people 'caught up' in the global flows of goods, technologies and 'lifestyles', and focus on the possibilities for new, unstable or destabilising, 'youth' identities (see Wildermuth and Dalsgaard, 2006; Baulch, 2008). On the other, the subaltern migrant is often depicted as the 'unaccompanied minor' whose narrative reflects both the determination and difficulties of overcoming the friction of transnationality. The poster for Sonia Nazario's film 'Enrique's Journey' shows the back of a young boy on top of a train looking into a misty future along the tracks. The film's subtitle – 'the story of a boy's dangerous odyssey to reunite with his mother' – speaks to a Homeric quality, a journey of (self-)discovery amidst danger, the maternal bond that drives it all, and the strong sense that despite the train from Guatemala through Mexico being known as the 'train of death' that it all works out well in the end. Some research, however, expresses unease that young people who grow up 'apart' from parents may face difficulties with intimacy and norms (Salazar Parreñas, 2005), others that parental pressure to maintain links with 'home' through family occasions, religion, or being 'sent' back may put strain on relations (Orellana et al., 2001; Menjívar, 2002).

Among the young people of our project 'moving' was a constant allusion, even if the actual act appeared to be rather more an illusion. Many respondents made reference, often quite fleeting, to their desire of experience of getting out of Puebla[5] and going to the United States or elsewhere. While we were able to find evidence that some had come to the city from the countryside, or had spent time in Mexico City, most accounts of going further afield were difficult to substantiate or were fantasy. One of our first contacts recounted his travels at some length, claiming to have been to the United States on several occasions and to have lived in Beverley Hills where he said he had a family. On a much later occasion Moises also hinted that he had been to Europe, although it was clear that he had no real idea where Europe was or how to get there. Mobility, however, was clearly a vital component to a young person's identity that, more mundanely, had involved years in and out of state and non-governmental institutions. Others too 'performed' mobility, for our benefit but with an authenticity of articulation that suggested a need to be believed. Sitting in the Jardineras one afternoon the usual patterns of work, drug taking, and conversation were disrupted by the deep rumble of an oncoming train. Dividing the Jardineras from the market was a barely used track that linked a number of industrial sites in the city, and which went further north. On board were young men sitting on the roof. On this and other occasions some of the group would jump onto the train and wave a faked goodbye. The first time Gareth asked Mateo if he had ever jumped the train for real. His answer was affirmative, he had 'been north' many times, but said with little conviction. How far had he gone? To Apizaco came the response. Apizaco is about 40 kilometres outside of Puebla, barely an hour's journey by bus. Mateo presented an imagined mobility, not to impress us with the idea of travel but to indicate his desire and efforts to 'get out', meaning to change a life marked by poverty, drugs, violence, and loneliness.

A very different insight was offered by Ramon. We had learned from a more formal interview that Ramon had been brought up in Tierra Blanca, Veracruz, and came to Puebla before spending time in Mexico City where he became involved with a gang, before returning to Puebla. When asked whether he had been north he would answer that he had got as far as the border, indicating variously between Tampico in the east and Tijuana to the west. He had not crossed however, claiming that he had run out of money and been homesick. In general terms his accounts were always consistent. But, on our last visit to the Jardineras in 2008, Ramon suddenly confided that he had lived in Los Angeles, and had spent time in prison there for involvement in a gang. Like many young people on the streets, Ramon may have been reluctant to reveal too much about himself to outsiders, and to offer instead a series of credible 'personas'. We are not sure the reason for the sudden revelation, except that perhaps it relates to the fact that he came back. He could not make it in the United States, despite his gang and the life that awaited him in Mexico. It was not that he was reluctant to tell us about being a mobile Mexican, but that he was embarrassed about being a 'failed globaliser'.

Travelling identities

We met Jiménez in Bensonhurst, at the corner of 20th and 86th in Brooklyn, New York, on Tuesday 23rd October 2007. Surfacing from the subway at mid-day, we phoned his mobile number, as he had instructed, and five minutes later there he was – jogging easily up the street, grinning. Now 19, Jiménez was a fit, muscular, tanned and handsome young man, quite changed from the chubby, asthmatic 16 year old interviewed 3 years before by Sarah in a Pueblan care home for street children. Jiménez had agreed to meet us (both Gareth and Sarah) today, on his day off, for a lunch to catch up on 3 years of news. We were keen to learn about his move to the United States, his life in New York and his plans for the future. And Jiménez wanted to show us where he lived, on the second floor of a four-storey apartment block in a quiet leafy suburban avenue, just 5 minutes from the subway station. As we strolled towards his apartment, he told us about his job in the kitchen of a nearby pizzeria, working from 11am to 11pm, Wednesdays through Mondays, earning 550 dollars a week preparing pizza dough. He had been working in the same restaurant for the past 2 years, basically since he had arrived in New York, had been promoted from washing dishes in his first year and now aspired to a move from the kitchen to front of house where the cooks made pizza. A conscientious worker, he had not missed a day's work in 2 years – except for yesterday, when his younger brother Antonio had arrived.

Antonio's arrival was a stunning piece of news. The 15 year old had just spent 5 days travelling from Puebla in central Mexico to north-eastern United States, including an illegal border crossing – through the 'killing deserts' from Sonora into Arizona. When we reached Jiménez's apartment we found Antonio accompanied by another brother, 17-year-old Federico, and Rocío, a girl of the same age who had shared the journey with Antonio. Rocío we discovered was the sister of Jiménez's girlfriend – who lived and worked as a teacher in Puebla. The brothers compared their experiences of the Mexico–USA journey: back in 2005 Jiménez had taken 9 days to complete the crossing; Federico had managed in 4 days in early 2007; Antonio and Rocío got through in 5 days, looking dazed and raw-skinned from the experience. Jiménez explained that all had taken the same route, arranged by an uncle of theirs who belonged to a ring of 'coyotes' or people smugglers, but his trip had taken longer when the group's 'coyote' did not show up at the pre-arranged meeting point in Mexico and they had had to wait several days for his replacement to arrive. Each had travelled from Puebla to Mexico City by bus, taken a plane to Hermosillo, Sonora, and hooked up with a larger group in a hotel to be taken by pick-up truck close to the US border. Walking only in the dark, they had taken three punishing nights to make the border crossing, under strict instructions about clothing (black), jewellery, lamps and mobile phones (none), equipment (1 light rucksack, sand-coloured blanket), food (tins of tuna, biscuits) and water. A pick-up truck on the other side took them to a hotel in Phoenix, where they cleaned up and rested before taking a bus to New York.

There were stories of exhilaration and adventure. Antonio told of a 'migra' policeman coming within feet of where he was hiding, as he held his breath; Jiménez recounted how they had lain still as helicopters circled overhead, aware that they could be picked up if someone was transmitting a mobile phone signal; Federico said muggings by gangs on the US side were rumoured to be common. But underlying the adventure was a more calculated tale of risk assessment, of coordinated planning and organised execution. Jiménez had not allowed his girlfriend Sonia to make the journey – he had assessed the dangers as too great for her and was mindful that his investment in her college fees back in Puebla would be jeopardised. He had paid $50,000 Mexican pesos (about US$5,000) for each brother to make the crossing under the guidance of an experienced coyote, each trip taking months to prepare. A certain mental attitude was necessary for the dangerous border crossing, Jiménez explained. He had advised his brothers 'don't think about where you're coming from or going to, just do it for yourself, concentrate on where you are right now' (interview notes, 27/10/07). This, he told us, had been his approach and it had worked for him. In all, these had been anything but impulsive or reckless border crossings. Rather, they suggest that Jiménez has a highly organised view of himself and the world around him.

We were given tantalising glimpses of the Brooklyn-based world into which Jiménez had negotiated his own entry and also that of his two younger brothers – and to which he intended to bring his Mexico-based mother. They reflect common Mexican experiences of illegal migration to the United States. He had, for example, a significant network in the United States of family members who had emigrated from Puebla – uncles, aunts, his father and older brother were all now resident in and around New York City (a popular destination for Mexicans from Puebla state) – some were reportedly now legal joint US–Mexican citizens, others were legal residents, relative newcomers had lived and worked illegally for several years.

In New York, Jiménez had quickly settled into a latino social network, finding work in a pizzeria owned by an Argentinean and staffed by Guatemalans and other inhabitants of Jiménez's birth place – Cholula town, close to Puebla City. Seventeen-year-old Federico had also been found a job by Jiménez in the same pizzeria chain – and Antonio was to be similarly placed by his brother. Jiménez assessed restaurant work to be ideal, providing meals to save money and a refuge from police as they worked out of sight in the kitchens. They were also likely to be able to negotiate the same day off, allowing them to spend Tuesday together as a family. The latino social network extended to their living accommodation – an apartment owned by a Guatemalan woman, Elena, and shared by seven illegal residents from Mexico and Guatemala. Jiménez's day was highly structured, beginning at 08:00 with 2 hours at the gym (US$45 per month for unlimited use) followed by a 12-hour working day from 11am to 11pm. He watched a little TV and used Internet-enabled mobile phones to keep in touch with other news in Spanish. With little need for English in his daily life, Jiménez had quickly given up on his 'English for Latinos' book purchased on arrival over 2 years earlier, although was keen to press Antonio into learning more to improve his options in New York. On arrival in New York in 2005 as a minor, Jiménez had enrolled for health and dental care, careful to have all the health checks and all the dental treatment available free to minors. On turning 18, his health care plan had become preventive, consisting of a careful diet, plenty of exercise, no cigarettes, coffee, alcohol or illegal drugs. A picture of clean living, Jiménez, was, at 19, a hard-working young man who had assumed responsibility for his younger brothers' well-being. Saving most of his earnings, Jiménez had bought a plot of land back home in Cholula, intending to return to Mexico in 2009 when, he calculated, he would have enough money to build a home for himself and his girlfriend.

Jiménez's story echoes the aspirations of many young Mexicans hoping to use illegal entry to the United States as a way to earn enough money to return as landowners, homeowners, successful businessmen. But Jiménez's new identity as highly organised, ambitious and farsighted seems remote from his 'street' child identity of a few years earlier.

> At the age of 9 I left home and was living for 2 years on the streets. I spent 4 years...3 years in a [NGO] care home...maybe 5...then I was in a Welfare home for a few months, and I left again and was in the street. Really I don't remember how long I lived in the street [...] Then they took me to the borstal...No, they took me back to the Welfare home...and when I behaved badly there they sent me to the borstal. And from there they brought me here [a second NGO care home] and here I've spent 2 years
>
> (Interview 19/11/04, p. 2)

His story of early mobility, of moving on to the streets, was a typical 'street child' story of family disintegration and abuse:

> So my mum decided to go off with this other man. And my dad stayed with us and drowned himself in alcohol. [...] And he hit us a lot [...] and my brother – the one after me – sometimes he would leave him tied up in a sack [...] When I arrived here in JUCONI house, I still had, after all that time [...] the marks from being hit with wire [...] and with the lead of an iron [...] and with rope (ibid, p. 19)...

I was 9 when my mother left and I didn't see her again.... my dad, when my mum went off with the other man, my dad, well we stayed with him but it's like.... Well it made my dad uncomfortable, he could only stand 2 years with the 4 of us and then he had a son with another woman (ibid, p. 2)... and then when my grandmother died, my dad decided to leave us and he went (ibid, p. 21)... My dad goes to the United States and we stay with a teacher and that teacher divided us up, she didn't put us together in the same place. I think the agreement with my dad, he told me this recently when he called, was that she was going to look after us – she was going to have all 4 of us in her house. Anyway, this woman takes me and leaves me in a care home, another brother was left in another care home and another in another and the oldest ran away...

(ibid, p. 2)

Jiménez's early moves foster the notion of a 'reluctant' mobility – buffeted by traumatic family circumstances, with movements between street and institutions reflecting not choice but unhappiness about his treatment and frustrated attempts to be with his family:

When I was in the Welfare home... because well, according to the Convention [on the Rights of the Child, 1989] we have the right to freedom, but we never went out [...] You're never allowed to go out when you're in Welfare.... and the thing was, like I wanted to search for my brothers, but they don't let you out, so I escaped time and again

(ibid, p. 16)

Intriguingly, Jiménez's job of tracking down his younger brothers, each in a different care home, was made easier because all were known simply as 'Jiménez' – by-product of an institutional device in busy homes to identify children by their surnames.

'Reluctant' mobility was similarly evident in the story of Esteban, who, like Jiménez, reached a time when he was able to 'harness' his mobility to use it to further his career. But at the age of 7, his moves between home and street were hardly signalling an adventurous spirit:

My specific problem: family disintegration. My mum left my dad when I was little, from then I had a stepfather (interview with Esteban, 25/08/06)... I remember that when they punished me, at 6, 7 years of age, it was with a cable with the plastic peeled back, with the pure metal and with that they beat me. It split the skin, it marked you, first it made you all swell up where they hit you and then the skin split…And…. well, nothing, just nothing. And I used to have to work, I was working and going to school, I used to sell chewing gum at first, then I shined shoes and the first time that I left home for the street, my first experience of living on the street I remember really, really well because it was caused by pure fear, I was working in the street, selling chewing gum, but all my earnings were taken by my stepfather, right? (ibid, p. 1)…On that occasion I had sold all my chewing gum and there was a travelling fair, there in Salina Cruz [Oaxaca], so I went to play roulette and I lost all my cash. I was excited, there were coins worth 20 pesos and I got excited about winning them, I got excited putting money on. You bet on the red or the green. I got so excited, I started to win and saw my money increase and then I lost it all at the end, like always happens, always. And there I was in Salina Cruz's mini Las Vegas and I was terrified they were going to beat me, right? And I was frightened about staying away from home too, I was frightened of both things, but I was more frightened of going home to be beaten than of staying out…

(ibid, p. 2)

Esteban and Jiménez manifest time and again a 'reluctant' mobility in their early lives, Jiménez restricting his mobility to within Puebla City, Esteban moving through various localities in Oaxaca, to Veracruz and Puebla with numerous return journeys. Each spent time on the streets in the company of other young people, but links formed on the street were tacitly understood as transitory, being instrumental to the immediate job of survival. Both opted to spend their teenage years in more settled environments, each in a different care home in Puebla City, each choosing, despite their earlier experiences of reluctant mobility, a settled existence to complete their schooling.

the only thing we had to do was study and that was it. I mean, they didn't make us work or anything. So we used to go to school and arriving home we'd do the cleaning. Each of us had a job – the patio, bedroom or bathroom. When they put us to cleaning – there were 4 of us – 2 of my friends said: no, they're going to make us work, let's go, let's go. But 2 of us wanted to stay (interview with Esteban, 25/08/06, p. 4)…and after a month and a half, my mum arrived. Because the 2 boys who had run away had gone back to Salina Cruz and they told where we were. So our mums arrived and everything, the other boy, Néstor he was called, my friend, he'd been my friend since the first year of primary, he went home. His sister was friends with my sister, which was why we spent so much time together. And he went home after a month and a half, but when my mum came I didn't want to go home. I was better off (in the care home). I mean, I was not OK in my family home, I was definitely not OK there, there was nothing more than abuse there, I would have done nothing there and I was no fool...

(ibid, p. 5)

Jiménez and Esteban took journeys not simply within the spatial dimension, but also moving from early identity ascriptions as 'abandoned' or 'street' children, in a way we began to think of as 'harnessing' their abilities to negotiate public and other spaces to deploy them in the interests of furthering socio-economic ambitions. Leaving Mexico they left behind their labels, living abroad simply as 'Mexicans', planning for an eventual return 'home' as successful travellers. With no family home to return to, they nevertheless identified 'Mexico' as home and more specifically localities they had known as children: Jiménez had bought land within spitting distance of his parental home; Esteban returned to Veracruz where he had spent his first years off the street in a care home. They understood their experiences of movement outside Mexico as preparatory to their successful returns to familiar corners of central Mexico. Jiménez had 'made it' from 'street' child to a steady job in the United States which allowed him to reunite his family and held the expectation of returning to his home town as a land owner and marriage to a local teacher. Esteban's social mobility traversed red light districts, care homes, private university, a year travelling in Europe, to become a lawyer and university teacher embarking on his doctoral studies in Spain.

I know how to fight and I so know how to fight that I looked for the opportunity to do a doctorate in Spain. And, yes, these are opportunities given to one in a thousand, but I didn't get it through luck, nor did they give it to me on a plate: I had to work for it. They didn't say: Right, we're going to look for a lad from Hogares (care home) or someone that has these certain characteristics. No. I earned it. I went and worried away at it and I made it. [...] And, well, life in Veracruz is treating me well, see now, I belong to the one percent of Mexicans who go abroad to do a doctorate, life is treating me well....

(interview with Esteban 23/01/08, p. 16)

While Esteban and Jiménez's early lives hardly fit the mould of idealised, cosmopolitan mobility – indeed their younger lives conjure all the elements of social exclusion – they nevertheless worked at turning themselves into subaltern cosmopolitans: Jiménez through his family connections in the United States, Esteban in the welfare home in which he spent much of his adolescence. But are Esteban's and Jiménez' simply idiosyncratic life histories or can they tell us something about the social identities of (mobile) children and youth more generally? A shared reluctance to become mobile, to leave the family home and move on to the street, echoes much research about 'street' children leaving home because of fear of abuse rather than in search of adventure. A subsequent harnessing of spatial mobility to follow personal ambitions suggests a transformational period in which spatially mobile young people increasingly identify and pursue opportunities involving socio-economic mobility. Both our research subjects have used technology to pursue multiple social lives: Jiménez through his two expensive mobile phones, one used for sustaining his distance romance with a Mexican girlfriend, the other (we suspect) for helping his uncle orchestrate border crossings; Esteban using the Internet to maintain and grow his network of friends in Europe and to educate himself. Each displays a highly organised view of self and the world around, after being subjected to family disorganisation (within a history of family migration) and living an unsettled, unhappy young life. Both spent adolescent years settled in care homes, valuing their educational opportunities.

> Nowadays, I feel more Pueblan than anything because in Puebla I spent... well in Puebla I grew up. All the rest were just stages, stages in my life, which shaped me. But in Puebla I became who I am today. In Puebla I had great experiences, with the priests and lads at the care home [Esteban lived in Hogares Calasanz, Puebla from the age of 13 through to University]
>
> (interview with Esteban 23/01/08, p. 12)

Both indicate ambitions of economic security, a family and a successful return 'home', considered almost stereotypical of Mexicans abroad. They seek not to change Mexican society, but rather to improve their own standing within a society which abandoned them, their transnational living representing less resistance to exclusion and oppression 'at home' than a means to join the 'included'. Esteban relates his ambitions to religion and morality, but also to his business acumen and opportunities to 'do a deal', Jiménez relates his to working hard, saving and taking opportunities presented by a family network. For both, 'clean living' is valued, not just in terms of being drug free but also through stable relationships with partners. In this sense, 'family' for both young men relates to constructions in which they are central figures shaping their family destinies, rather than contemplating a return to the parental home. Both Esteban and Jiménez desire – and have prepared for – their return to Mexico.

> My idea is to get to know about things – my studies are kind of the vehicle, right? They are pretext to leave, but really it's so I can get to know, see, do, live other cultures, understand them, have things to recount to my grandchildren: Spain is like this, look, it's like that, have things to tell them and to become better, to be a better person. My life project is to have a family, have my wife, my children and to be good for them, not for myself. I mean, it's no good if it's just for yourself is it? It's no use to me that my University certificate is on the [care home's] office wall. It does nothing for me really. But having a wife and children, when it's all for other people not just for yourself, then it's great
>
> (interview with Esteban 23/01/08, p. 25)

Esteban and Jiménez experienced mobility in a number of different ways, moving with reluctance onto the streets, experimenting with mobility between institutions, before harnessing mobility to pursue personal ambitions. Our interviews reveal two young people deeply aware of how they have become 'global' travellers, networked into flows of information and responsibilities, expressed as their knowledge of education grants and the Internet, to the payment of remittances and arrangements for family to follow behind.

Conclusion

Colloquially all Mexicans abroad are referred to as *hijos ausentes* (absent children), a turn of phrase that suggests both infantilisation and loss to the paternalistic nation, 'la patria'. For the two people at the centre of this paper, neither family nor nation would seem, on their merit, to demand much loyalty. Both left home in childhood and spent time on the streets and various institutions, 'movements' that we describe as reluctant, before becoming transnational actors. Getting to New York and Seville entailed a shift across and mixing with worlds that would have seemed distant, physically, socially and culturally not long before. In so doing both shifted from being, or being ascribed identities as, 'street children' with the notions of immobility/deterioration to becoming youth and 'subaltern cosmopolitans'. Both harnessed the opportunities presented to them by civil society organisations, and in different ways by family, signalling the material and emotional importance of home to the act of departure. Once abroad, both Jiménez and Esteban's narratives present pride in their respective achievements but also an awareness of their 'difference' from hosts and a continued presence that requires negotiation.[6] Hovering in the background of both narratives – as we suspect is especially true of all subaltern cosmopolitans – is the register of previous identities. Their cosmopolitanism is heavily caveated by their responsibilities to themselves, to brothers and girlfriends, and preparation for going back. In traversing borders two 'mobile Mexicans' and successful globalisers, once streets kids but now confident young men, have reconciled mobility and identity.

Notes

1. We are grateful to participants of the panel *Urban Youth: Cultures, Identities and Spatialities* at the 2008 Annual Conference of the Association of American Geographers, and especially co-chair Lorraine van Blerk and discussant Craig Jeffrey.
2. The 'street children' nomenclature is often stretched to include young people over 18, a move that is misleading in Mexico, and much of Latin America, where in contrast with the 1980s, when unaccompanied 8-, 9- and 10-year olds were a common sight on the streets, older teenagers and youth are more prominent (see UNYP, 2008).
3. The project research assistant, Elsa Herrera, was the most consistent point of contact.
4. Although we believe that friendship was formed with most participants, there was always a niggle of voyeurism and mutual performances (see Thomas de Benítez et al., forthcoming).
5. Puebla State, our main fieldwork site, ranked sixth poorest of Mexico's 32 States and registered the fourth largest decrease in income attributable to migration, after Oaxaca, Veracruz and Chiapas (UNDP, 2007).
6. Jiménez relates this to his good conduct and hard work, Esteban to his social networking and academic record.

References

Ahmed, S. (1999) Home and Away: Narrative of Migration and Estrangement. *International Journal of Cultural Studies* 2(3): 329–47.
Amoore, L. (2006) Biometric Borders: Governing Mobilities in the War on Terror. *Political Geography* 25: 336–51.

Baulch, E. (2008) *Making Scenes: Reggae, Punk, and Death Metal in 1990s, Bali*. Durham: Duke University Press.

Bauman, Z. (1995) *Life in Fragments; Essays in Postmodern Morality*. Oxford: Blackwell.

Beazley, H. (2002) Vagrants Wearing Make-up: Negotiating Spaces on the Streets of Yogyakarta, Indonesia. *Urban Studies* 39(9): 1665–83.

Benhabib, S. (1999) Citizens, Residents, and Aliens in a Changing World: Political Membership in the Global Era. *Social Research* 66: 709–44.

Butler, J. (1993) *Bodies that Matter: On the Discursive Limits of 'Sex'*. New York: Routledge.

Castles, S. (2002) Migration and Community Formation under Conditions of Globalization. *International Migration Review* 36(4): 1143–68.

Chamberlain, M. and Leydesdorff, S. (2004) Transnational Families: Memories and Narratives. *Global Networks* 4, 227–41.

Chavez, L.R. (2008) *The Latino Threat: Constructing Immigrants, Citizens, and the Nation*. Stanford: Stanford University Press.

D'Andrea, A. (2006) Neo-Nomadism: A Theory of Post-Identitarian Mobility in the Global Age. *Mobilities* 1(1): 95–119.

Ennew, J. and Swart-Kruger, J. (2003) Introduction: Homes, Places and Spaces in the Construction of Street Children and Street Youth. *Children, Youth and Environment* 31(1): http://cye/colorado.edu.

Gidwani, V. (2006) Subaltern Cosmopolitanism as Politics. *Antipode* 38: 7–21.

Gigengack, R. (1999) The Buca Boys from Metro Juarez: Leadership, Gender and age in Mexico City's Youthful Street Culture. *Etnofoor* 12(1): 101–24.

Gilroy, P. (2008) *Postcolonial Melancholia*. New York: Columbia University Press.

Glick Schiller, N., Basch, L. and Blanc-Szanton, C. (1992) Transnationalism: A New Analytical Framework for Understanding Migration. In N. Glick Schiller, L. Basch and C. Blanc-Szanton (eds.) *Toward a Transnational Perspective on Migration*. New York: New York Academy of Sciences.

Golbert, R.L. (2001) Transnational Orientations from Home: Constructions of Israel and Transnational Space among Ukrainian Jewish Youth. *Journal of Ethnic and Migration Studies* 27(4): 713–31.

Gómez-Pena, G. (1996) *The New World Border: Prophecies, Poems and Loqueras for the End of the Century*. San Francisco: City Lights.

Gupta, A. and Ferguson, J. (1992) Beyond Culture: Space, Identity and the Politics of Difference. *Cultural Anthropology* 7(1): 6–23.

Hannam, K., Sheller, M. and Urry, J. (2006) Mobilities, Immobilities and Moorings. *Mobilities* 1(1): 1–22.

Hannerz, U. (1969) *Soulside: Inquiries into Ghetto Culture and Community*. Chicago: University of Chicago Press.

Hannerz, U. (1996) *Transnational Connections: Culture, People, Places*. London: Routledge.

Herrera, E., Jones, G.A. and Thomas de Benítez, S. (2009) Bodies on the Line: Identity Markers among Mexican Street Youth. *Children's Geographies* 7(1): 67–81.

Jeffrey, C. and McFarlane, C. (2008) 'Performing Cosmopolitanism: Introduction to the Special Issue'. *Environment and Planning D: Society and Space*, 26(3): 420–7.

Jones, G.A., Herrera, E. and Thomas de Benítez, S. (2007) Tears, Trauma and Suicide: Everyday Violence among Street Youth in Puebla, Mexico. *Bulletin of Latin American Research* 26(4): 462–79.

Kothari, U. (2008) Global Peddlers and Local Networks: Migrant Cosmopolitans. *Environment and Planning D: Society and Space* 26: 500–16.

Levitt, P. and de la Dehesa, R. (2003) Transnational Migration and the Redefinition of the State: Variations and Explanations. *Ethnic and Racial Studies* 26(4): 587–611.

Martínez, R. (2002) *Crossing Over: A Mexican Family on the Migrant Trail*. New York: Picador.

Menjivar, C. (2002) Living in Two Worlds? Guatemalan-Origin Children in the United States and Emerging Transnationalism. *Journal of Ethnic and Migration Studies* 28(3): 531–52.

Orellana, M.F., Thorne, B., Chee, A. and Lam, W.S.E. (2001) Transnational Childhoods: The Participation of Children in Processes of Family Migration. *Social Problems* 48(4): 572–91.

Parkin, D. (1999) Mementos as Transitional Objects in Human Displacement. *Journal of Material Culture* 4(3): 303–20.

Quinones, S. (2007) *Antonio's Gun and Delfino's Dream: True Tales of Mexican Migration*. Albuquerque: University of New Mexico Press.

Rosas, G. (2006) The Managed Violences of the Borderlands: Treacherous Geographies, Policeability, and the Politics of Race. *Latino Studies* 4: 401–18.

Salazar Parreñas, R. (2005) *Children of Global Migration: Transnational Families and Gendered Woes*. Stanford: Stanford University Press.

Scheper-Hughes, N. and Hoffman, D. (1998) Brazilian Apartheid: Street Kids and the Struggle for Urban Space. In N. Scheper-Hughes and N. Sargent (eds.) *Small Wars – The Cultural Politics of Childhood*. Berkeley: University Of California Press.

Thomas de Benítez, S., Jones, G.A. and Herrera, E. (forthcoming) Ethnography as Team Performance: Youth and Researchers on Mexican Streets. *Ethnography*.

UNDP (2007) *Informe sobre Desarrollo Humano México 2006–2007: migración y desarrollo humano* [Human Development Report, Mexico (2006–2007): Migration and Human Development] UNDP, Mexico.

UNYP (2008) Youth on the Streets, www.un.org/youth.

Van Blerk, L. (2005) Negotiating Spatial Identities: Mobile Perspectives on Street Life in Uganda. *Children's Geographies* 3(1): 5–21.

Vertovec, S. (2001) Transnationalism and Identity. *Journal of Ethnic and Migration Studies* 27(4): 573–82.

Wildermuth, N. and Dalsgaard, A.L. (2006) Imagined Futures, Present Lives: Youth, Media and Modernity in the Changing Economy of Northeast Brazil. *Young* 14(1): 9–31.

Young, L. (2003) The Place of Street Children in Kampala: Marginalisation, Resistance and Acceptance of the Urban Environment. *Environment and Planning: Society and Space* 21: 607–27.

Part II
Interactions and Institutions

5
Accomplishing Social Action with Identity Categories: Mediating and Policing Neighbour Disputes

Elizabeth Stokoe and Derek Edwards

This chapter examines the relationship between social action and identity using the methods of conversation analysis, and shows how social actions such as complaints about transgressions, or denials of culpability in events, bring into play self- and other-categorizations of the persons involved. Drawing on data collected as part of our study of neighbourhood disputes, we demonstrate how ascribed identity categories (e.g. 'I'm a single mother') and category-implicative descriptions (e.g. 'she's eighty three') function systematically as constituent features of members' methods for accomplishing action. Studying the recurrent ways through which categories are deployed in interaction permits the empirical investigation of, and sheds light on, the social organization of cultural knowledge.

Neighbour disputes are a familiar social problem and media topic. Over the past 15 years, the number of mediation centres in the United Kingdom has increased rapidly, as more and more neighbours find that they can not resolve their disputes without the help of a third party. Perhaps surprisingly, then, academics have paid little attention to the nature and causes of neighbour disputes. Existing reports come from the government, local councils, mediation centres and related sources (e.g. Citizen's Advice Bureau, 2007; DirectGov, 2007). These reports list the causes of neighbour problems as 'noise', 'children', 'abuse', 'boundaries and fences', 'trees', and 'parking space'. However, our pilot study of publicly available dispute discourse (e.g. on television and radio call-ins) and a small number of recorded interviews between mediators and their clients suggested that although these may be the official causes of disputes, people's complaints often hinge on the *types of person* they and their neighbour are (Stokoe, 2003; Stokoe and Wallwork, 2003).

In other words, the identities of the disputing parties, something not coded for in official reports, may play an important role in neighbour conflict. We wanted to investigate how social identities figure in the discourse of neighbour conflict, and what the implications might be for understanding dispute initiation, escalation and resolution.

Although 'neighbour relationships' themselves are under-researched, there is a large literature on neighbour*hood-relevant* topics in community and environmental psychology, sociology, and cultural geography. This work is generally conducted via surveys and interviews, designed to gather information about, for example, residents' reactions to changes in their neighbourhood, causes of pleasure and stress, sources of dispute and conflict, and subjective experiences of 'community' (e.g., for a review, see Bridge, *et al.*, 2004). Some studies correlate variables such as 'environmental satisfaction', 'sense of community', and 'place attachment', levels of physical and psychological well-being, or 'levels of neighbouring activity' (e.g. Prezza, *et al.*, 2001; Vallance, *et al.*, 2005). In addition to these sorts of studies, there is plenty of theoretical commentary about 'neighbourhood', 'community', and related concepts, as well as political critique and analysis of the discourse of 'social inclusion', 'cohesion', and other recent government policy rhetoric (e.g. McGhee, 2003; Worley, 2005; Lupi and Musterd, 2006).

Despite this large and diverse literature there has been little (if any) work that examines actual encounters between neighbours as they live their lives, or that studies the situated contexts where such relations are worked out (an exception is Laurier, *et al.*'s, 2002, ethnographic description of neighbouring). In contrast, our project studies neighbour relationships involving *actual interaction between neighbours*, gathered independently of researcher intervention or manipulation. This meant finding settings where ordinary people make complaints about, and argue with, their neighbours. We identified three such settings:

1. Telephone calls to neighbourhood mediation centres, and subsequent interviews between mediators and their clients;
2. Police interviews with suspects, recorded as part of everyday police practice;
3. Telephone calls to local council environmental health and 'antisocial behaviour' units.

Access to these settings enabled us to record and examine people interacting with each other and various institutional professionals. It is in these conversations that people formulate complaints, display their understanding of what it means to be a 'good' or 'bad' neighbour, explain what counts as legitimately 'complainable' behaviour, and demonstrate how identity is used as a resource for making complaints, narrating events, denying accusations, or justifying actions. Our project aimed to provide insights into the sorts of daily conflicts, disputes, and resolutions that occur between neighbours and the professional bodies that deal with them.

Reformulating identity and social action: The study of interaction

Rather than approaching identity as a 'given' cognition or social structure, we sought to discover the identity categorization resources and practices used in real settings of social interaction. We also approached 'identity' in broader terms than the narrow set of traditional academic categories (e.g. 'class', 'gender', 'race', although see Speer, this book, for an explicit focus on gender), by focusing additionally on people's own character-based ('bully', 'nasty person') and other identity-relevant descriptions ('parent', 'slag'). We aimed to discover *which* identities appeared in people's complaints; their *salience*, and their relevance to the *persistence* or *resolution* of conflict. We examined how speakers describe themselves and others; that is, how categories are 'ascribed' (to others) and 'avowed' (in self-description). In addition to looking at overt categorial reference, we examined more subtle features such as how identity categories are implied in descriptions of people's actions, appearance, tendencies and dispositions. Our approach to identity therefore builds upon Sacks's (1992) groundbreaking work on membership categorization (see also Jayyusi, 1984; Watson, 1997; Hester and Eglin, 1997a; Antaki and Widdicombe, 1998), in which analysis unpacks the logic and function of social category descriptions in particular interactions or documents.

We focused both on the sequential organization of social actions performed in talk and on the social categories embedded in the turns of talk that accomplish those actions. In so doing, our analysis provides evidence against a common assumption about the 'capturability' for research and analysis, of identity topics such as 'gender', 'ethnicity', 'age', and so on (Stokoe and Edwards, 2007; Stokoe, 2008, 2009). For example, writing about ethnic identity, van Dijk (1987: 18) argued that 'recording everyday conversations is one thing, but collecting "real" conversations about ethnic minority members is quite another... [it would] be a very inefficient way of collecting data when we would record hundreds of hours of talk in order to get perhaps a few hours of talk about ethnic groups'. He goes on to suggest that we cannot 'simply go into the field and observe how, when, where, and with whom people talk with others about ethnic groups...Finding data...would amount to a search for the proverbial needle in the haystack' (1987: 119). As a data-gathering source, then, interviews are advantageous as they enable researchers to collect guaranteed 'content' about their research questions. However, as has been argued elsewhere, accounts elicited in interviews comprise post-hoc reflections on participants' own or others' identity memberships, rather than how they are occasioned within, and for, the practices of everyday life. As Sacks (1992: 27) observed, researchers end up 'studying the categories Members use, to be sure, except at this point they are not investigating their categories by attempting to find them in the activities in which they're employed'.

Writing from a conversation analytic perspective, Pomerantz and Mandelbaum (2005) argued that because of the kind of phenomenon they are, we cannot predict when categories will crop up in interaction, nor that when a category is used, it will be an instance of the same interactional phenomenon, nor doing the same kind of action. Pomerantz and Mandelbaum therefore claim that 'because we cannot know in advance when a person will explicitly invoke a...category, there is no way to plan data collection of them' (p. 154). A key aim of our work has been to counter such claims by demonstrating that seemingly elusive phenomena do indeed occur, somewhat predictably, in the same sequential kinds of environments, in the same kinds of turns, doing the same kinds of actions. Overall, this chapter develops our understanding of how the ascription and disavowal of identity categories are embedded systematically in the social actions of everyday life.

Our data comprised approximately 120 hours of neighbour dispute interaction: 20 hours of neighbour mediation, 230 telephone calls to mediation centres, 30 calls to antisocial behaviour units, and 122 police interrogations of suspects. The data were collected in four different regions of the United Kingdom. Appropriate consent was obtained for the use in research and publications of anonymized data recordings and transcripts. The data were transcribed using Jefferson's (2004) system for conversation analysis (CA) (see Appendix B at the end of this book). Our analytic approach draws on CA's basic principles of turn design, action formation, and sequence organization; MCA's (Membership Categorization Analysis) focus on 'the organization of common-sense knowledge in terms of the categories members employ in accomplishing their activities in and through talk' (Francis and Hester, 2004: 21); and discursive psychology's (DP) key concerns with how talk manages subject-object, or mind–world relations when dealing with psychological considerations such as identity and motive (e.g. Edwards, 2005). We take as our starting point the notion that talk is 'the primordial scene of social life... through which the work of the constitutive institutions of societies gets done' (Schegloff, 1996: 4). It is largely through talking that we live our lives, build and maintain relationships, and establish 'who we are to one another' (Drew, 2005: 74). Both of these points are strongly suggestive of why *analyzing talk* is particularly useful for analyzing identity. We worked by conducting repeated readings of the transcripts in conjunction with audio-recordings, aiming to identify robust patterns in the way identity-relevant conversational phenomena and practices are *occasioned*: where they are located in the sequential unfolding of talk, how they are formulated within a turn's design, how they are taken up by recipients, and how they are made to matter for the trajectory of the talk.

Accomplishing social action in neighbour disputes

The analysis is divided into five short sections, each illustrating a key finding about how identity can be central to, or implied within, the accomplishment of social action. Full analyses of each phenomenon can be found in our other published work. Some sections draw mainly on the mediation subset of data while others draw mainly on the police interrogation materials. The first section explores the institutional relevance of identity matters at the start of telephone calls to mediation helplines. The second section examines the use of categories in formulating complaints and enhancing grievances, and the third focuses on examples of 'category-based denials' (Stokoe, 2006) and defences against complaints. Fourth, we examine the way identity figures in accounts for why previous attempts to solve neighbour problems, before calling mediation, had failed; this is followed by a related section on how callers resist offers of mediation using identity and characterological descriptions.

Identity and institutional alignment in telephone call openings

In the first of three brief examples of calls to mediation centres, C is the caller and M is the mediator taking the call.

1. DC-27

```
        ((Phone rings))
1   M:  Mediation in Churchbrough g'd morning:
2   C:  .hh ↑Oh good mornin'.=um: (.) I don't know where
3       to sta:rt.=↑I've gotta dispute with my
4       nei::gh[bour.
5   M:         [.hh ↑Okay can I jus' [...]
```

It is a feature of telephone call opening sequences that greetings and identification are the first order of business (e.g. Schegloff, 1979). Such identifications are intrinsically identity-relevant, but are also relationship-relevant, and the relationship between the caller and called is established in the types of greeting and identifications that are done. Also relevant to what happens at the start of calls is whether it is a domestic or institutional call, and whether each party understands the type of interaction – the business to be accomplished – that the call is for. At line 1, M, in providing self-identification, does not say who she is personally, nor her role, but names the service and what it provides: mediation for the local area. In response, the caller provides no formal self-identification – she does not give her name nor say from where she is calling. It is implied in the 'turn-generated' category (Psathas, 1999) provided in M's opening turn that if M is the institutional representative, C is the client of, or caller to, that institution, and no further work is done. In C's first turn, she does a greeting ('↑Oh good mornin'.') and, after formulating the possibly complex or involved nature of her story ('I don't know where to sta:rt'), she formulates a 'headline' for the problem she will go on to unpack: '↑I've gotta dispute with my nei::ghbour.' Note that M comes in just before the end of C's turn, at a point where she can project an end of the turn and its action: M has heard 'dispute' and 'neigh-' and can now proceed with the next order of business in the call, which is to ask the caller's permission to record it.

The next example shares several features with Extract 1.

2. DC-12

```
        ((Phone rings))
1   M:  Mediation in Churchbrough g'mo↑rning,
2           (0.6)
3   C:  Hello:: I'm ju- I've ↑just been given this
4       number↓ an' I just wanted to talk a↓bout like
5       we've got really terrible neighbours.
6           (0.3)
```

```
7   M:   .Hhh yeh sure ye- (0.3) y've rung right place.
8   C:   Ri::ght.=
9   M:   =.Hhh can I just tell you b'fore we start [...]
```

As in Extract 1, M starts with an institutional self-identification, and C returns with a greeting but no identification. However, immediately following her greeting she says 'I've ↑just been given this number↓'. This immediately signals potential alignment trouble. The caller is not calling because they need a specific kind of help and know where to get it. It implies that they may have been passed on from somewhere else, that they may be unsure of who or what they are calling. This type of formulation was very common at the start of calls. It is a feature of neighbour mediation service calls, unlike calls to emergency services or doctors' receptionists, that callers did not always know much about the service. So misalignments between what the caller wants, and what is on offer, are a possible problem early in these calls.

At line 5, the caller provides an initial gloss on the problem: 'we've got really terrible neighbours.' This may look like a typical way of introducing and formulating a problem between neighbours, but in fact it is more interesting than it looks. It does not actually define a problem between neighbours, such as not getting on with them, having an ongoing feud with them, or having broken off relations with them. Unlike the caller in Extract 1, who states she has a 'dispute', this caller formulates a one-sided complaint: 'We've got really terrible neighbours.' So, before the call has started, there are already signs of potential trouble for the service providers. (Indeed, this call ends with the caller resisting repeated offers of mediation.) However, the fact that C has used the category 'neighbours' is enough to signal to M that this is the right type of call for her to deal with. She affirms that C has rung the right place, although not without some perturbation to the smooth progressivity of the call – that is, there is some delay, an audible in-breath, a repair initiator and re-start on 'y've rung right place'. It might be that M is already picking up signs of trouble and her response symmetrically fits C's. As in Extract 1, M then delivers the ethical permission script.

In the final example in this section, C has left a message on the mediation centre's answer machine, and M is returning the call.

3. DC-65

```
        ((Phone rings))
1   C:   .hhh Churchborough three: two double three one two.
2   M:   Hello is that mister Can:ley.
3   C:   Speaking.
```

```
 4   M:   Hi:. my name's Jill. I'm ringing from: Mediation in
 5        Churchto:wn. you left us a couple of messages.
 6   C:   I did ye:ah.
 7   M:   Yes. how can I he:lp.
 8   C:   .hhh next door ne- uh- let me just turn t- telly off
 9        >hold on a minute please.<
10              (7.2)
11   C:   Sorry about 'at.
12   M:   That's okay.
13   C:   Next door neighbour. [.hhh
14   M:                        [↑Oh uh- sorry jus' before ...
          ((6 lines omitted - ethics script))
22   C:   Next door nei:ghbour. (0.7) um:: (0.2).hhhhh is::
23   →    >Indian.<
24              (1.6)
25   C:   I've no: problem with Indians: bu' unfortunately he's
26        >lower caste< so he doesn't do any work.
27              (0.2)
28   C:   An' that's not ra:cist.
29              (0.4)
30   M:   pt. What so: (0.6) ((tape pitch squeal))
31        wha' has him [being Indian got to- do:    ]=
32   C:                [W- the prob- the problem is,]=
33   M:   =[with it then.]
34   C:   =[I mean,       ]
```

The opening lines are somewhat different in this call, as both speakers
provide their names (although notably M does not give her surname).
However, as in Extracts 1 and 2, M also provides an institutional identification and offer of help as an invitation to C to explain his problem.
C begins to formulate his complaint at line 8 ('.hhh next door ne-'),
but cuts off to insert a short sequence about turning off his television
(lines 8–12). He begins again, recycling the same words, 'Next door
neighbour..hhh', but this time, having heard the word 'neighbour' M,
like M in Extract 1, overlaps the end of C's turn to start the ethics
script. This done, C restarts for a second time to formulate his complaint, again using the same formulation 'Next door nei:ghbour.', but
this time continuing to specify the problem with the neighbour: '(0.7)
um:: (0.2).hhhhh is:: >Indian.< '.

In our corpus of over 400 telephone calls, this is a unique opening, in that the caller begins his complaint with an ethnicity category,
'>Indian.<'. Note the pauses, hesitation, delay, and speeded up delivery of the actual category indicating trouble in this turn (lines 22–23).

After a long gap (line 24) in which there is no uptake from M, C produces a turn that accounts for his first, displaying his understanding that he is possibly being heard as racist, something that he then explicitly denies following a further absence of response from the mediator (line 27). At lines 30–33, M challenges the relevance of C's categorization of his neighbour, and the call (about car-parking problems outside their houses) proceeds without mentioning 'Indian' again.

In this first section we have shown how identity categories are made relevant at the start of calls, primarily the institutional category of the call-taker, and the relevance of being 'neighbours' for the caller and their complainee. These self-identifications provide an initial basis for further identity work to be done with regard to complainant and complainee in relation to the complaint itself, as we show in the next section.

Category-based complaints

The next extract comes from another mediation centre call. C has been complaining about excessive noise from her next-door neighbour's child.

```
4. HC-31
1   C:    Um:: an' some- uh- [sometimes:
2   M:                       [((sniffs))
3             (0.6)
4   C:    Because I- I: have a little girl who's the s-
5         (.) exactly the same age actually.
6   M:    Oh ri:ght.
7   C:    Um: (0.3) an'- an:, (.) an' I usually get her
8         into bed for half past eight.
9             (0.2)
10  C:    An,=
11  M:    =Yeah.
12            (0.3)
13  C: →  By that ti- a- cos I'm a single mother,
14  M: →  M:mm.=
15  C: →  =By that time, (0.3) I'm ti:red
16            (0.2)
17  C:    .hhh
18  M:    Yeah.=
19  C:    An' I don't have many resources left for
20        co:ping with things.
```

C is describing circumstances that enhance her grievance: that by 8:30 in the evening she is tired and cannot cope with additional problems created by the people next door. One feature of her account is the contrast between what *she* does to get her daughter to bed (lines 7–8) and what her neighbour by implication does not do: put his child to bed at what, for C, is a reasonable hour. C begins to describe the consequences of the noise for her, 'By that ti- a-' (line 13), but halts the production of this 'turn constructional unit' (TCU[1]) to insert the account 'cos I'm a single mother'. The placement and 'continuing' function of M's response at line 14 ('M:mm.') displays his understanding that C had not completed the original action launched at line 13 and, importantly, his recognition of the category and what it might mean to be 'a single mother' – he does not, for instance, treat it as an object for repair ('huh?', 'single mother?'). C then reinstates her description, recycling the original framing words 'By that time, (0.3) I'm ti:red'.

It is notable that C's categorial phrase 'I'm a single mother' performs self-attributed category membership directly, rather than ascribing membership via category-implicative description (e.g. 'I'm on my own with my daughter'). The use of the indefinite article 'a' produces the category as something with known-in-common meanings (Stokoe, 2009). C ties 'being tired' and 'not having many resources for coping' to the category 'single mother', moving from naming a category to unpacking its incumbent features or 'predicates'. The category 'single mother' works to explicate why C does not have 'resources' for 'coping' – she has no partner to share the load of additional problems. This is not to say that the category 'single mother' always indexes the same meaning (Stokoe, 2003). Rather, the orderliness of categories and their predicates, 'their "going together", is achieved and is to be found in the local specifics of categorization as an activity' (Hester and Eglin, 1997b: 46).

In Extract 5, C is a local council worker calling on behalf of a woman whose house backs onto cricket club grounds. The woman has complained to the council that balls from the club are damaging her roof, and make it unsafe to sit in her garden. C wants the mediation centre to mediate between the woman and the club.

```
5. DC-16
1  C:   [...] she can't go in 'er ga:rden an' it's dam- she's
2       paid for: (.) tiles bein' fixed on 'er roof:. without
3       even contactin' them,=she's says- she knows they're re-
4       (0.2) they kno:w they're responsible [hh     ] but she
5  M:                                        [.pt Yeh.]
6  C: → doesn't want to confront them: she's [eighty three]
```

```
 7   M:                              [.hhh ↑↑No: I]'d be uh
 8   M:   ↑ye:[ah.]=it's not *i-* uh y'know: *i-* b- *i-*
 9   C:      [(Um)]
10           (0.5)
11   M: →  Obviously age: (.) c- *i- i-* (.) could [be an i:ssue]
12   C:                                           [Ye:ah:     ]
13   M:   with'er but-.hh [↑y'know] it's ↑not something that-=
14   C:                   [(Yeah) ]
15   M:   =(0.3) a lo:t of people: um: do: easily.
```

C is narrating the woman's circumstances and complaints: not being able to use her garden – a mundane entitlement for someone who owns one – and having to pay for damage caused by the club. At lines 3–4, C reports that the club knows that they are responsible for the damage. Note the repair from 'she knows they're re-' to 'they kno:w they're responsible' (lines 3–4), replacing the pronoun 'she' with 'they'. The repair fixes any notion that it is only the woman's version of events that the cricket club caused damage: the club itself accepts responsibility. M acknowledges this (line 5), and C provides an account for why her client has not 'confronted' the club herself: 'she's eighty three' (line 6). The account formulates an *attribute* of the client but does not explicitly categorize her as, say, 'old'. However, 'eighty three' invokes a host of possible *category resonances* (Schegloff, 2007a) relevant to why this person does not want to complain directly to the cricket club (e.g. 'too old', 'frail', 'intimidated', etc.). M's response, 'Obviously age: (.) c- *i- i-* (.) could be an i:ssue' (line 11) shows that she has 'heard the categorial resonances' of 'she's eighty-three', thus converting an 'individual attribute to membership category' (Schegloff, 2007a: 445); that is, turning *description* into *categorization* (Stokoe, 2009). C's overlapping response 'Ye:ah:' treats M's recognition of C's category-resonant description as evidence of intersubjectivity and shared category knowledge. However, M suggests that although age might be the category in play for C, in fact 'a lo:t of people:' (line 15) do not find confrontation easy. Thus M displays her understanding of the categorial basis of C's complaint, but does not fully align with it, replacing 'age' with 'people in general'.

The examples in this section have shown how people forge 'a link between the complainability of the conduct and the category membership of those implicated in it – whether amplifying or qualifying that complainability' (Schegloff, 2005: 453). We have also begun to see cadences in the way categories are used to complain and, simultaneously, implicate the moral characters of the perpetrators of trouble. That is, perpetrators are not just causing damage (etc.), but are insensitive to their victims' category memberships as people who are not equally competent, fit, or healthy. In the next section, we examine cases in which speakers use categories to *deny* the accusations and complaints made against them.

Category-based denials

Extract 6 comes from a police interrogation of a suspect (S) aged 15, arrested for assaulting his neighbour. S has said that he entered his neighbour's garden to retrieve a football and this caused a confrontation. He admits swearing at the man, but denies assault. P is the police officer conducting the interview.

```
6. PN-33
 1    S:    Yeh I did walk towards 'im.
 2              (0.6)
 3    S:  → Cos I walked towa:rds 'im >an' I says< "if you weren't
 4        → old then I woulda wha:cked yuh."
 5              ((---19 secs cut---))
 6    P:    He's sayin' that when you've walked towar:ds 'im you've
 7          lunged forward and he:ad butted 'im on 'is no:se.
 8              (0.5)
 9    P:    Has that 'appen:ed
10              (0.2)
11    S:    Wha- I've ↑'it 'im:.
12              (0.2)
13    P:    You've head butted 'im. You've lunged forward an'
14          [head butted 'im.
15    S:    [NO::: no I ain't at a:ll.
16              (0.3)
17    S:    Unless y'cn ge' any proof then:
18              (1.5)
19    S:  → I'v- (.) headbutted 'im ↑wha' ↑w'd ↑I ↑wanna ↑head butt
20        → an old bloke fo:r.
21              (2.0)
22    S:    Shtu:pi:d.
```

At lines 2–3, S admits saying to the man that if he were not old then S 'woulda wha:cked' him. Edwards (2006: 475) has shown how suspects use such modal verb phrases 'to claim a disposition to act in ways inconsistent with whatever offence they are accused of', their value being that the 'semantics provide for a sense of back-dated predictability with regard to the actions in question'. Here, S makes a dispositional claim that because he does not 'whack' old people *in general*, he did not 'whack' this old man in particular – although leaving the implication that he may 'whack' 'young' people! S thereby constructs a contrast-class of categories in which 'old' people constitute the un-whackable group. However, P pursues the assault charge by presenting the aggrieved's testimony (lines 6–7), that S 'lunged forward and he:ad butted 'im on 'is no:se'. Note how P's formulation of this testimony incorporates actions that S has already admitted to, 'walking towards' the neighbour. After no response from S, P asks a direct question, 'Has that 'appen:ed'. S's response ('Wha- I've ↑'it 'im:.'), with its 'incredulous' prosody, treats the accusation of 'head butting' as 'news', although he formulates 'head butting' as the more general action of 'hitting'. His turn initiates a repair sequence in which P reformulates the accusation, repeating the specific action of 'headbutting' which S denies in overlap at line 15. At line 17, S suggests that the case is a matter of evidence, and his word against the neighbour's. After a long gap, S then produces a 'category-based denial' incorporating 'would' plus a categorial item ('old bloke') to complete the action.

As Edwards (2006) has shown, the clause 'I wouldn't hit an X' appears routinely in police interrogations. The 'X' categorial item is used indexically with regards to the category memberships of the speaker, such that 'adults' might say 'I wouldn't hit a child', but 'men' do not say, at least in the data collected, 'I wouldn't hit a man' (see Stokoe, 2006). Category-based denials therefore tell us about the symmetrical–hierarchical organization of a culture's categories: who the 'vulnerable' and 'powerful' members normatively are. S's denial is designed indexically with regards to his own age as a 'teenager', for whom it is unclear what counts as 'old': categories may not have an objectively defined meaning outside the local context of their use.

Extract 7 comes from a call to a mediation centre. The caller has been describing a long-standing dispute with her neighbour, but is here recounting *his* complaint about *her*.

```
7. EC-9
1   C:   I was doing gardening in ga:rden?
2   M:   ((clears throat))
3   C:   And: suddenly I: heard a very:.hhh (.) bad BANGing the door,
4        and I rushed to door?.hhh and I saw th- that this guy,.hhh
5        (.) wit- 0.2) half naked, in front of my door, (.) with=
6   M:   =↑Oh.=
7   C:   =finger: .hhh (.) mm- gesture: and putting his finger to me:
8             (0.3)
9   C:   Nnuh-.hhh "Put your music down."=I said "Who you are:,".hhh
10       (.) to sho:ut at me. and m- put your finger to me..hhh
```

```
11      this is not the m- my music is <not lo:ud.>.hh I am <not
12   →  l- like you:> to listen to reggae music. I'm a- I'm just
13   →  sixty two years old.=I have no.hhh Ti::me. an' I have to-
14   →  <no:: mo:od> to listen high music. [...]
```

C's first turn in this sequence sets the scene, with her doing 'being ordinary' (Sacks, 1984), and so nothing complainable, at the start of her narrative ('doing gardening in ga:rden?'). This is in contrast to what happens next, 'suddenly' and without occasion: 'a very:.hhh (.) bad BANGing the door'. C reports an incident between herself and her neighbour, in which she describes his complaint about C's loud music. As part of a denial, C reports herself saying that her music is '<not lo:ud.>' (line 11). She offers a contrast between herself and the neighbour, 'I am <not l- like you:> to listen to reggae music', which contains the implied accusation that her neighbour, not her, is the cause of music-related problems. Finally, she utters a denial based on a category-implicative attribution; that she is 'sixty two years old'. Note the repair segment within which this description is embedded, from a possible self-categorization ('I'm a-') to a self-description ('I'm just sixty two years old'), blurring the boundaries between the two practices. C then spells out the relevance of being sixty two: '=I have no.hhh Ti::me. an' I have to- <no:: mo:od> to listen high music.' This description trades on a normative expectation that 62 year olds do not listen to loud music, in which case C could not be the party at fault in the dispute by virtue of her category membership.

Speakers regularly invoke or make inferences about their own and other people's identity categories when denying actions of which they are accused. As we show in the next section, they also recruit identity matters to accomplish other social actions.

Accounting for failure to help oneself

Extract 8 comes from hear the start of a call to a mediation centre, following the ethics script.

```
8. DC-73
1   M:    Hi. How can I hel:p.
2   C:    U:m (0.5) I've complained about- (0.3) u-the girl
3         downstairs with 'er mu:sic.
4   M:    .h Right.
5   C:    t'the council an' they've give me:*: your number.
6   M:    .hh Right. Okayhh.
7               (0.3)
```

```
 8  M:   U*h *i:*i*i is it loud noise that you're
 9        con[cerned about.]
10  C:       [Ye:h I've  ] ph:oned security again last
11        nigh[t. that *i-it's it's (0.6) from morning=
12  M:        [Righ'.
13  C:   =t'↓night it's on (.) no:w.
14            (0.5)
15  M:   Right.
16            (0.3)
17  C:   U::m (0.4) I have ta:lked to 'er about it but
18    →  sh' one o' these people: (0.6) y'can't talk to.
19            (0.3)
20  M:   R:i:ght. O:k[ay.
21  C:→              [She's twenty one year ↓old with an
22    →  att(h)it(h)u(h)de.
23            (0.2)
24  M:   .hhh Rhigh[ht
25  C:             [You know what they're like at that
26        a:ge?
27  M:   .h Ri:ght. I see: right.= *An' *is tha*t* (0.3)
28        music being played uh- all the ↓time y'[thin:k.]=
29  C:                                           [Yes love]
30        =[it is yeh.]
31  M:   =[.hhhh     ] Rhighht. Okahy..HHHh U::m *u- I'll
32        °u-u-w-° I'll tell y'a little bit about mediation
33        an' how we can he:lp [an' then I'll] l-let you=
34  C:                         [°Yeh sure°   ]
35  M:   =decide if you want to go ahead..hhhh
```

A key point about this extract is the precise location of C's description of her neighbour as 'twenty one year ↓old with an att(h)it(h)u(h)de'. C starts her call formulating her as 'the girl downstairs', an institutionally oriented description that provides M with the information that C is calling, appropriately, about a near neighbour's late night music.

Edwards and Stokoe (2007) analysed numerous instances like this one, in which either callers or mediators talk about what callers may expectably have done, prior to seeking outside help, to try to resolve the problem themselves. This is a particular instance of a general norm, outside of exploitative practices of various kinds, that one should not seek help for something one can readily do oneself. In the case of neighbour disputes, and relevantly to their resolution via mediation, self-help generally amounts to trying to first talk things through with the neighbour. Unusually in this case, C does not wait to be asked about it. Her first orientation comes at lines 17–18, characterizing her neighbour as 'one o' these people: (0.6) y'can't talk to'. After a slightly delayed receipt from M, C further specifies this characterization with the target lines, 'she's twenty one year ↓old with an att(h)it(h)u(h)de'. Notice that C does not start her call complaining about 'a twenty-one year old with an attitude', but refers instead to 'the girl downstairs with her music'. Being aged 21 with an attitude is an identity formulation specifically designed not for defining the complainable matter itself (playing late night music), but for accounting for failed efforts at obtaining a cooperative response from her. So characterological and identity matters figure at particular interactional junctures, where they are formulated for particular interactional contingencies – in this case, accounting for why expert intervention is being sought.

In the final section, we consider another regular social action which is accomplished via characterological formulations of the persons involved, which is when callers resist or refuse an offer of mediation.

Resisting offers of mediation

Extract 9 comes from a mediation centre call; here the mediator is describing the mediation process.

```
9. HC-7
 1   M:   We wouldn't take si:des, we wouldn't- (0.7) try and
 2        decide who's right or wrong but would.hh would try
 3        to help you both um:: (0.8) sort out uh: the
 4        differences between: (0.2) between you.
 5             (2.5)
 6   C:  → Well I- (1.2) to be qui:te honest I don't think
 7        she'd cooperate.
 8             (0.4)
 9   M:   N:o:.
10             (0.6)
11   C:   You know:.
12             (1.0)
13   C:   Um:,
14             (1.2)
15   C:   I- I just don't- don't know what to do:.
16             (0.8)
17   C:   I mean when she's- (0.6) threatenin', (0.8)
18        to put me in a HO:me,
19             (1.4)
20   C:   I mean what right has she to do say things like
```

```
21            ↑↑tha:t!
22               (0.2)
23    M:    .hhh well none at all: I mean she's got- (.) she's
24          got no power. to do that. has she.
25               (0.6)
27    C:    No:¿
28               (0.5)
29    C:    But uh- (0.8) I mean.k
30               (0.7)
31    C:    Other pe:ople have heard it.
32               (0.4)
33    M:    Mmm.
34    C:    This music my neighbour beLO:W.
35               (0.8)
36    C:    Uh: bu- a-appar- the- they're on holiday at the
37          moment.
38    M:    Right,=
39    C:    =There's no:body dare approach her,
40               (0.3)
41    M:    Mmm[.
42    C: →     [Because she's such a nasty per:son.
43    M:    Right..hhh ((coughs))
44               (1.5)
45    M:    .hhh
46               (1.7)
47    M:    So would you- would you like us to um:: (1.9) to
48          give it a go:?
```

It is clear from the numerous lengthy gaps in this extract that it is saturated with interactional trouble. At lines 1–4, M formulates (i.e., provides a particular description of) the mediation process, emphasizing the neutral approach adopted that typifies at least an idealized version of mediation (see Cobb and Rifkin, 1991; Jacobs, 2002; Heisterkamp, 2006). As we regularly observed, such an approach is often assessed negatively, either implicitly or explicitly, by callers. Here, by formulating the process of mediation, M is implicitly offering the service, and C is in a position to respond positively, accepting the offer, or negatively, rejecting it. Several features of the talk indicate an upcoming dispreferred response, a rejection of the offer: the 2.5-second gap before C's response, and her turn-initial 'Well' which starts an account for rejecting the offer, which also functions as a rejection: 'Well I- (1.2) to be qui:te honest I don't think she'd cooperate.' As Edwards and Fasulo (2006) have observed, parenthetical 'honesty phrases' such as 'to be honest' typically frame dispreferred actions such as offer rejections, invitation refusals, and failures to provide expected answers to questions.

C's account, of course, puts the blame for mediation failure squarely on her neighbour's shoulders: she is someone who would not cooperate. By implication, C's neighbour is not a cooperative person; and the characterological aspects of her are further specified towards the end of the extract 'she's such a <u>nas</u>ty per:son.' A clear case of misalignment follows, in which M continues to push C to 'give it a go:?' despite C's clear resistance throughout the conversation.

Concluding remarks

In this chapter, we have presented several sections of analysis that illustrate key findings from our studies of neighbour disputes. We have provided evidence of the centrality of identity matters to such disputes, and shown how they arise in regular ways, designed at and for particular kinds of interactional moments and in the service of particular social actions. Of course, our analyses have broader implications for the study of identity and social action than the study of neighbour relationships. We hope to have demonstrated a method for studying identity using a robust empirical approach that provides clear evidence for warranting claims about *how* matters of identity become relevant for people, and *what* they can do with it in terms of accomplishing social action.

As we noted earlier, our approach to identity has been to conceive of it in broader terms than the traditional academic set (e.g. 'class', 'gender', 'race'), focusing on these where they are made relevant but additionally on people's own character-based ('bully', 'nasty person') and other identity-relevant descriptions ('parent', 'slag'), which occur much more frequently. Our analyses have shown that whereas matters of gender, ethnicity, age, and so on do feature as topics regularly across the data, it is the more mundane characterological forms that find their way into disputes, impacting on the nature of complaints, the likelihood of offers of mediation being taken up, and so on. Being a 'nasty person', or 'the type of person you can't talk to' or a 'neighbour from hell' accounts for what makes a person's actions complainable, and also for what makes the situation intractable, difficult to resolve, prone to reprisals following any complaint being made public, or else rendering the prospect of mediation 'pointless'. Characterological descriptions might not be quite what some think of, theoretically, as 'identity', but they feature in important and compelling ways in the neighbour conflicts we have collected, and are highly consequential for the effective operation of mediation processes and services.

Note

1. 'Turn constructional units' are 'the building blocks out of which turns are fashioned' (Schegloff, 2007b: 3).

References

Antaki, C. and Widdicombe, S. (eds.) (1998) *Identities in Talk*. London: Sage.
Bridge, G., Forrest, R. and Holland, E. (2004) *Neighbouring: A Review of the Evidence*. University of Bristol: ESRC/Centre for Neighbourhood Research.
Citizen's Advice Bureau (2007) Neighbour Disputes. www.adviceguide.org.uk (accessed 31 December 2007).
Cobb, S. and Rifkin, J. (1991) Practice and Paradox: Deconstructing Neutrality in Mediation. *Law and Social Inquiry* 16, 1: 35–62.
DirectGov (2007) *Home and Community: Neighbour Disputes*. www.direct.gov.uk
Drew, P. (2005) Conversation Analysis. In K. L. Fitch and R. E. Sanders (eds.) *Handbook of Language and Social Interaction*. Mahwah, NJ: Erlbaum.
Edwards, D. (2005) Discursive Psychology. In K. L. Fitch and R. E. Sanders (eds.) *Handbook of Language and Social Interaction*. Mahwah, NJ: Erlbaum.
Edwards, D. (2006) Facts, Norms and Dispositions: Practical Uses of the Modal *would* in Police Interrogations. *Discourse Studies* 8, 4: 475–501.
Edwards, D. and Fasulo, A. (2006) 'To be Honest': Sequential Uses of Honesty Phrases in Talk-in-Interaction. *Research on Language and Social Interaction* 39, 4: 343–76.
Edwards, D. and Stokoe, E. (2007) Self-help in Calls for Help with Problem Neighbours. *Research on Language and Social Interaction* 40, 1: 9–32.
Francis, D. and Hester, S. (2004) *An Invitation to Ethnomethodology*. London: Sage.
Heisterkamp, B. L. (2006) Conversational Displays of Mediator Neutrality in a Court-Based Program. *Journal of Pragmatics* 38: 2051–64.
Hester, S. and Eglin, P. (eds.) (1997a) *Culture in Action: Studies in Membership Categorization Analysis*. Washington, DC: University Press of America.
Hester, S. and Eglin, P. (1997b) The Reflexive Constitution of Category, Predicate and Context in Two Settings. In S. Hester and P. Eglin (eds.) *Culture in Action: Studies in Membership Categorization Analysis*. Washington, DC: University Press of America.
Jacobs, S. (2002) Maintaining Neutrality in Dispute Mediation: Managing Disagreement while Managing not to Agree. *Journal of Pragmatics* 34: 1403–26.
Jayyusi, L. (1984) *Categories and the Moral Order*. London: Routledge.
Jefferson, G. (2004) Glossary of Transcript Symbols with an Introduction. In G. H. Lerner (ed.) *Conversation Analysis: Studies from the First Generation*. Amsterdam: John Benjamins.
Laurier, E., Whyte, A. and Buckner, K. (2002) Neighbouring as an Occasioned Activity: 'Finding a Lost Cat'. *Space and Culture* 5, 4: 346–67.
Lupi, T. and Musterd, S. (2006) The Suburban 'Community Question'. *Urban Studies* 43, 4: 801–17.

McGhee, D. (2003) Moving to 'Our' Common Ground: A Critical Examination of Community Cohesion Discourse in Twenty-First Century Britain. *Sociological Review* 51, 3: 376–404.

Prezza, M., Amici, M., Roberti, T. and Tedeschi, G. (2001) Sense of Community Referred to the Whole Town: Its Relations with Neighbouring, Loneliness, Life Satisfaction and Area of Residence. *Journal of Community Psychology* 29, 1: 29–52.

Pomerantz, A. and Mandelbaum, J. (2005) Conversation Analytic Approaches to the Relevance and Uses of Relationship Categories in Interaction. In K. L. Fitch and R. E. Sanders (eds.) *Handbook of Language and Social Interaction*. Mahwah, NJ: Lawrence Erlbaum Associates.

Psathas, G. (1999) Studying the Organization in Action: Membership Categorization and Interaction. *Human Studies* 22: 139–62.

Sacks, H. (1984) On Doing 'Being Ordinary'. In J. M. Atkinson and J. Heritage (eds.) *Structures of Social Action: Studies in Conversation Analysis*. Cambridge: Cambridge University Press.

Sacks, H. (1992) *Lectures on Conversation*, Vols. I & II, G. Jefferson (ed.) Oxford, UK: Basil Blackwell.

Schegloff, E. A. (1979) Identification and Recognition in Telephone Conversation Openings. In G. Psathas (ed.) *Everyday Language: Studies in Ethnomethodology*. New York: Irvington.

Schegloff, E. A. (1996) Issues of Relevance for Discourse Analysis: Contingency in Action, Interaction and Co-Participant Context. In E. H. Hovy and D. R. Scott (eds.) *Computational and Conversational Discourse: Burning Issues – An Interdisciplinary Account*. New York: Springer.

Schegloff, E. A. (2005) On Complainability. *Social Problems* 52, 4: 449–76.

Schegloff, E. A. (2007a) Categories in Action: Person-Reference and Membership Categorization. *Discourse Studies* 9, 4: 433–61.

Schegloff, E. A. (2007b) *Sequence Organization: A Primer in Conversation Analysis, Volume 1*. Cambridge: Cambridge University Press.

Stokoe, E. H. (2003) Mothers, Single Women and Sluts: Gender, Morality and Membership Categorisation in Neighbour Disputes. *Feminism and Psychology* 13, 3: 317–44.

Stokoe, E. (2006) On Ethnomethodology, Feminism, and the Analysis of Categorial Reference to Gender in Talk-in-Interaction. *Sociological Review* 54, 3: 467–94.

Stokoe, E. (2008) Categories and Sequences: Formulating Gender in Talk-in-Interaction. In L. Litosseliti, H. Saunston, K. Segall and J. Sunderland (eds.) *Language and Gender Research Methodologies*. Basingstoke: Palgrave Macmillan.

Stokoe, E. (2009) Doing Actions with Identity Categories: Complaints and Denials in Neighbour Disputes. *Text and Talk* 29, 1: 75–97.

Stokoe, E. and Edwards, D. (2007) 'Black this, Black that': Racial Insults and Reported Speech in Neighbour Complaints and Police Interrogations. *Discourse and Society* 18, 3: 355–90.

Stokoe, E. H. and Wallwork, J. (2003) Space Invaders: The Moral-Spatial Order in Neighbour Dispute Discourse. *British Journal of Social Psychology* 42: 551–69.

Vallance, S., Perkins, H. C. and Moore, K. (2005) The Results of Making a City more Compact: Neighbours' Interpretations of Urban Infill. *Environment and Planning B* 32, 5: 715–33.

Van Dijk, T. (1987) *Communicating Racism: Ethnic Prejudice in Thought and Talk.* London: Sage.

Watson, R. (1997) The Presentation of Victim and Motive in Discourse: The Case of Police Interrogations and Interviews. In M. Travers and J. F. Manzo (eds.) *Law in Action: Ethnomethodological and Conversation Analytic Approaches to Law.* Aldershot: Ashgate Publishing.

Worley, C. (2005) 'It's Not About Race. It's About the Community': New Labour and 'Community Cohesion'. *Critical Social Policy* 25, 4: 483–96.

6
Passing as a Transsexual Woman in the Gender Identity Clinic

Susan A. Speer

In this chapter I report findings from research undertaken as part of a large-scale study of the construction of transsexual identities in a British National Health Service Gender Identity Clinic (Speer and Green, 2008). Drawing on a single case conversation analysis of one minute of videotaped and transcribed interaction from an assessment session between a male consultant psychiatrist and a pre-operative male-to-female transsexual[1] patient attending the clinic, I investigate the interactional practices associated with the social action of 'passing' as female.

On passing

'Passing' is a concept of long-standing interest in social science research on identity (Butler, 1993; Goffman, 1963; Ginsberg, 1996; Ahmed, 1999; Sánchez and Schlossberg, 2001). However, the first studies to set about identifying the social practices associated with passing as male or female were conducted by the ethnomethodologists, Harold Garfinkel (1967) and Suzanne Kessler and Wendy McKenna (1978). Unlike much research on passing which treats it as involving deception of some kind – that the passing individual is presenting themselves as a member of a group that is *not their own*[2] – ethnomethodologists adopt a broader definition of passing which entails a person 'doing something in order to be taken as she/he intends' (Kessler and McKenna, 1978: 19). From this perspective, 'everyone is passing' (1978: 19): passing is an activity that we *all* engage in as part of our everyday lives.

Although for most of us, the practices that we deploy in order to pass go 'unnoticed', ethnomethodologists believe that for transsexual persons, passing as a 'normal' or 'natural' male or female is an 'enduring practical task' (Garfinkel, 1967: 118), which requires constant work and 'active deliberate management' (1967: 139) on their part. By studying transsexuals' passing practices, and the way members attribute gender to ambiguously gendered individuals, we can begin to uncover the taken-for-granted, cultural and normative ways through which we recurrently *do* sex and gender (West and Zimmerman, 1987).

The approach to gender exemplified in these studies was remarkably ahead of its time (Crawford, 2000). Indeed, Garfinkel's (1967: 181) claim that 'normally sexed persons are cultural events' can be considered a radical comment on the social construction of sex more typically credited to the post-feminist philosopher, Judith Butler (1990), more than two decades later. One of the main limitations of both studies, however, is that although they placed great emphasis on members' 'everyday interactions' (Kessler and McKenna, 1978: 115), 'actual witnessed displays of common talk and conduct' (Garfinkel, 1967: 181), and 'the ways transsexuals talk about... transsexualism, the language they use' (Kessler and McKenna, 1978: 114), there is remarkably little by way of first-hand evidence of participants' talk-in-interaction included in their analyses. The vast proportion of the data used in the texts consists of short, decontextualized (i.e., typically monologic, one speaker, one line) excerpts from transcripts of interviews with trans individuals, and the researchers' post hoc recollections and reports of events. What is missing from both studies is a systematic analysis of transsexual persons' 'naturally occurring' interactions and accounts, and their contribution to those very practices of gender construction that Garfinkel and Kessler and McKenna intended to analyse (for an extended overview and critique of this work, see Speer, 2005 and Speer and Green, 2007). My aim in this chapter is to update these studies and develop and extend what we know about transsexuals' passing practices with reference to a fragment of just such data drawn from a psychiatric assessment session in the distinctive institutional environment of the Gender Identity Clinic (GIC).

Passing in the gender identity clinic

Of course, as clinic insiders with full access to patients' medical histories, psychiatrists will already know whether patients were born male or female. In this sense, patients cannot possibly pass with psychiatrists in the GIC in the same way they might with others outside the clinic environment who do not know about their transsexual status. Nonetheless, the institutionally ratified, diagnostic remit of the clinic psychiatrist, and the precarious, essentially contested nature of members' gender identities in this setting, makes the GIC an extremely rich site for the exploration of passing as a social action.

Clinic psychiatrists are essentially 'gatekeepers' to hormones and surgery (Speer and Parsons, 2006, see also Johnson, 2007). They assess patients according to a pre-defined set of medical criteria, and aim to produce a 'differential diagnosis' (i.e., to accurately diagnose the type of gender identity disorder and to determine that patients are not suffering from some related or unrelated mental health problem). Patients must be assessed by, and obtain the approval of, at least two psychiatrists before they can be referred to the surgeon. Constantly attuned to the possibility that patients may have learnt, and simply be repeating, the 'necessary life-history required for successful "passing"' (Hird, 2002: 583), psychiatrists monitor patients' actions extremely closely.

Although the internationally recognized Standards of Care for Gender Identity Disorders (HBIGDA, 2001) does not treat physical appearance or success in passing in the preferred gender role as a formal criterion in the assessment process, there are numerous reports in the literature that gender professionals 'have judged transsexuals' authenticity on their ability to pass' (Lev, 2004: 264). Certainly, it is not uncommon (as I go on to show below), for psychiatrists, as well as patients, to comment on, or allude to, the patient's physical appearance and overall ability to pass *as* a man or a woman, during their assessment sessions. It is hardly surprising given this context that patients may interpret their success at the clinic (i.e., whether or not they will be diagnosed as transsexual and obtain the treatment they desire) as dependent on them showing, through their talk, bodily comportment, appearance and gestures, that they can pass as a convincing, 'always have been, always will be', male or female, in their interactions with the psychiatrist. (For more on the diagnosis and treatment of transsexualism, see Green, 2005, 2007, 2008; Barrett, 2007.)

Analysing gender identity in the clinic

The approach to gender identity I adopt in this chapter is strongly influenced by Emanuel Schegloff's (1991, 1997, 1998) conversation analytic remarks on the role of demographic variables in interaction. According to Schegloff, gender, like other features of identity such as age, class, and race, should not be treated analytically as external, independent variables that condition and constrain behaviours. Rather, they are emergent and locally occasioned resources which may or may not be 'made relevant' in interaction, 'indexed' (Ochs, 1992) or 'oriented to' as participants' concerns (for examples of research that exemplifies this approach, see Hopper and LeBaron, 1998; Speer, 2005; Kitzinger, 2007; and Speer and Stokoe, forthcoming). One routine conversational means through which gender gets indexed in the GIC, and through which the social action of passing gets done, is via the use of what I am calling 'appearance attributions' – that is, references to what the patient *looks* like. In my data, these attributions are typically evaluative, involving positive or negative assessments of some (implicitly or explicitly gendered) appearance-relevant attribute. Appearance attributions are initiated by both parties, and take a range of forms. Some examples of patient-initiated appearance attributions from my data include:

[T11]
I've got good legs.

[T13]
'I don't look as a guy, all my features are female.

[T11]
I'm realistic enough to realize that I'll never look like Pamela Anderson or a woman like that, but I do look feminine a bit.

Some examples of psychiatrist-initiated appearance attributions include:

[T11]
My first impression would be that you're a long haired man...I would think you're a guy with long hair. I wouldn't think that you're a woman

[T12]
Since you look like a young woman...they wouldn't really have any legal basis to deny you contact under the paediatric service.

[T10]
Well you look like a woman. The only giveaway thing is your voice.

In this chapter, I explore the role that such attributions play in the patient's attempts to pass as female, and to be treated *as* a trans woman in this distinctive institutional setting. Although I have presented these attributions in a decontextualized fashion above, it is important to note that they do not exist in an interactional vacuum. Just as Kessler and

McKenna (1978: 136–7) stressed the central role of the recipient, or the 'perceiver' of a gender display in transsexuals passing as male or female, I adopt the view expressed by C. Goodwin and M. Goodwin, that nobody is ever building an utterance, or an action alone. Indeed, speakers will often change what they are saying or doing in the course of a spate of talk on the basis of the response that they are getting from their recipient(s) (M. Goodwin, 1980; C. Goodwin 1981; C. Goodwin and M. Goodwin, 2004). Part of the distinctiveness of what I aim to show here, then, is that gender is a thoroughly embodied and *co-constructed* practice in interaction, and an analysis of the interrelation of the talk and gestures *of both speakers and hearers* is absolutely fundamental to our understanding of how members 'do', and 'display' gender in an interaction, and pass as male or female (Speer and Green, 2007). Thus, in addition to exploring the vocal and gestural means by which the patient works to pass as a transsexual female, and do gender in this setting, I am equally concerned to ask, how does the psychiatrist orient towards and treat these 'gender displays'? Does he co-participate in, ignore, or reject them? How does the psychiatrist's response shape the patient's next interactional move, and what is the relationship between these displays and responses?

I intend this chapter to contribute to social scientific research on passing, identity management, and appearance, as well as to broader debates around the social construction of gender and how it gets 'done', 'displayed' and 'oriented to' in interaction.

Data and setting

The data excerpt I analyse below derives from a corpus of more than 156 transcribed audio-recordings and 38 video-recordings of psychiatrist–patient consultations in a large British National Health Service GIC.[3] The clinic in the study is the largest GIC in the world. Ninety-five percent of all NHS referrals are dealt with here, and psychiatrists at the clinic accept approximately 500 new patients each year (Green, 2008). Ethical approval for this study was granted by the NHS Central Office of Research Ethics Committee. The data were transcribed verbatim in the first instance by a professional transcriber. Detailed transcripts were then worked up by me using conventions developed within CA by Gail Jefferson (2004). A simplified version of these conventions can be found in Appendix B. I have marked the relevant appearance attributions on the transcript in bold. Bodily movements and gestures are noted in the left-hand margin. Still images are included below to exemplify these gestures and their interlacing with the talk, where relevant to the analyses. (For a full account of the methods and materials used in this study, see Speer and Green, 2007, 2008.) The clip I have chosen is from an exit interview, and the patient identifies as a pre-operative male-to-female transsexual.[4] I have chosen this excerpt for analysis for two main reasons: First, it contains examples of both patient-initiated and psychiatrist-initiated appearance attributions. As such, it permits investigation of the interactional circumstances in which the patient deploys appearance attributions in order to pass as a transsexual female, *and* those circumstances in which she is apparently treated as having passed successfully by the psychiatrist. Second, it contains a chain of *multiple* descriptions concerning the patient's appearance. This allows us to track how such descriptions develop incrementally over time, with each successive turn in the interaction, and in response to the recipient's actions. The patient has been taking female hormones for over a year, and, she presents 'in role', in traditional female attire. At her last visit to the clinic this patient obtained her first approval for surgery from one of the psychiatrists, and this interaction is taken from her session with a second psychiatrist. Four minutes prior to the start of the excerpt, the psychiatrist announces to the patient that he and his colleagues will be sending a letter to the surgeons endorsing her for surgery. This 'green light announcement' is a momentous occasion for this patient – who has been trying to obtain her surgery for 12 years (the psychiatrist tells the patient that until now she has not been deemed psychologically stable enough to proceed to surgery). The excerpt begins one minute prior to the end of the assessment session.

```
[Speer Video 4 Male-to-Female Pre-op. Exit interview]
1    Psy:              As long as you're absolutely convi:nced we'll let
2    Pt simultaneously you do it.
3    engaged with bag  (.)
4    Pt:               W'll ye::ah- I mea- I mea:n there's no good puttin'
5                      any more obstacles in the way, I might aswell j's:t
6                      sort of get it done when I know I can sti::ll- you
7                      know- hopefully maybe I mean,
8    Pt sweeps hair both  I- I do: (0.4) you know people at wo:rk think I've
9    sides of face        got a lovely figure >I mean I've got that going for
10   Psy smiles, Pt       me I (look/got)quite nice,<
11   gestures hand across chest
12                      (0.8)
13   Psy:               [°Okay°.
14   Pt:                [(because/figure) slight- you know- kind of- you
15                      know- dependin',
16                      (.)
17   Pt: Psy nods       >An- that's the men(h)< (h)ri(h)ght(h) I'm not(   )
```

```
18                      say that (    ) so.hhh you kno::w uh:m,
19                      (0.4)
20  Pt: Pt gestures    I mean my face is- I c'd do with putting a ba:g
21  bag over head      over my head b't.hhh uh:m,
22                      (0.4)
23  Pt:                .Pt as a ru:le- you know like as I say the lo:nger
24  Psy nods           I leave it the harder it's gonna ge:t,you know (°l-°)
25  Psy:               Okay but whether or not you have the genital
26                      surgery, [sitting here right now,
27  Pt:                         [Ye:ah,
28                      (.)
29  Pt:                Yeah,
30                      (.)
31  Psy:               I don' know whether you've had surgery.
32                      (1.0)
33  Pt:                You don't kno:w.
34  Psy: Psy hands     [(        I'm) here looking at you who]=
35  Pt: out-stretched, [Oh r:ight     yes that's what I'm]=
36  Psy: shakes head   =[who w'd know?=
37  Pt: and shrugs     =[saying.       Yeah. Yeah. (Sure).
38  Psy:               This is not a (nudist) interview.
39                      (.)
40  Pt:                No. Su:re. [Su:re.]
41  Psy:               [You ] look like a woman.
42                      (.)
43  Pt:                Yea:h, n[o, that's right. (Yeah that's)
44  Psy:               [You don't have to have surgery to
45                      continue looking like a woman [(of course).
46  Pt:                [Yeah but- I- I- s- I-
47                      (0.6) I- I want to have relationsh(h)ip(h) so(h)
48                      wi[th a ma:n or whatever..h[h
49  Psy:                 [Okay.               [Okay.
50  Pt:                An' (0.4) whatever.
51  Psy:               [Okay.
52  Pt:                [You know so,
53  Psy: Gets up       Okay, we will send a let[ter of referral
54  Pt:                                        [Yeah, okay
```

Let us start by taking a closer look at the first few lines of the excerpt. What can we say about the interactional environment in which the first, patient-initiated appearance attribution takes place?

The psychiatrist's opening declarative and the patient's response

```
1  Psy:                As long as you're absolutely convi:nced we'll let
2  Pt simultaneously   you do it.
3  engaged with bag    (.)
4  Pt:                 W'll ye::ah- I mea- I mea:n there's no good puttin'
5                       any more obstacles in the way, I might aswell j's:t
6                       sort of get it done when I know I can sti::ll- you
7                       know- hopefully maybe I mean,
8  Pt sweeps hair both I- I do: (0.4) you know people at wo:rk think I've
9  sides of face       got a lovely figure >I mean I've got that going for
```

At the start of the excerpt the psychiatrist re-issues the endorsement he had given earlier, this time in the form of a declarative that acquiesces to giving permission for surgery subject to the patient meeting the condition, and reassuring him, that she is 'absolutely convi:nced' that she wishes to proceed (lines 1–2). Notice that 'We'll let you do it' (lines 1–2) is a clear orientation to the institutionalized, gatekeeping role of the psychiatrists at the clinic. It makes relevant and 'prefers' (Pomerantz, 1984a; Sacks, 1987) a response in which the patient shows herself to agree with the formulation that she is 'absolutely convi:nced' – to produce a 'no doubts' response. However, the patient's initial 'W'll ye::ah' (line 4) indicates that her response will not be straightforward (Schegloff and Lerner, 2004), and treats the underlying supposition of the question – that she may have some remaining doubts about proceeding to surgery – as inapposite. She goes on to produce a rather hedged account for why she is convinced, and which explains why she needs the surgery now (the 'I mean' (line 4) is dedicated to launching this task). So what does the patient's account for 'why now' consist of?

Her 'I mea:n there's no good puttin' any more obstacles in the way' (lines 4–5) clearly orients to the psychiatrist as gatekeeper, and indexes the views of many patients who see the assessment process as an inconvenient hoop they must jump through in order to get what they need. In lines 5–7 she seems to be having some trouble formulating her response. She says, 'I might as well j's:t sort of get it done when I know I can sti::ll'. But still what? This turn is clearly moving towards explicating some time or age-limited activity which surgery would allow her to participate in, but it trails off. Indeed, it may be designedly doing so in that it relies on the psychiatrist to project where the patient might be going with this turn, and specifically to infer what age-limited activity she is explicitly *not* stating. The patient's 'hopefully maybe' (line 7) is taking up a stance of desire towards this world of activities. However, here again, the precise specification of this world is aborted in favour of further unpacking ('I mean' – line 7).

The utterance that comes exactly next is the patient's first appearance attribution 'I- I do: (0.4) you know people at wo:rk think I've got a lovely figure' (lines 8–9). In combination, the hedging, the temporalizing of 'sti::ll' (line 6), the stance taking of 'hopefully maybe' (line 7), and the appearance attribution (lines 8–9), provide clues which help the psychiatrist to indexically fill in or infer what the patient is getting at here: that she wants the surgery now while she is still young and attractive enough to get a partner. Indeed, lines 5–9 can be heard as possibly suppressing what they are going towards, and which we arrive at only eventually after the psychiatrist's challenge, 'Yeah but- I- I- s- I- (0.6) I- I want to have relationsh(h)ip(h) so(h) with a ma:n or whatever..hh' (lines 46–8). So, for this patient it is all about having the appropriate genital equipment for a heterosexual relationship.

The patient's appearance attributions

```
 8    Pt sweeps hair both    I- I do: (0.4) you know people at wo:rk think I've
 9    sides of face          got a lovely figure >I mean I've got that going for
10    Psy smiles, Pt         me I (look/got)quite nice,<
11    gestures hand across chest
```

Let us now take a closer look at the first appearance attribution (lines 8–9). The first thing I want to note is that the launching of the attribution coincides precisely with a 'self-groom' in which the patient sweeps her hair away from both sides of her face, as exemplified in Figures 6.1a, 6.1b and 6.1c.

That these actions coincide so precisely indicates that the self-groom may not be entirely random (i.e., that the patient's hair is in the way of her face and needs moving at just this moment). Rather, it may constitute a gender display that is designedly fitted to the vocal elements of the interaction. By 'designedly fitted' I mean that as a distinctly feminine, normatively recognizable way that women groom their hair

Figure 6.1a   Lines 8–9: Pt: I- I do: (0.4) you know people at wo:rk think I've got a lovely figure

Figure 6.1b Lines 8–9 cont'd

Figure 6.1c Lines 8–9 cont'd

(especially, perhaps, during heterosexual interactions[5]), it works as an implicit indexing of gender, and a 'seen but unnoticed' background (Garfinkel, 1967) through which the psychiatrist will frame and interpret the vocal element of what the patient is saying. In combination, the vocal (appearance attribution) and the visual (self-groom) aspects of the interaction can be regarded as mutually elaborative and reinforcing elements of the same phenomenon – that is, of the patient showing the psychiatrist that not only is she treated by others outside of the clinic environment as a woman, but that she is also able to behave like one within it.

The second thing to note about the appearance attribution is that the turn in which it appears is launched with 'I- I do:'. This seems to be the beginnings of some kind of positive self-assessment (e.g., it could be going towards 'I do think I look nice', or 'I do have a lovely figure'), but it is self-repaired (Schegloff, Jefferson and Sacks, 1977) in favour of the reported compliment of a third party: 'people at wo:rk think I've got a lovely figure' (lines 8–9). This repair from 'I do:' to 'people at wo:rk think' constitutes a shift in the patient's footing (Clayman, 1992; Clayman and Heritage, 2002). This footing shift appears to be in the service of avoiding what Pomerantz (1978) has termed 'overt self-praise' or a 'self-brag' – something that might be associated with the patient assessing her own figure. By reporting the affirmation of others in the third party assessing her figure, the patient increases the epistemic distance between herself and the praise, invoking the comments of people who are *entitled* (Sacks, 1984) (and perhaps more entitled than she is) to make an objective assessment of her appearance. This way of building the appearance attribution is clinically consequential in that the patient is currently being assessed by the psychiatrist in part for whether she has a realistic view of herself in her new role. If she can convince him that she passes with others (both men and women) outside the clinic environment – others who notice and comment on feminine aspects of her appearance, thus *treating her as a woman* – then she can show that she is hardly deluded about her transsexual status.[6]

The patient's '>I mean I've got that going for me' (lines 9–10) unpacks what she meant by, and her stance towards, the embedded compliment, showing that she affiliates with it. This is followed with a second appearance attribution: 'I (look/got)quite nice'< (line 10). Although this is clearly framed as a positive self-assessment, it is also a *downgraded* assessment ('quite nice' is not as strong as 'lovely figure'). Why might the patient downgrade her assessment in this way? One clue lies in the reactions of the psychiatrist who remains steadfastly non-responsive throughout lines 8 and 9. He does not co-participate in the patient's assessments, affiliate with, or ratify what she is saying. He does smile at line 10, as the patient starts to voice her second appearance attribution. However, this is a 'grimacy' smile that is

Figure 6.2   Line 10 Pt: I (look/got)quite nice, <

strongly mitigated by him placing his hand in front of his face (see Figure 6.2).

This smile appears to show that the psychiatrist is responding to what the patient is saying, but without explicitly agreeing or disagreeing with it.

In my view, each of the three components of the patient's turn in lines 8–10, the reported compliment (appearance attribution 1), the displayed alignment with the reported compliment, and the downgraded self-assessment (appearance attribution 2), seem to work incrementally to pursue a particular kind of response from the psychiatrist (Pomerantz, 1984b). Indeed, as conversation analysts have shown, recipients of first assessments often co-participate in those assessments by producing agreeing and upgraded second assessments (Pomerantz, 1984a; C. Goodwin and M. Goodwin, 1987; Heritage and Raymond, 2005). I want to suggest that in this instance the patient uses each of the three elements of her turn in lines 8–10 to exploit this normative feature of the sequential organization of assessments, and to secure just this kind of recipient uptake from the psychiatrist. With the downgraded assessment and each added unit of her turn-so-far, she seems to be working to encourage, and make it easier for the psychiatrist to affiliate with, validate or ratify what she is saying.

The psychiatrist's response to the appearance attributions

```
8   Pt sweeps hair both   I- I do: (0.4) you know people at wo:rk think I've
9   sides of face         got a lovely figure >I mean I've got that going for
10  Psy smiles, Pt         me I (look/got)quite nice,<
11  gestures hand across chest
12                         (0.8)
13  Psy:                   [°Okay°.
14  Pt:                    [(because/figure) slight- you know- kind of- you
15                         know- dependin',
16                         (.)
17  Pt: Psy nods           >An- that's the men(h)< (h)ri(h)ght(h) I'm not(   )
18                         say that (   ) so.hhh you kno::w uh:m,
19                         (0.4)
```

However, instead of affiliating with the patient, the psychiatrist says a rather quiet '°Okay°' (line 13), which is very delayed (note the 0.8-second gap at line 12 that projects a 'dispreferred' response (Pomerantz, 1984a)). Just like the smile at line 10, this okay acknowledges but does not align or dis-align with what the patient has said. It is certainly not doing enthusiastic uptake or acknowledgement.[7] This apparent failure on the part of the psychiatrist to participate in the way the patient is working towards here, appears to be oriented to by the patient, whose turn at lines 14 and 15 ('(because/figure) slight- you know- kind of- you know- dependin'), contains overt signs of trouble. Her repetitive, affiliation seeking 'you knows' (lines 14–15) hold the import of the prior assessment in place, providing further opportunities for the psychiatrist to ratify or validate what she is saying. That he does not do so may be an instance of the psychiatrist exemplifying the kind of *professional distance* one might expect in such a setting, and I will return to discuss this possibility in the conclusion.

As if orienting to the psychiatrist's lack of affiliation as an indication that something is problematic in her prior talk, the patient says '>An-that's the men(h)< (h)ri(h)ght(h) I'm not() say that ()' (lines 17–18). This utterance appears to index directly back to, and locate as a possible trouble source, her earlier reported compliment and subsequent alignment with it. Through it the patient clarifies that it is the *men* at work who say she has a lovely figure and it is not *her* who is saying this about herself, hence deflecting any potential imputation that she was bragging.

The psychiatrist fails to respond vocally to this, but emits an almost imperceptible nod on completion of the word '(h)ri(h)ght(h)' (line 17) – a nod that I take to be an 'I've heard you' nod, rather than an affiliative or agreeing nod (c.f. Stivers, 2008).

The patient's self-deprecation

```
19                      (0.4)
20  Pt: Pt gestures    I mean my face is- I c'd do with putting a ba:g
21  bag over head      over my head b't.hhh uh:m,
22                      (0.4)
23  Pt:                .Pt as a ru:le- you know like as I say the lo:nger
24  Psy nods           I leave it the harder it's gonna ge:t,you know (°1-°)
```

In the absence of the kind of response from the psychiatrist that she appears to be working towards, the patient goes on to produce a third appearance attribution – this time in the form of a negative assessment or *self-deprecation* of her appearance: 'I mean my face is- I c'd do with putting a ba:g over bag over my head' (lines 20–21). This self-deprecation is accompanied by an intricate gesture whereby the patient points to her face and, just ahead of vocalizing the self-deprecation, exemplifies the act of putting a bag over her head.

This self-deprecation does two things: It serves to deflect any remaining imputation that the patient is engaging in a self-brag and it represents a further attempt on the part of the patient to get a more active kind of response or participation from the psychiatrist. Indeed, as CA work on negative self-assessments or self-deprecations has shown, they usually prefer some sort of *disagreement* by the recipient (Pomerantz, 1984a). The 'b't.hhh uh:m' at line 21, and the 0.4-second gap at line 22 both provide further opportunities for the psychiatrist to participate. However, here again, he remains steadfastly non-responsive.

Having moved through a chain of progressively downgraded appearance attributions ranging from the very positive 'lovely figure' (line 9), through the downgraded 'quite nice' (line 10), right through to the self-deprecating 'my face is- I c'd do with putting a ba:g over my head' (lines 20–21), the patient seems to have nowhere else to go to get the kind of participation from the psychiatrist that she appears to be pursuing. Indeed, she has already worked hard in her prior talk to locate and rectify any potential sources of trouble that may account for the psychiatrist's non-participation.

The psychiatrist's challenge

```
23  Pt:       .Pt as a ru:le- you know like as I say the lo:nger
24  Psy nods  I leave it the harder it's gonna ge:t,you know (°1-°)
25  Psy:      Okay but whether or not you have the genital
26            surgery, [sitting here right now,
27  Pt:                [Ye:ah,
28            (.)
29  Pt:       Yeah,
30            (.)
```

```
31   Psy:                      I don' know whether you've had surgery.
32                             (1.0)
33   Pt:                       You don't kno:w.
34   Psy: Psy hands           [(        I'm) here looking at you who]=
35   Pt:  out-stretched,      [Oh r:ight       yes that's what I'm]=
36   Psy: shakes head         =[who w'd know?=
37   Pt:  and shrugs          =[saying.        Yeah. Yeah. (Sure).
38   Psy:                      This is not a (nudist) interview.
39                             (.)
40   Pt:                       No. Su:re. [Su:re.]
```

When she continues her turn at line 23, the patient produces a series of
cliches: 'as a ru:le' and 'the lo:nger I leave it the harder it's gonna ge:t'
(lines 23–4). As instantly recognizable 'truisms', these utterances are easily and perhaps normatively 'agreeable with' (especially when combined
with the participation-seeking 'you knows' at lines 23 and 24). However, instead of agreeing with the patient, the psychiatrist's 'Okay but'
(line 25) seems to work to bracket off what the patient has just said, stop-
ping the activity in progress in order to shift to something else. With
it the psychiatrist launches a challenge to what the patient is saying,
which extends over lines 25, 26 and 31: 'Okay but whether or not you
have the genital surgery, sitting here right now, ... I don' know whether
you've had surgery'. This challenge is one of a series that involve the psychiatrist voicing his 'here and now' experience of the patient in order
to counter what she has been alluding to up to this point; that genital surgery may affect her outward appearance, and (by implication),
that she may be more able to attract a man when she has had the
operation.

Although the psychiatrist clearly *does* know that the patient is pre-
operative, on the face of it, his comments could be interpreted as an
indirect compliment – and a proposal that the patient passes. Indeed,
instead of treating the psychiatrist's turn at lines 25–31 as something
that challenges her account for 'why surgery now', the patient's 'yes
that's what I'm saying. Yeah. Yeah. (Sure)' (lines 35 and 37) transforms it
into something that potentially aligns with, or ratifies her own position
(hence treating it as something that is already evident to her).

The psychiatrist's appearance attribution

```
38   Psy:  This is not a (nudist) interview.
39         (.)
40   Pt:   No. Su:re. [Su:re.]
41   Psy:             [You ] look like a woman.
42         (.)
43   Pt:   Yea:h, n[o, that's right. (Yeah that's)
```

```
44   Psy:                    [You don't have to have surgery to
45                     continue looking like a woman [(of course).
46   Pt:                                          [Yeah but- I- I- s- I-
47                     (0.6) I- I want to have relationsh(h)ip(h) so(h)
48                     wi[th a ma:n or whatever..h[h
49   Psy:              [Okay.                      [Okay.
50   Pt:               An' (0.4) whatever.
51   Psy:              [Okay.
52   Pt:               [You know so,
53   Psy: Gets up      Okay, we will send a let[ter of referral
54   Pt:                                        [Yeah, okay
```

The psychiatrist continues to elaborate his 'here and now' experience of the patient, this time with an explicitly gendered appearance attribution: 'You look like a woman' (line 41). This appearance attribution differs from those of the patient in that it does not contain any subjective, assessing terms like 'lovely' or 'nice' (c.f. lines 9 and 10). Instead, it is produced as an objective, *clinical* statement about the patient's female appearance. However, here again, instead of treating 'You look like a woman' as part of a challenge, the patient accepts it, transforming it into a potential compliment that validates her own, position: 'Yea:h, no, that's right. (Yeah that's)' (line 43).

The psychiatrist now shifts away from detailing aspects of his 'here and now' experience of the patient, towards formulating the import or upshot of these experiences for his challenge: 'You don't have to have surgery to continue looking like a woman (of course)' (lines 44–45). It is only now that the patient treats what he is saying as a challenge and produces her own, 'bottom line' account for why she wants the surgery now: 'Yeah but- I- I- s- I- (0.6) I- I want to have relationsh(h)ip(h) so(h) with a ma:n or whatever..hh' (lines 46–8). This bottom line account alludes to what I suggested the patient might be suppressing right at the start of this excerpt: that she needs the surgery now because she wants the appropriate genital equipment for a heterosexual relationship. That the psychiatrist now treats this account as acceptable and wishes to bring the session rapidly to a close is evidenced by his repeated, sequence closing 'okays' at lines 49, 51 and 53 (Schegloff, 2007).

On treating someone *as* a woman

I have analysed an excerpt that contains a chain of multiple descriptions concerning the patient's appearance. These appearance attributions were progressively downgraded by the patient in order to attract a response in which the psychiatrist co-participates in, and ratifies her performance by treating her *as a woman.*

Of course, one might suggest that the psychiatrist's resultant *failure* to participate in the interaction in the way that the patient appears to be working towards here can be accounted for, in part, by reference to his status as a professional expert who is expected to exemplify just the kind of *professional distance* or *clinical neutrality* that we see here (Drew and Heritage, 1992; Clayman and Heritage, 2002; Heritage and Maynard, 2006). However, this argument cannot provide a complete explanation, because the psychiatrist's own, subsequent appearance attributions: 'You look like a wo̲man' (line 41), and 'You don't ha̲ve to have su̲rgery to continue lo̲oking like a woman (of course)' (lines 44–45) show that he is not averse to making explicitly gendered comments about the patient, or commenting on her appearance.

So what might account for this seemingly contradictory behaviour on the part of the psychiatrist? In particular, why might he appear reluctant at first to ratify or validate the patient's position, only to subsequently state that she does indeed look like a woman? I want to suggest that there are some sequential features of the appearance attributions that have consequences for the way in which they get produced and managed. Crucially, the patient's reported compliment (lines 8–9) and subsequent downgraded appearance attributions (lines 10 and 20–21) are relatively informal, 'lifeworld' descriptions (Mishler, 1985: 81–2) which place the psychiatrist in *second position* (that is – a *responsive* position) to the patient's assessments (Sacks, 1995; Schegloff, 2007). Thus, if he were to agree with them (and to disagree with the self-deprecation (Pomerantz, 1984a)), it would require him to respond by co-participating in treating the patient as a woman in a non-clinical way – agreeing with her view of her appearance. By contrast, the psychiatrist's description 'You look like a wo̲man' (line 41), devoid as it is of the kinds of evaluative terms (e.g., 'lovely' and 'nice') evidenced in the patient's lifeworld narrative, is delivered in *first position* in order to fulfil the *clinical,* and hence formal, professional task of informing the patient that an operation will not affect her outward appearance. Now the patient is in the responsive position, and must affiliate or disaffiliate with his (clinical) view of her appearance. This shows that the psychiatrist is not averse to telling the patient that she looks like a woman – that she 'passes'. Rather, he *is* averse to being placed in *second position* to a lifeworld narrative in which he must agree or disagree with, ratify or validate *her view of her appearance.* It follows that the precise composition and position of the psychiatrist's appearance attributions is bound up with his efforts to sustain a relatively neutral, medical definition of the situation in the face of the pursuit by the patient of 'counter themes' (Emerson, 1970). And this order of things is very much in line with the psychiatrist's role as gatekeeper in this setting (Speer and Parsons, 2006).

Conclusion

I want to end by reflecting on some of the implications of these analyses for gender identity research. Part of the distinctiveness of what I have tried to show here is that gender identities are a collaborative product of the interaction between both speakers and hearers, and that the precise form the patient's gendered descriptions, displays, and passing practices take is highly contingent on the type of participation that is shown by the psychiatrist. Clearly, parties are able to exploit the normative sequential features of interaction (e.g., whether one is in first position, initiating a course of action, or in second position, responsive to a course of action), in order to seek ratification of, or avoid being placed in the role of having to ratify, a particular identity. However, when we consider the detailed turn-by-turn construction of this interaction, it becomes clear that passing as female, and 'doing gender', 'indexing gender' and 'orienting to gender', is not the primary activity of either party, or the most salient thing about what they are doing with their talk at that moment. Neither patient nor psychiatrist is, first and foremost, engaged in the act of displaying or ratifying gender. Rather, the appearance attributions are delivered primarily in the service of other business not focally concerned with doing gender. Thus, the patient's implicitly gendered appearance attributions at lines 8–10, and 20–21, are produced in order to account for why she is 'absolutely convi:nced' (line 1) that she wants the surgery now, while the psychiatrist's explicitly gendered appearance attributions at lines 41 and 44–5 are deployed as part of a counter-argument designed to challenge the patient's account, and in particular her alluded-to view that surgery will alter her appearance.

That the patient's attempts to pass and be treated by the psychiatrist as a woman, may be subservient, or subsidiary to, these other, more focal activities, does not mean that gender and passing are not relevant here, or that gender is not getting done, indexed or oriented to. Rather, in the GIC, gender is a fairly pervasive, 'omnirelevant' category that gets indexed and talked about much of the time (Klein, in press). It makes sense that doing, indexing and orienting to gender co-exists with, and gets woven relatively seamlessly into the texture of interactional slots whose primary or focal purpose is the accomplishment of other actions (Speer and Green, 2007: 362). It is this multi-layered nature of social action which accounts for how it is that in the GIC (as, elsewhere), telling a patient that they 'look like a woman' – that they 'pass', does not necessarily involve *treating* them as one. Talking about and indexing gender, on the one hand, and doing gender or treating someone as gendered, on the other, are very different things. Just as explicitly articulating a gender category does not automatically make gender relevant to what is going on in the talk, so too, gender can be relevant and consequential for an interaction even where a gender category is not explicitly articulated (Raymond and Heritage, 2006; Kitzinger, 2007). (For more on the relationship between focal and subsidiary actions, and their role in doing gender, see Kitzinger, 2008, and Speer, in press.)

Clearly, the social action of 'passing' has special relevance for transsexual patients in the somewhat unique institutional environment of the GIC where gender identities are fought over and contested. More work is needed to establish whether there are similar patterns of participation in other settings (such at dating interactions, for example), where participants strive to have their displayed identities affirmed and ratified by others. Nonetheless, I hope to have demonstrated that considerable insights can be gained from examining real-life empirical materials in their turn-by-turn detail – considering both the composition of the speaker's turn, its position in a sequence of turns, and the mutually elaborative relationship of the talk with embodied action. Identity researchers might benefit from closer engagement with videotaped materials of interactions in real-life settings. It is this kind of analysis, rather than abstract theorizing, that I believe offers the most promising set of tools with which to develop a systematic, empirically grounded form of identity research.

Notes

1. Transsexualism is formally designated in the Diagnostic and Statistical Manual of Mental Disorders (DSM-IV, 1994) as a 'Gender Identity Disorder' (GID). Persons with GID are said to exhibit 'a strong and persistent cross-gender identification and a persistent discomfort with their sex or a sense of inappropriateness in the gender role of that sex' (The Harry Benjamin International Gender Dysphoria Association (HBIGDA) 'Standards of Care for Gender Identity Disorders', 2001: 4). Throughout this chapter I use the medical term 'transsexual' as opposed to the more political term, 'transgender', to describe the research participants, because this research deals specifically with individuals who seek medical treatment to change their sex. The notion of

transgender is often used in a political context by transgender activists in order to avoid medical categorization.

2. For example, according to the Oxford English Dictionary (2006: passing, n. 8), passing involves 'being accepted, or representing oneself successfully as, a member of a different ethnic, religious, or sexual group'.

3. Richard Green arranged access to the field site, coordinated data collection on site, and provided brief explanation on the clinical management of patients.

4. The majority of patients attending the clinic are male-to-female transsexuals. Although statistics on such matters are notoriously problematic, this reflects the much larger incidence of transsexualism amongst males in the population (some of the latest figures from the Netherlands suggest transsexualism affects 1 in 11,900 males and 1 in 30,400 females (HBIGDA, 2001: 2)).

5. Of course, we do not know the sexual orientation of the psychiatrist in this data, but this does not rule out the possibility that the patient is treating the interaction from within a heteronormative framework as a heterosexual interaction (Kitzinger, 2005). Indeed, being treated as a woman *by a man* in a heteronormative culture may be the ultimate validation of one's passing.

6. In other words, by referring to her recognizably feminine attributes, she shows herself to be, and to be recognizable by others as, a *bona fide* member of the category 'woman' (Sacks, 1995).

7. See C. Goodwin and M. Goodwin (1987) for how recipients can refuse to co-participate in assessments.

References

Ahmed, S. (1999) She'll Wake up One of These Days and Find she's Turned into a Nigger' – Passing through Hybridity. *Theory, Culture and Society* 16, 2: 87–106.

Barrett, J. (ed.) (2007) *Transsexual and Other Disorders of Gender Identity: A Practical Guide to Management.* Oxon: Radcliffe.

Butler, J. (1990) *Gender Trouble: Feminism and the Subversion of Identity.* New York: Routledge.

Butler, J. (1993) *Bodies That Matter: On the Discursive Limits of 'Sex'.* London: Routledge.

Clayman, S. (1992) Footing in the Achievement of Neutrality: The Case of News Interview Discourse. In P. Drew and J. Heritage (eds.) *Talk at Work: Interaction in Institutional Settings.* Cambridge: Cambridge University Press.

Clayman, S. and Heritage, J. (2002) *The News Interview: Journalists and Public Figures on the Air.* Cambridge: Cambridge University Press.

Crawford, M. (ed.) (2000) A Reappraisal of *Gender: An Ethnomethodological Approach. Feminism & Psychology* 10, 1: 7–72.

Drew, P. and Heritage, J. (eds.) (1992) *Talk at Work: Interaction in Institutional Settings.* Cambridge: Cambridge University Press.

DSM-IV (1994) *Diagnostic and Statistical Manual of Mental Disorders.* 4th Edition. Washington, DC: American Psychiatric Association.

Emerson, J. P. (1970) Behaviour in Private Places: Sustaining Definitions of Reality in Gynecological Examinations. *Recent Sociology* 2: 74–97.

Garfinkel, H. (1967) *Studies in Ethnomethodology.* Englewood Cliffs, NJ: Prentice-Hall.

Ginsberg, E. K. (ed.) (1996) *Passing and the Fictions of Identity.* Durham, North Carolina: Duke University Press.

Goffman, E. (1963) *Stigma: Notes on the Management of Spoiled Identity.* Englewood Cliffs, NJ: Prentice Hall.

Goodwin, C. (1981) *Conversational Organization: Interaction Between Speakers and Hearers.* New York: Academic Press.

Goodwin, C. and Goodwin, M. H. (1987) Concurrent Operations on Talk: Notes on the Interactive Organization of Assessments. *IPrA Papers in Pragmatics* 1, 1: 1–55.

Goodwin, C. and Goodwin, M. H. (2004) Participation. In A. Duranti (ed.) *A Companion to Linguistic Anthropology.* Maldan, MA: Blackwell.

Goodwin, M. H. (1980) Processes of Mutual Monitoring Implicated in the Production of Description Sequences. *Sociological Inquiry* 50, 3–4: 303–17.

Green, R. (2005) Gender Identity Disorders. In B. Sadock and V. Sadock (eds.) *Comprehensive Textbook of Psychiatry.* 8th Edition. Philadelphia: Lippincott Wiliams.

Green, R. (2007) Gender Development and Reassignment. *Psychiatry* 6, 3: 121–4.

Green, R. (2008) Potholes in the Interview Road with Gender Dysphoric Patients: Contentious Areas in Clinical Practice. *Sexologies* 17, 4: 245–57.

HBIGDA (2001) The Harry Benjamin International Gender Dysphoria Association. *Standards of Care for Gender Identity Disorders,* Sixth Version. [Online document] Available from: <http://www.hbigda.org/Documents2/socv6.pdf> [Accessed September 2006].

Heritage, J. and Maynard, D. (eds.) (2006) *Communication in Medical Care: Interactions Between Primary Care Physicians and Patients.* Cambridge: Cambridge University Press.

Heritage, J. and Raymond, G. (2005) The Terms of Agreement: Indexing Epistemic Authority and Subordination in Talk-in-Interaction. *Social Psychology Quarterly* 68, 1: 15–38.

Hird, M. (2002) For a Sociology of Transsexualism. *Sociology* 36, 3: 577–95.

Hopper, R. and LeBaron, C. (1998) How Gender Creeps into Talk. *Research on Language & Social Interaction* 31, 1: 59–74.

Jefferson, G. (2004) Glossary of Transcript Symbols with an Introduction. In G. H. Lerner (ed.) *Conversation Analysis: Studies from the First Generation.* Amsterdam: John Benjamins.

Johnson, K. (2007) Transsexualism: Diagnostic Dilemmas, Transgender Politics and the Future of Transgender Care. In V. Clarke and E. Peel (eds.) *Out in Psychology: Lesbian, Gay, Bisexual, Trans and Queer Perspectives.* Chichester: Wiley.

Kessler, S. J. and McKenna, W. (1978) *Gender: An Ethnomethodological Approach.* New York: John Wiley and Sons.

Kitzinger, C. (2005). Heteronormativity in Action: Reproducing the Heterosexual Nuclear Family in 'After Hours' Medical Calls. *Social Problems* 52, 4: 477–98.

Kitzinger, C. (2007) Is 'Woman' Always Relevantly Gendered? *Gender & Language* 1, 1: 39–48.

Kitzinger, C. (2008) Developing Feminist Conversation Analysis: A Response to Wowk, *Human Studies* 31, 2: 179–208.

Klein, N. L. (in press) Doing Gender Categorization: Non-Recognitional Person Reference and the Omnirelevance of Gender. In S. A. Speer and E. Stokoe (eds.) *Conversation and Gender*. Cambridge: Cambridge University Press.

Lev, A. I. (2004) *Transgender Emergence: Therapeutic Guidelines for Working with Gender-Variant People and Their Families*. Binghampton, NY: The Haworth Clinical Practice Press.

Mishler, E. G. (1985) *Discourse of Medicine: Dialectics of Medical Interviews*. Norwood, NJ: Ablex.

Ochs, E. (1992) Indexing Gender. In A. Duranti and C. Goodwin (eds.) *Rethinking Context: Language as an Interactive Phenomenon*. Cambridge: Cambridge University Press.

Oxford English Dictionary (2006) *The Oxford English Dictionary*. Available from: http://www.oed.com/ [Accessed July 2006].

Pomerantz, A. (1978) Compliment Responses: Notes on the Co-operation of Multiple Constraints. In J. Schenkein (ed.) *Studies in the Organization of Conversational Interaction*. London: Academic Press.

Pomerantz, A. (1984a) Agreeing and Disagreeing with Assessments: Some Features of Preferred/Dispreferred Turn Shapes. In J. M. Atkinson and J. Heritage (eds.) *Structures of Social Action: Studies in Conversation Analysis*. Cambridge: Cambridge University Press.

Pomerantz, A. (1984b) Pursuing a Response. In J. M. Atkinson and J. Heritage (eds.) *Structures of Social Action: Studies in Conversation Analysis*. Cambridge: Cambridge University Press.

Raymond, G. and Heritage, J. (2006) The Epistemics of Social Relationships: Owning Grandchildren. *Language in Society* 35, 5: 677–705.

Sacks, H. (1984) On Doing 'Being Ordinary'. In J. M. Atkinson and J. Heritage (eds.) *Structures of Social Action: Studies in Conversation Analysis*. Cambridge: Cambridge University Press.

Sacks, H. (1987) On the Preferences for Agreement and Contiguity in Sequences in Conversation. In G. Button and J. R. E. Lee (eds.) *Talk and Social Organisation*. Clevedon: Multilingual Matters.

Sacks, H. (1995) *Lectures on Conversation* (vols 1 and 2 combined, G. Jefferson, ed.). Oxford: Blackwell.

Sánchez, M. C. and Schlossberg, L. (eds.) (2001) *Passing: Identity and Interpretation in Sexuality, Race, and Religion*. New York: NYU Press.

Schegloff, E. A. (1991) Reflections on Talk and Social Structure. In D. Boden and D. Zimmerman (eds.) *Talk and Social Structure*. Cambridge: Polity Press.

Schegloff, E. A. (1997) Whose Text? Whose Context? *Discourse & Society* 8, 2: 165–87.

Schegloff, E. A. (1998) Reply to Wetherell, *Discourse & Society* 9, 3: 413–16.

Schegloff, E. A. (2007) *Sequence Organization in Interaction: A Primer in Conversation Analysis I*. Cambridge: Cambridge University Press.

Schegloff, E. A., Jefferson, G. and Sacks, H. (1977) The Preference for Self-Correction in the Organization of Repair in Conversation. *Language* 53, 2: 361–82.

Schegloff, E. A. and Lerner, G. (2004) Beginning to Respond. Paper presented at the *Annual Meeting of the National Communication Association*. Chicago, IL, November.

Speer, S. A. (2005) *Gender Talk: Feminism, Discourse and Conversation Analysis.* London: Routledge.

Speer, S. A. (in press) On the Role of Reported, Third Party Compliments in Passing as a 'real' Woman. In S. A. Speer and E. Stokoe (eds.) *Conversation and Gender.* Cambridge: Cambridge University Press.

Speer, S. A. and Green, R. (2007) On Passing: The Interactional Organization of Appearance Attributions in the Psychiatric Assessment of Transsexual Patients. In V. Clarke and E. Peel (eds.) *Out in Psychology: Lesbian, Gay, Bisexual, Trans and Queer Perspectives.* Chichester: Wiley.

Speer, S. A. and Green, R. (2008) *Transsexual Identities: Constructions of Gender in an NHS Gender Identity Clinic.* End of Award report. Award No: RES-148-25-0029. Economic and Social Research Council.

Speer, S. A. and Parsons C. (2006) Gatekeeping Gender: Some Features of the Use of Hypothetical Questions in the Psychiatric Assessment of Transsexual Patients. *Discourse and Society* 17, 6: 785–812.

Speer, S. A. and Stokoe, E. (eds.) (forthcoming) *Conversation and Gender.* Cambridge: Cambridge University Press.

Stivers, T. (2008) Stance, Alignment and Affiliation During Story Telling: When Nodding Is a Token of Preliminary Affiliation. *Research on Language in Social Interaction* 41, 1: 29–55.

West, C. and Zimmerman, D. (1987) Doing Gender. *Gender & Society* 1, 2: 125–51.

7
Identity at Home: Offering Everyday Choices to People with Intellectual Impairments

Charles Antaki, W. M. L. Finlay and Chris Walton

What does it mean to be 'intellectually impaired'? At one level the answer is quite clear: there are official criteria for the term, enshrined in psychological and psychiatric classification schemes, and given weight in the provision of education, health and social services. Give the individual a battery of tests (of memory, verbal fluency, comprehension, adaptive functioning and so on) and compare the results to the average scores for people of their age; if the individual is at a certain distance below, then apply the label. Thereafter, things happen to the individual on the basis of that diagnosis – she or he now has a legal 'identity' which opens some doors and closes others. A new, shifting set of rights, obligations and less-definable social expectations come into play.

This chapter is pitched at just those less-definable social expectations. We are not concerned with the scientific evidence for, or the scientific practices of, the diagnosis of intellectual impairment. Nor are we able to comment on the history, or indeed the legitimacy, of such scientific work, nor on the legal basis for the institutional care that comes in its wake, nor on the budgeting of welfare, nor the scarcity or generosity of its provision. What we do want to do, though, is to see how the identity of 'the intellectually impaired person' cashes out in the simple realities of everyday life. Being intellectually impaired in a testing situation is, supposedly, straightforward – you either answer enough standard questions correctly or you do not (though see Maynard and Marlaire, 1992, for reasons to doubt this complacent picture). But in the more obviously ambiguous and negotiable world of real life, to 'be intellectually impaired' is in part a matter of who asks you what question, how, when, and what they accept as a valid answer. Words, actions and identities wrap around each other.

In the project on which this chapter's report is based, we undertook to look, in detail, at what is said to intellectually impaired people in some typical British residential homes in which they live. Once we started the ethnographic work, and started to look at the week's video footage as it came in, a number of issues came very readily to mind: to what degree was the staff's interaction with the residents 'ordinary', and to what degree was it influenced by their impairment? If it was so influenced – which would hardly be surprising – was it positive, merely mechanical, routine, or empowering? Did it mitigate the residents' impairments, ignore them, respect them, or indeed actively perpetuate or construct them?

The sharpest question that emerged was what it meant for the residents to have a choice in what they did around the home. To have the power to decide when to go to the toilet, when to eat, what to wear and how to spend one's day is the unremarked right of those with a 'normal' identity. Adults – adults without intellectual impairment – do not normally need to ask each other if and when they want to do such things. Yet it was common around the residences. Moreover, there was a backstory to the asking of such questions. Each residence, and the health trust which ran it, had a formal commitment to 'offering choice' as part of their way of 'empowering' their clients. So offering choice loomed large, both interactionally and ideologically.

Choice

In 2001 the UK Department of Health issued *Valuing People*, a much-cited manifesto which called explicitly for people with intellectual impairments to be given more say in what they did and what happened in their lives. That call eventually came to be enshrined in statute, in the UK's Mental Capacity Act of 2005, and the talk of choice and control has echoed down through regional health authorities to local service-providers, and indeed to individual units such as care homes. 'Choice' and 'personal control' are now pervasive aspirations of mission statements at all official levels.

Mission statements are one thing, but reality may be another. Certainly it would seem, in principle, easy for staff to find time to give the people they support a choice; and it may seem equally easy for a resident in a home to take full advantage of any offer of choice that comes her or his way. But support staff have responsibilities for service targets, health and safety, and the constant worry of getting things done on time, all of which can conflict with their role as facilitator, supporter and choice-giver. What choice does one give a resident, when the local authority minivan – which has taken weeks to arrange, and will not come back for a fortnight – is now waiting outside the door, ready to take people off on a day's outing? Conversely, people with intellectual disabilities have to negotiate the contradictory identities assigned to them within different discourses of care. If they have become used to being relatively passive recipients of services, advice and education, it may be hard to take wing and fly as an empowered and informed consumer of services. What to make of being encouraged to make choices, and then find one's choice ignored because it conflicts with a service routine, a learning agenda, or a health and safety concern? In many cases, being given, and making, a choice may not be straightforward.

The question, then, comes down to what happens on the ground. To answer these questions, we shall need to look closely at the details of talk in interaction, with all its complexities and consequences. Conversation Analysis (CA), our method of choice, has already been used to study the communicative strategies of people with an intellectual disability (e.g., Wootton, 1989), the practices of their assessment (e.g., Antaki, 1999), the interactional production of 'acquiescence' and 'incompetence' (Rapley, 2004) and the manner in which people manage their identities in interviews (e.g., Rapley, *et al.*, 1998). More pertinently for the study we report here, we have also successfully used CA to open up a number of the working practices of staff supporting people with intellectual impairments: in building social relationships (Antaki, *et al.*, 2007b), in encouraging people to talk (Antaki, *et al.*, 2007a), in playing a game (Finlay, *et al.*, 2008c), in overlooking non-verbal communication (Finlay, *et al.*, 2008a) and in dealing with residents' refusals (Finlay, *et al.*, 2008b).

Conversation analysis, identities and social action

Conversation Analysis can help uncover the relationship between identity and action in two ways. One is to show up the play between category terms (teacher, motorist, partner and so on) and their rhetorical implications in use: for a great deal more on that, as well as exemplary research that shows how it is that categories can bring off social actions, see Stokoe and Edwards (this book). The other way CA can help is to examine the categorical *implications* of people's words. To ask anyone a question (or to offer them a choice and so on) is necessarily to presume, in the question, something about their abilities, desires, powers and so on, if only at that moment. Questions, among other utterances, can very strongly hint at a person's 'categorical membership', as Sacks put it (see, e.g., his account of 'inference-rich' categories in one of his earliest collected lectures, Vol. 1, 1992: 40–48). Of course, the exact words used are crucial. So getting a clear verbatim record, on tape, of what staff ask the residents of a care home is an unambiguous source of evidence about what they presume. Such contemporary and unabridged evidence is more reliable, richer and amenable to more subtle analysis than the kind of thing available from informants in retrospective interviews, or even to the watching ethnographer as she or he struggles to keep up with the race of words in everyday speech.

The second thing that CA promises is more subtle, and to do with not just what is said, but how and when it is said – the format of the question, where it comes in the stream of talk, and what happens to the answer that it gets. In these details we find identities becoming more complex – quickly shifting and contradictory as staff and residents manage simultaneously a range of different service agendas. Here the value of a contemporaneous video record is still more precious than in the case of a capture of the mere words, important though that is. Memory for streams of talk is wholly unreliable, let alone memory for quite exactly how those streams of words were delivered, in what order, with what reply, and with what further extension, perhaps to dozens of turns at talk. No; here, CA, with its insistence of inspection of talk as it happened – or its partial but still useful record on tape – is irreplaceable. It allows the deployment of CA's now impressively varied set of keys for unlocking what talk does (only a very few of which will feature in this chapter; see, in this book, the chapters by Speer and by Stokoe and Edwards for yet more illustration).

Let us see, then, an example of each of those identity implications in choice-giving that CA reveals. In the following two sections, we shall be drawing on some of the publications that our project has yielded; where we skimp on detail, we shall refer the reader to the more complete account elsewhere. A word, first, is in order about the residents and staff members at two residential homes in the south of England who were good enough to let us into their lives for some eight months, on and off, for weekly filming sessions. We filmed them around the table, in planning meetings, in the kitchen and on outings. We had made sure that they gave informed consent before we started, and they were always asked again at the start of any filming session (indeed, this produced a series of blanks at a third venue, where permission, though given in principle, was always denied on any given occasion). The particular extracts we use in this chapter come from meetings at one particular residential home, where the residents had a degree of verbal fluency.

Presuming a limited identity

It was a frequent experience of the residents in the homes we studied to be asked whether they wanted to engage in this activity or that. Such a choice would often come up in planning sessions, when the staff had to fill out an activity sheet for the coming week; part of those activities would be discretionary, and it was a matter of official policy that the residents should be given a choice in what to do.

Offering any person a choice between this or that activity is not quite entirely unexceptional: for one thing, it presumes that the person asked requires alternatives be put to them, and that the person making the offer has it in their power to grant their wish. How often this obtains in everyday adult life, outside of service encounters where the outcome depends on going through a script of choices, is hard to say. So the very act of offering a choice to an adult, especially about what the sort of thing that they might be expected to have their own ideas about and follow them up themselves (like, e.g., what they want to do in their leisure time), already implies something unusual for adult speakers.

But what struck us was one particular variant that seemed even less likely to be used when presenting a choice to a person without an impairment. Instead of (and sometimes as well as) presenting the resident with the description of the activity in general terms (say, e.g., 'do you want to go to concert on Friday, at Ashdown'?), or in terms of its inherent attractions ('do you want to go to concert on Friday – it's a jazz band'?), the staff member would ask 'do you want to go to concert on Friday, *with Bill?*' (emphasis added). Extract 1 gives an example. Note that all place names and personal names have been altered, for the sake of confidentiality. The notation on the transcript, which is meant to help reproduce the actual delivery of the words, is explained in Appendix B to this book.

Extract 1. VD03-230206. 07.60 'Concert with Bill'

```
01  →   Dave    There's a-, °I'll go round°, ((to Alec)) there's a concert
02  →           next week [with Bill.]=Do you want to go to the concert
03      Alec              [(eh ah). ]
04  →   Dave    next week with [Bill?     ]
05      Alec                   [er=yeah,]
06  →   Dave    ((to Dominic)) Do you want to go with [Bill        ]
07      Alec                                         [((to Chris))
08              Chris.]
```

In principle, Dave, the staff member, could have listed the musical attractions of the concert – and much else besides – rather than choose to make Alec's choice turn on the presence of Bill (who was not one of the house's residents, and who didn't feature at any other point in the talk). Notice that Alec had indeed already started to give his answer at line 3, without the need to be told about Bill; nevertheless, Dave repeats the offer, and once again Alec answers it before Bill is mentioned (line 5). In line 6, Dave repeats the offer to another resident (Dominic), but now the activity itself is dropped and Bill becomes the only feature mentioned. What does the (apparently unnecessary) addition of a person's name presume about what Alec needs to know? And what does the omission of the activity presume about Dominic?

The answer comes out vividly in this exchange between Dave and another resident, Henry, at the same planning meeting. Dave wants to know if Henry wants to go to one of two alternative venues, pseudonymised as Stern Grange and Life Care Change Network.

Extract 2. CHW-VD03-230206. 11.44 'With Lenny'
((n.b. Dave is holding his fists out towards Henry on the table))

```
01    Dave    ((to Henry)) which is better,
02            [Stern Grange, (.3) Li:fe Care Change Network meeting,]
03            [          ((points to each fist alternately))            ]
04    Alec    ((glasses off, rubbing his eyes)) (°o:hm°)
05    Henry   (oh. (.) [this)
06                     [((points to Stern Grange hand))]
07            (.5)
08    Dave    Stern [Grange.
09    Henry         [Stern Grange with Oliver ((pointing to Oliver))
10    Dave    [Do you'n want to go to your meetings any more ] on a
11    Alec    [((still rubbing eyes)) (                      )]
12    Dave    Friday?
13            (1.0)
14    Henry   no [more ner.
15    Alec       [((still rubbing eyes)) ((turns to Dominic)) (eyes)
16 →  Dave    with Lenny.=
```

At line 14, Henry explicitly confirms that he does not want to go to the Life Care Change Network meeting. At this point, Dave now refers to a named individual whom he associates with the meeting: *with Lenny* (line 16). Notice now how the interaction proceeds:

```
17      Alec     =(eyes yer).
18      Dave     why not, zit- (.) jus boring?
19               (.5)
20      Henry    boring.
28      Dave     don't like it? ((shakes head))
29      Henry    no, (    [    ).
30 →    Dave               [>wha' about the other people there that< like you.
31               (3.0)
32 →    Dave     all the other people like you: there, (.5) they'll miss you.
33               (.)
34      Henry    (uh-er uh like me).
35      Dave     is that, (.) [duzzat make you happy or sa:d.]
36      Alec     [()]
37      Henry    (ve'y sad). ((signs tears))
38      Dave     [so do you want to see 'im], yes or no.
39      Alec     [()]
40      Henry    no:,
41      Dave     okay, fair °enough°.
```

Why 'with Lenny'? Dave offers two candidate answers (Pomerantz, 1988) to solicit what Maynard calls a 'perspective display' (1991) – that is, to get the other person to say what he or she thinks about the matter at hand, before playing one's own trump card. That trumper is the generalised company of the Lennys of Henry's world: 'the other people there' who, crucially, 'like you' and 'who'll miss you'. Henry is being asked to confirm that he is willing to disappoint his friends. Indeed, he is asked (line 35) whether that will name him happy or sad (line 35). The latter. But he sticks to his guns.

All this has revealed something very suggestive about the roles that Lenny, in Extract 2 above, and Bill, in Extract 1 earlier, play; these are the 'other people' in the residents' world to whom – according to the staff – they are bound by ties of friendship and community. They are what is attractive about the activities that the staff propose to the residents. A concert may turn out to be musically enjoyable, and a Life Care Change meeting might be turn out to be inspiring; but for the staff, the way to get the residents there is to promise good fellowship.

There is surely nothing wrong with this. But it implies an identity limited just to one main factor. As we put it in a fuller account of the phenomenon,

> repeated appeal to the social aspect of activities might have the unwelcome effect of negating the residents' abilities to choose activities on other grounds. It disqualifies them from choosing on such rational criteria of the activities such as their location, ease or difficulty, familiarity or unfamiliarity, intellectual challenge, aesthetic appeal, and so on.
>
> (Antaki, *et al.*, 2007b: 407)

In other words, it presumes that the most that the residents might get from an activity is the chance to be with other people. However happy and fulfilling that might be, the assumption that they will not benefit from much else perpetuates their limited identity, rather than challenge it.

Responding to choices in ways that produce problems

We found, in 30 hours of videotape, six fairly robust ways in which staff formatted choices for the residents. Space precludes us listing them all (which are more fully described in Antaki, *et al.*, 2008), so we will concentrate on two, to bring out a pervasive problem with the formats: they could cause serious confusion in the resident. But before we do list those two examples, the reader might like to just look back for a moment at the form used by staff member Dave in Extract 2 above. You will see, in lines 2–3, that Dave helps Henry see the alternatives by physically putting out his two fists on the table in front of him. This makes the two options visibly present as alternatives in parallel, just in case Henry's memory might not cope with keeping them in mind in series. Interestingly, this seems to have been a practice that Dave invented for himself; useful as it is, no other staff member used it. Now for two less successful (but much more common) formats which illustrate a more complex relationship between identities and real-life choice situations. In the first example, we will see how the level at which a choice is drawn can make the difference between competent and incompetent, independent and acquiescent. In the second, we see how choice and instructional agendas might shift quickly from one another, with corresponding shifts in the actors' identities.

Multiplying available options

The scene is a menu-planning meeting, in which staff member Kath has to record each resident's preferred meals for the coming week. This can be a drawn-out process for all concerned, as the residents must study a set of picture cards and nominate seven days' worth of choices for breakfast, lunch and dinner. Kath has reached Alec:

```
Extract 3. VC-12; 10:34 minutes. Bacon butties.
 1       Kath:   ((holds picture-cards in front of Alec))
 2       Alec:   [that one there,               ] (.) bacon
 3               [((points to a picture Kath is holding))]
 4               (.5)
 5       Kath:   You want bacon,
 6       Alec:   w'ye:h=
 7 →     Kath:   =In toast.
 8       Alec:   w-w'ye:h,
 9 →     Kath:   Yeh? [bacon buttie, in a ro:ll ((mimes 'roll' minimally))]
10       Alec:        [(uhm) ((lifts mug and drinks))]
11             (1.0)
12 →     Kath:   Or just bacon on its own.
13       Alec:   [(Jus' bacon)                       ]
14 →     Kath:   [D'you want th' bread with it]
15               (.3)
16       Alec:   Er >y- yeh<
17               (.4)
18 →     Kath:   Bacon butties.
19               (.3)
20       Alec:   Bu'ies yeh
21 →     Kath:   [Bacon in a:- in a (.) toasted sandwich.   ]
22               [((mimes, hand in claw shape; palm down)) ]
23               (.5)
24       Alec:   >Y- yeh [yeh yeh<]
25       Kath:           [>Is that what °you want°.<]
26       Alec:   >Y- yeh<
27       Kath:   O:kay ((picks up pictures)) °that's he- (.4) he's sorted°,
28               ((walks back to seat))
```

Kath wants to find out just exactly how Alec wants his bacon. The arrowed lines show her pursuit of the various possibilities that are on the picture card available to everybody around the table (bacon on its own; in toast; as a "bacon buttie" in a roll; in a toasted sandwich). But these multiple options have the effect of occasioning Alec to produce a series of inconsistent affirmatives, as if he has changed his mind with each new option. Of course, there is a wholly well-meaning sense to what Kath is doing. She wants to be sure that she records exactly what Alec wants, and that Alec is given the opportunity to review all the possibilities, similar though they might be.

But Alec has pointed to bacon (line 2) and confirms 'bacon' as his choice in line 6. If that is what he wants, and if he is indifferent to the varieties of ways in which the bacon might be served, then Kath's pursuit may be counter-productive. If he has already issued a definitive answer, then giving him what sounds like a further option strongly implies that he ought to consider changing his mind. That danger is all the starker in the last of our examples, below.

Reissuing the choice question

The other risky practice that staff had was to simply reissue the question even after the resident had made a clear and decisive choice. In the example below, Tim and Alec are in the kitchen, and Alec is about to peel some potatoes. There are two peelers available.

Extract 4. VC-08; 04:12. Potato peeler.
```
 1      Tim:    Which one do you wanna use (0.2) thi:s one or
 2              [this one
 3 →    Alec:   [That one that one                             ]
 4              [((points toward peelers, which are out of shot))]
 5      Tim:    °Go on°
 6 →    Alec:   ((picks up one of two peelers now in shot and inspects it))
 7      Tim:    [Are you gonna use that one          ]
 8              [((points toward peeler Alec is holding)) ]
 9              [or this one                      ]
10              [((points to peeler on the worktop))]
11              (.3)
12 →    Alec:   >That one< ((puts down the peeler in his hand and picks
13              up the one that Tim is pointing to))
14      Tim:    ((turns away)) (°well y'go on°)
```

Tim, the staff member, asks Alec which of the two peelers he wants to use; Alec motions towards where the peelers lie on the worktop, and picks one of them up (line 6). We pause at this point. As we said right at the start of this chapter, people with intellectual impairments often get asked to make choices which seem odd to non-impaired adults. Possibly, while working in the kitchen, one staff member might have been asked by another to choose a peeler, but it seems to us unlikely. One could speculate about the multiple meanings of asking Alec to make this sort of choice. But we leave that to the reader, and instead we start the tape up again, after Alec has made his choice. Now (line 7) Tim reissues the question, as if Alec had made no choice at all. 'Are you going to use that one [i.e. the one that Alec now holds in his had, ready to use], or this one?' Tim asks.

One might say that Tim is treating Alec as having made only a provisional choice, and is merely inspecting one candidate before finally choosing. But Alec did say 'that one, that one' at line 3. So this looks very much like the classroom teacher's reissue of a question to a pupil who has got their first answer wrong. It demonstrates unequivocally that the answer is not ready for acknowledgement of receipt (which is the conventional way in which satisfactory answers get treated; see Houtkoop-Steenstra, 2000), without actually going so far as to say that the answer is wrong. But the upshot is the same: the pupil will change their answer, or admit ignorance. In the case of making a choice, ignorance is hardly an option; so it is not surprising that Alec accedes to Tim's implied criticism of his choice, and changes it. He picks up the other peeler without demur (line 12) and is rewarded by Tim's receipt and acknowledgement that he may now proceed (line 14).

We should say a word in the staff member's defence. Ethnographic work around the house suggests that the first peeler that Alec picked up was, in fact, one that he had had trouble with before. He may have forgotten that. Tim might be discreetly helping him avoid peeler trouble again. Indeed, why else would Tim care which peeler Alec used?

That is a fair point. But we are at pains to say that the staff are well-meaning. What we point to is that they use choice-formats to do something that might be done more transparently. If Tim wanted Alec to change his mind, why not give him the rational grounds for doing so? He could be reminded that he has previously found this peeler awkward, or he could be shown the likely source of trouble in its handle, and so on. It was too often the case that a staff member used the discourse of 'choice' simply to issue an instruction, where a moment of reflection and education might have been more suited to the staff's own Mission Statement mandate to respect and empower. In this extract, then, we see a quick shift in identities: the initial offer of a choice positions Alec as an actor able to make his own decision; the reissue of the choice followed by Alec's change of mind seem to turn him into a compliant learner. The interesting feature is that although there appear to be two institutional agendas apparent (choice and learning independence skills), the content of the worker's utterances seem to be only about choice. What is crucial to the outcome of the interaction (and the identity of Alec) is the point at which a choice becomes accepted.

Concluding comments

At the head of the chapter we asked what it meant to be intellectually impaired. In trying to come to at least a partial answer we avoided issues of definition and categorisation, and we invited the reader to join us in an empirical survey of just how (some) people with an intellectual impairment lived and were treated by those around them. We wanted to see to what degree their identities as intellectually impaired were ignored, worked round, or perhaps consolidated by what was said to them, and how it was said.

Aware of the complex and politically sensitive debate in social policy circles about personal control and dignity, we decided to concentrate our attention on the issue of choice. What would a video record, addressed with the insights of CA, tell us about how staff offer choices? How do staff give residents control over the routines of food preparation, holiday planning, evening entertainment and the other miscellany out of which their lives are made up? We have presented here two things of particular interest: what staff *presumed* in the offer of a choice (concentrating on the curious case in which the staff member used a third party's name as an enticement to do some activity) and in the *interactional ambiguity* of some common choice formats that the residents had to decipher.

In both cases, identities loomed large. In the first case, the type of choice offered, the way the real events are turned into words, implies something about the person to whom it is offered. In the second we see the complexity of choice as it occurs in interaction. In both cases we tracked the ambiguous and changing identities which come into play as staff try to work out what choice means in practice and how it relates to other service agendas. The reader may recall that in the example in which resident Alec was being asked what sort of bacon he wanted for breakfast, the staff's efforts were well-intentioned, but had the effect of turning Alec from a competent choice-maker into an actor who could be seen as acquiescent or incompetent. The production of different identities seems to hinge on what level of specificity the staff insist on, and what level of generality they accept. The episode of the potato-peeler exemplified the second case. Here we see how different agendas can be served using the discourse of choice, how the identity of the resident can be dependent on how decisions are responded to, and crucially, when choices are accepted in an interaction.

The examples in this chapter show some of the ways the identity of a person with intellectual disabilities is played out in the physical context of residential care. We might also say that the identities play out in the context of interactions which might officially and institutionally be considered empowering. The CA as such stands or falls by how persuasive it is as an account of what is going on; but of course 'what's going on' is arguably rather different in the two contexts. We have tended in this chapter to see what is going on as the latter context, and make CA count as a contribution to our understanding of official stories of empowerment. If the aim of public policy is to promote a view of people with intellectual disabilities as people able to exercise power over their lives, then the close inspection of real-life interactions has something to say. What we have said here is that being allowed to exercise control is hardly a straightforward matter. An ethnographic study, backed up by the close analysis of interaction that CA can provide, gives us the instruments for measuring just how difficult it can be.

The focus of this chapter, then, has been on the identity implications of talking in certain ways (specifically, of course, ways of offering choices to people with intellectual impairments). It is worth stepping back and seeing the lines of convergence with the other chapters in this section of the book. Susan Speer cast her eye over the wary exchanges between patient and psychiatrist in a sex-change clinic; Liz Stokoe and Derek Edwards listened in to people appealing to the police and the local council for help with bothersome neighbours. All of us use CA; that is, we all find great profit in attending very minutely to the exact details of people's dealing with each other, down to the most inconspicuous choice of words and the smallest pause between them. As we have seen, it is out of this cloth that ordinary social life is woven. If the reader stands back, they can compare that way of doing social science with the other ways represented in other chapters of this larger book. To some degree, CA and other ways of proceeding are complementary: CA does not claim the empire. Readers will make their own judgements about what territory CA concedes and what it claims. But insofar as the claims that a social scientists wants to make about identities can be grounded in the facts of the matter – in the to-and-fro of people's dealings with each other, whether in the sex-change clinic, the police station or the residential home – then CA has the advantage of taking us straight to where the facts lie thickest. We live, and play out our everyday business, in a forest of words and actions; looking very closely at those words and actions will reveal, like no other method, how we actually make our identities work in a society built on interaction and social exchange.

References

Antaki, C. (1999) Assessing Quality of Life of Persons with a Learning Disability: How Setting Lower Standards may Inflate Well-being Scores. *Qualitative Health Research* 9: 437–54.

Antaki, C., Finlay, W.M.L., Jingree, T. and Walton, C. (2007) 'The Staff are Your Friends': Conflicts between Institutional Discourse and Practice. *British Journal of Social Psychology* 46: 1–18.

Antaki, C., Finlay, W.M.L. and Walton, C. (2007a) Conversational Shaping: Staff-Members' Solicitation of Talk from People with an Intellectual Impairment. *Qualitative Heath Research* 17: 1403–14.

Antaki, C., Finlay, W.M.L. and Walton, C. (2007b) How Proposing an Activity to a Person with an Intellectual Disability can Imply a Limited Identity. *Discourse and Society* 18: 393–410.

Antaki, C., Finlay, W.M.L., Walton, C. and Pate, L. (2008) Offering Choices to People with an Intellectual Impairment: An Interactional Study. *Journal of Intellectual Disability Research* 52: 1165–75.

Antaki, C., Finlay, W.M.L., and Walton, C. (in press) Choice for People with an Intellectual Impairment in Official Discourse and in Practice. *Journal of Policy and Practice in Intellectual Disabilities*.

Department of Health (2001) *Valuing People*. London: Her Majesty's Stationery Office.

Finlay, W.M.L., Antaki, C. and Walton, C. (2008a) On not being Noticed: Learning Disabilities and the Non-Vocal Register. *Intellectual and Developmental Disabilities* 45: 227–45.

Finlay, W.M.L., Antaki, C. and Walton, C. (2008b) Saying no to the Staff – An Analysis of Refusals in a Home for People with Severe Communication Difficulties. *Sociology of Health and Illness* 30: 55–75.

Finlay, W.M.L., Antaki, C., Walton, C. and Stribling, P. (2008c) The Dilemma for Staff in 'Playing a Game' with People with a Profound Intellectual Disability. *Sociology of Health and Illness* 30: 531–49.

Houtkoop-Steenstra, H. (2000) *Interaction and the Standardized Interview. The Living Questionnaire*. Cambridge: Cambridge University Press.

Maynard, D.W. (1991) The Perspective-Display Series and the Delivery and Receipt of Diagnostic News. In D. Boden and D.H. Zimmerman (eds.) *Talk and Social Structure: Studies in Ethnomethodology and Conversation Analysis*. Cambridge: Polity Press, pp. 162–92.

Maynard, D. and Marlaire, C. (1992) Good Reasons for Bad Testing Performance. *Qualitative Sociology* 15: 177–202.

Pomerantz, A. (1988) Offering a Candidate Answer: An Information-Seeking Strategy. *Communication Monographs* 50: 360–73.

Rapley, M. (2004) *The Social Construction of Intellectual Disability*. Cambridge: Cambridge University Press.

Rapley, M., Kiernan, P. and Antaki, C. (1998) Invisible to Themselves or Negotiating Identity? The Interactional Management of 'Being Intellectually Disabled'. *Disability and Society* 13: 807–27.

Sacks, H. (1992) *Lectures on Conversation*. Oxford: Blackwell.

Wootton, A. (1989) Speech to and from a Severely Retarded Young Down's Syndrome Child. In M. Beveridge, G. Conti-Ramsden and I. Leudar (eds.) *The Language and Communication of Mentally Handicapped People*. London: Chapman-Hall.

Part III
Communities, Cities and Nations

8
Identity Making for Action:
The Example of London Citizens

Jane Wills

In recent years there has been growing moral panic about alienation in our inner city communities. Such places are argued to be less engaged in the democratic polity than they were in the past while simultaneously being fractured by widening divides between people and groups. Exemplified by the increasing numbers of young men being stabbed to death on the streets of London, our inner city communities are popularly understood as politically disenfranchised and turning in on themselves. In response, there have been a plethora of new ideas from Government and beyond to re-enchant citizens with the political process and to heal the divisions within. In this context, however, we need to know more about the relations between identity and civic engagement. We need to know how people come to identify with each other and how they might be mobilised and supported to act. In order to explore these issues, this chapter looks at one example in detail. I explore the work of a broad-based community alliance called London Citizens that connects a wide range of different community-based organisations and seeks to engage their members in political action over common concerns.

London Citizens is worthy of attention for a number of reasons. It is now recognised as being the largest and most diverse community-based alliance operating in the United Kingdom and it has pioneered a number of successful campaigns. It is particularly note-worthy for the diversity of its membership which at the time of writing involved more than 100 different educational, faith, labour and community groups. The alliance has also facilitated the political participation of otherwise marginalised people with particularly important roles for youth, women, minority ethnic communities, the low paid and new migrants. The living wage campaign has been London Citizens' most celebrated success, winning major improvements in the wages and conditions of approximately

5000 workers and redistributing an estimated £20 million towards the low paid (Wills, 2004, 2008).[1] This campaign has been successfully translated from hospitals to banks, universities, hotels and art galleries. It has cemented the reputation of the organisation and has facilitated a positive link with the Mayor. At the time of writing, other ongoing campaigns sought to win regularisation for irregular migrants, improve access to social housing and create safer streets. Such campaigns involve members of London Citizens developing relationships (sometimes after collective action or media pressure) with elected politicians, unelected public sector officials and corporate leaders to implement change.

This chapter explores the identity-work that is involved in this form of politics. Drawing on the work of social psychologists, the chapter considers the way in which London Citizens engages people on the basis of mutual differentiation (fostering 'unity across difference') while also allowing them to enlarge their affiliations, creating a new super-ordinate identity as members of London Citizens (Brewer and Gaertner, 2001; Hewstone *et al.*, 2002; Vertovec, 2007a). This is done by engaging people on the basis of their *existing identifications* and attachments (to faith, trade union, school, university or community group) and then, through finding common ground and sharing experiences of collectivity, nurturing an *enlarged – and additional – identity* as a member of London Citizens. Through the careful management of relationships between different groups of people, coupled with sharp attention to the need for results and the emotional impact of collective experience, London Citizens has found the means to make political and social capital out of internal divisions. In this case, solidarity is a product – rather than a victim – of difference in the city today. The organisation has hit upon an organisational formulae that makes a virtue of the multiple and diverse identities that are so often cast as a problem.

The chapter starts by providing a brief overview of contemporary knowledge and debate about citizenship in Britain's poorest communities. Turning residents into active citizens is argued to depend upon new forms of identity politics. If Britain's poorest are to be re-enchanted with democracy as well as each other, they will need to be inspired to take up new identifications as engaged, politically minded and mobilised people. In the context of our urban communities, this new identity politics will also need to reflect, respect and recognise the diversity of communities sharing space in the city. As such, the chapter also engages with current debate about living with difference and the desire for community cohesion. The chapter suggests that this can be done through action over shared goals but in so doing, public relationships do not have to be 'deep.' London Citizens has facilitated the creation of civic relationships that are mutually rewarding, but not necessarily particularly profound. The material presented in the main part of this chapter explores the work of London Citizens in nurturing an internal culture that reflects, respects and recognises different institutions, people and their traditions while simultaneously facilitating shared experiences and the emergence of a super-ordinate identity. The chapter suggests that London Citizens works because it is able to embrace different traditions while also securing the means of power. In so doing, it generates a new enlarged political identity that people come to inhabit.

Citizenship and identity-making

Contemporary democracy is built on the founding notion of citizenship. Citizens are those who belong to the polity, who are able to vote and who have the rights and responsibilities attached to any particular nation. The nature of citizenship shapes the terms on which people relate to each other and in practice, this stretches far beyond the technical aspects of belonging to a particular state. As Pattie *et al.* (2004: 22) explain, 'citizenship is a set of norms, values and practices designed to solve collective problems which involve the recognition by individuals that they have rights and obligations to each other if they wish to solve such problems.' While such 'norms, values and practices' are reproduced through the formal mechanisms of citizenship (belonging to a nation, having rights to vote, to reside and to use services for example) they also permeate more informal social relations (in institutions, community groups, neighbourhoods, public space and friendship groups). If people are to get along with each other, they need have at least some degree of overlap in their 'norms, values and practices' in relation to citizenship. If people are to avoid conflict, they need to have some shared expectations of collective behaviour. In this sense, citizenship is about identity. Broadly defined, citizenship refers to the way in which people think of themselves in relationship to others across multiple scales. The practices associated with citizenship reflect inherited and reworked traditions of moral order, social behaviour and collective responsibility and as such, they are closely connected to some shared sense of belonging.

There is currently great public concern that the 'norms, values and practices' traditionally associated with citizenship in Britain are being disrupted. Pundits highlight falling voter turnout, increased cynicism about politicians and the political process, urban riots, ethnic segregation, the apparent support for militant Islam, anti-social behaviour and rising knife crime as evidence of a crisis in citizenship. People are argued to be increasingly alienated from the political process as well as each other and the Government has launched a plethora of new initiatives to mount a response. New legislation has sought to bolster a stronger sense of 'Britishness' (through citizenship tests, ceremonies and English language requirements for would-be applicants as well as citizenship lessons in schools for all children, Muir, 2007); to encourage democratic engagement (through devolution, local Mayoralties, postal voting and experiments in Local Government); to foster community cohesion (through statutory reporting by schools and Local Government); to support local engagement (through lay participation in schools, social housing, Local Government and the NHS); as well as to increase social control (through the use of Anti-Social Behavioural Orders, penalties for tenants who engage in anti-social behaviour and the parents of truanting children).

As yet, there is little evidence that these initiatives will have any dramatic effect. Scholars have highlighted the deep-rooted structural processes that underlie this state of affairs. These include the erosive impact of globalisation on the power of the nation-state; the impact of a resurgent individualism associated with neo-liberal consumer capitalism; widening socio-economic inequality and its resulting exclusions; as well as higher rates of geographic mobility and immigration (Bauman, 2001; POWER enquiry, 2006). In practice, these processes are most intensely felt, and the possible solutions are least likely to be effective, in the poorest and most marginalised communities in the United Kingdom. Survey data indicate that it is the poorest who are most alienated from the political system while also being the most vulnerable to the effects of community conflict (Li *et al.*, 2005; Pattie *et al.*, 2004; Putnam, 2007). Widening socio-economic divides have had a direct impact on political engagement and those who need politics most are least likely to be fully engaged.

In this context, there is a growing 'identity gap' in political life in countries like the United Kingdom. Politics has become increasingly professionalised and the mediating institutions that once connected people to the political process – particularly in poor areas – have declined. Political parties, trade unions and faith organisations all used to be more significant in engaging people and articulating their interests in the wider polity. The decline of these organisations has created a political vacuum in many poorer communities and while the parties of the far right have made some running since the 1990s, their preoccupations with 'race' and immigration have little resonance in the context of multicultural Britain today. Indeed, given the diversity of peoples living in cities like Birmingham, London and Manchester, any successful political organisation would have to both reflect and accommodate very different cultural groups (Sennett, 1977; Young, 2000; Sandercock, 2003; Massey, 2005).

Ethnic diversity is often thought to pose particular challenges to political organisation. Sharing space and place in the city does not necessarily lead to the development of shared perceptions of common interests and the practice of solidarity (Amin, 2002; Dench *et al.*, 2006; Valentine, 2008; Vertovec, 2007a). Indeed, in this context, there is growing concern that prevailing policies to promote multiculturalism have tended to widen divisions between the divergent communities that share the space of the nation (Phillips, 2005). In the wake of the urban riots in northern England in 2001 and particularly after the terrorist attacks in July 2005 when 'home-grown' suicide bombers felt able to detonate large explosive devices on London's public transport system, Government ministers have trumpeted the need to break down the barriers between ethnic groups and foster greater cohesion. In a growing stream of initiatives that have become known as the Community Cohesion agenda, state bodies are now urged to promote integration and unity between different groups (Robinson, 2005; Commission on Integration and Cohesion, 2007). Public funding is now increasingly limited for those organisations that represent a 'single' identity group and the solution to community fracture is now argued to involve the creation of new identifications – forged through face-to-face encounter – that break down divisions between different groups.[2]

In so doing, interventions to foster community cohesion aim to 'scale-up' identifications, calling on individuals to join others in an enlarged social category to facilitate their engagement in political life. In the language of social psychology, these initiatives depend upon categorical argumentation to cement new 'in-groups' to which individuals feel able and willing to join (Hewstone, 1996; Hopkins and Reicher, 1997). Such exhortations echo ongoing government efforts to foster political participation more generally. Building politically engaged communities also depend upon people finding shared interests and regard for each other.

Both political agendas thus demand renewed attention to the politics of identity-making. Promoting active citizenship and cohesive communities involves an appeal to individuals to take an interest in their locality and each other. In one agenda the local issues come first and in the other, the divided community takes priority, but both actually call for similar things. Moreover, given the material hardships experienced by many people living in urban areas, political organising around shared material needs may well be a meaningful route to cohesion. In his review of community cohesion in six communities in the United States, Bach (1993: 49; see also Vertovec, 2007a) presents a relatively up-beat account of efforts to find common ground via an emergent politics over the nature of place. As he explains, 'Beyond interpersonal encounters, one shared interest persistently emerges as a rallying point for newcomers and established residents – controlling the character of community change.'

Social psychologists argue that this process of 'scaling-up' identity can take three different forms. First, through *de-categorisation* (or 'unity *despite* difference'), whereby existing divisions are replaced by a new identification, as is practiced by political parties, social movements and single issue campaigns. Second, through *mutual differentiation* (dual identity or 'unity *across* difference'), whereby existing divisions remain alongside ongoing cooperation, as has been practiced in coalitional politics. And third, through *re-categorisation* (or 'difference *and* unity'), whereby multi-layered identifications co-exist through the creation of super-ordinate identity categories, as has been practiced via the imagined community of 'nation' (Gaertner *et al.*, 1994; Brewer and Gaertner, 2001; Hewstone *et al.*, 2002; see also Vertovec, 2007a). On the ground, these three processes tend to overlap with each other; social movements are often internally divided despite their unity in the face of a common enemy (Drury *et al.*, 2003); and coalitional politics are sometimes unintentionally generative of a shared super-ordinate identity as people learn to work with each other.

In addition, however, there are scalar limits to these processes of identity-making for political ends. It is difficult for political groups to 'scale-up' identification beyond the limits of face-to-face relationships without losing their ability to engage and mobilise people. Many of the institutions that no longer 'work' in representing and mobilising poor Britons today have fallen foul of this fact. As they have centralised power and decision-making, concentrating their energies on the 'centre,' they have abandoned the roots of their organisations to die. Accelerated by a process of bureaucratisation and professionalisation, unions, political parties and many church groups have lost their grassroots and their political strength (Voss and Sherman, 2000; Osterman, 2003). To avoid these problems, reinvigorating local citizenship and cohesion would demand a political intervention to 'scale-up' identity sufficiently to mobilise and secure the ability to effect change without losing the necessary connections to people and place on which such power depends.

Equally, efforts to sustain new identifications that sit 'on-top' of cultural differences through a super-ordinate identity category can be too thin to impact on behaviour and/or fall foul of internal power differentials. As Valentine (2008: 333) puts it in relation to contemporary debates about community cohesion, there are significant dangers in ignoring real and perceived feelings of injustice that will tend to override any positive outcomes from 'contact.' As she suggests, 'people's accrued histories of social experiences and material circumstances may also contribute to their feelings about urban encounters from both sides (i.e. from the perspective of participants from both majority and minority groups).' For Valentine, organising 'contact' across difference will be transformative only when it facilitates genuinely mutual relationships (see also Hewstone, 1996; Dixon and Durheim, 2003). In practice, successful relationship building requires enough contact – of the right quality – to be meaningful. Super-ordinate identity categories like 'British' may be a focal point for unity but be too 'remote' to have much impact on daily behaviour.

As will be outlined below, London Citizens has proved particularly effective in tackling these issues by allowing individuals to live simultaneously in different identity-camps in organisations that operate at fairly local dimensions. People join the alliance as members of an existing civil society organisation such as a church, a school, a mosque or a trade union, and once unity is forged on the basis of existing identity groups – involving an active minority of those involved in any particular group – participation in shared activity works to create an enlarged identity to which people can also belong. Mutual differentiation co-exists with ongoing re-categorisation and the majority of 'members' remain in the former domain. Moreover, given that the organisation depends upon the quality of its relationships and its ability to mobilise its members, it generally operates at the sub-urban scale. The organisation works by linking people from 'vested' local institutions in particular areas of the city (East, South and West) with occasional city-wide events. This allows each area alliance to sustain meaningful face-to-face relationships between mutually differentiated organisations. In what follows, I outline the experience of London Citizens with a view to exploring what this tells us about the intersection of politics, community and identity in urban Britain today. I argue that London Citizens is novel in relation to the way it enables participation whilst also effecting – which in turn is affecting – political change.

(Re)Making political identities: The work of London citizens

An enabling organisation

London has an extraordinarily diverse population that now embraces an estimated 300 different languages and hundreds of different national groups (Vertovec, 2007b). In 1986, 18 per cent of Londoners were foreign-born (approximately 1.17 million people), three-quarters of whom came from the former colonies. Just 20 years later, the number of foreign-born Londoners had doubled, increasing to approximately 2.23 million people (or 31 per cent of the city's population), just over half of them coming from the ex-colonial world (LSE, 2007). This degree of diversity is particularly striking in the poorest parts of the city and Boroughs like Brent, Hackney, Haringey, Newham and Tower Hamlets have a plethora of different minority groups sharing space with each other. The oldest area-based alliance in London Citizens has its origins in these diverse communities. The East London Communities Organisation (TELCO) has operated in the Boroughs of Hackney, Newham, Tower Hamlets, Redbridge and Waltham Forest since 1996. During these years the alliance has attracted a wide range of different communities into membership, some of them more mono-cultural than others, including the London Buddhist Centre, the East London Mosque, a number of Catholic Churches, some Anglican Parishes, a Methodist Church, some union branches, schools and a University Department (Jamoul and Wills, 2008). As such, TELCO has come to reflect at least some of the divergent traditions of belief and practice that exist in London's east end.

Like its counterparts in the wider London Citizens alliance, TELCO has relatively low barriers to entry. Organisations can join on the basis of their willingness to 'act together for change.'[3] Organisations are not expected to alter their core beliefs or practices as a result of joining the alliance: they can carry on with business as usual while simultaneously belonging to TELCO and the wider alliance. Unlike many other political interventions that demand some 'sign up' to a core programme or common ideology, joining London Citizens just requires a willingness to work with others in pursuit of shared goals. As the 'Mission Statement' published as part of the agenda for TELCO's tenth anniversary assembly declared:

> As members of TELCO we are a diverse power alliance of communities organising for change and a better East London. We commit to building and training a TELCO leadership of different races, faiths

and ages that is committed to action for the common good. I am proud that my community is a TELCO member working in unity and fellowship with my neighbours for the greater good of all.

(TELCO's tenth anniversary assembly agenda, 16 November, 2006)

This approach makes it easy to append membership of London Citizens onto existing activities. Groups can secure the advantages of belonging without having to change what they do. As this head teacher of a Roman Catholic secondary school put it during interview: 'We are part of TELCO, TELCO is part of us, but we are not TELCO, if you see what I mean' (21.12.05). This school saw membership of TELCO as a useful adjunct to its ongoing work and activities. Belonging to the wider London Citizens was cost-free: it did not demand a great deal from the school, it had no impact on its core agenda, but it was very helpful in connecting the school to other organisations, as well as augmenting its work around citizenship. Likewise, those organisations that have a strong community ethos have been able to join TELCO to reinforce the things they already do. As this representative from Buddhist Centre explained, 'I think it fits very well because it feels like the issues are relatively clear at the local level...I can get involved without having to compromise any kind of principles... [TELCO are] about social justice and poverty and dignity of people' (2 February 2006).

Organisations joining an area-based alliance like TELCO were found to take part on the basis that this would impact very little on their internal affairs. While London Citizens organisers commit willingly to work with member communities in order to strengthen their internal culture and leadership development, this is not done unless it is wanted. This policy of 'non-interference' was reported to make membership less threatening as there were unlikely to be unanticipated or negative consequences within.

Since the mid-1990s, London Citizens has sought to construct a very broad alliance with a willingness to embrace all those wanting to join. The organisation tends to use readings, reflections and teachings from a very wide and divergent set of sources, including the sacred and secular, the political and the spiritual. This public display or performance of different traditions has helped to appeal to a wide range of groups while also reinforcing a shared respect for difference within. At the time of writing, the small leaflet produced to publicise the alliance in its dealings with 'outsiders,' included five quotes to illustrate its core political goals. Demonstrative of the desire for breadth, these quotes appeared in the following order:

> The cultural revolution of the late twentieth century is best understood as the triumph of the individual over society, or rather the breaking of the threads which in the past have woven human beings into social textures.
>
> (Eric Hobsbawm)

> To train citizens in the capacity for freedom and to give them scope for free action is the supreme end of all true politics.
>
> (Archbishop William Temple, 1943)

> If you want peace, you must work for justice.
>
> (Pope Paul VI)

> And to co-operate with one another in righteousness and piety.
>
> (The Quran – Al-Maidah, 5:2)

> We must learn to live together like brothers and sisters or perish together as fools.
>
> (Dr Martin Luther King)

London Citizens has thus adopted a self-consciously open door policy focusing on those committed to action rather than commitment to shared ideology or belief. As these quotes attest, the organisation simultaneously celebrates the traditions and teachings of Christianity, Islam, the civil rights movement and leftist scholarship.

Such efforts to reflect and respect difference are regularly reinforced at London Citizens' public events. In November 2006, TELCO held a large public assembly to celebrate its tenth anniversary with more than 1000 people attending. The meeting was carefully choreographed to reflect, respect and recognise the diversity of TELCO's membership. It began with performances from the choirs of St Antony's and St Helen's Roman Catholic Primary Schools, a dance group from Norlington Boys School and folk dancing by members of the Lithuanian chaplaincy of the London Diocese of the Roman Catholic Church. The meeting itself was then co-chaired by a representative from UNISON's Local Government branch in Tower Hamlets (a white middle-aged woman), a priest from a Catholic Church in Newham (a white middle-aged man), a young black student from a Catholic secondary school in Waltham Forest and an Asian man representing East London Mosque. The event was then opened with a reflection by the renowned Muslim scholar Professor

Tariq Ramadan before each community was publicly recognised by everyone else in the room. Each of the 45 member organisations had the chance to introduce their group from the front of the hall, ensuring that the assembled guests and fellow TELCO members knew they were there.

As the event unfolded, each bit of the 'business' between TELCO and its guests, covering campaigns for a living wage, affordable housing, an ethical Olympics and rights for irregular migrants, was introduced by representatives from different TELCO member communities that had been particularly active around that campaign. This brought more women and young people to the podium – many of them from minority ethnic backgrounds – further widening the diversity of those taking part. This meeting performed difference on stage and this had as much political impact as the details of the business demands that were made. Politicians, business and community leaders found it difficult to resist the demands made by such a large and diverse group of people. The performance of diversity was itself a key weapon in the struggle for change.

However, London Citizens' leaders were not naïve about the potential of diversity to divide. The leadership sought to control the performance of diversity by tightly managing public events and establishing a strong internal culture to foster public respect. As this ex-chair of the trustees who is also a Methodist Minister and an ex-Chief Executive of a community organisation in membership put it during interview: Diversity 'without [boundaries] would be a very dangerous exercise' (28.4.05). Echoing this concern, many respondents also argued that managing diversity was only possible if you had sensitivity for the issues that were known to divide. Issues relating to gender norms and sexuality were clearly contentious and participants knew they had to leave these matters alone. For those involved, solidarity depended upon respecting but not debating the divergent views of the others involved. Solidarity was built on the basis of shared interest's rather more than common beliefs.[4] Indeed, the fact that solidarity was possible despite the chasms of ideological difference that clearly exist over issues such as sexuality, individual freedom and the sanctity of the family was due to the way that people were able to put aside their differences in pursuit of common concerns.

This pragmatic politics tended to create public and civic relationships of mutual respect. In contrast to arguments about the need to foster community cohesion through articulating and understanding difference, London Citizens has created a powerful new identity that depends upon respecting rather than articulating the issues over which people are bound to divide. In pursuit of shared goals, individuals were prepared to put aside their (sometimes profound) differences in favour of the alliance. As this trade unionist put in when describing her involvement in London Citizens: 'If we can make progress on things like the living wage, why do you want to talk about abortion, you've got to take things where they are, you know?' (5 May 2005; see also Jamoul and Wills, 2008).

As outlined in relation to the performance of diversity at public events, participants came to recognise the power of diversity in delivering political goals. Support for the alliance came to 'trump' any need to articulate differences and threaten the coalition itself. In this regard, a number of respondents recalled their turbulent relationship with the ex-Mayor of London who had a rather traditional Leftist disposition towards religious people and religious belief. In those early days, and in common with many others on the Left, Ken Livingstone would regularly declare his hostility towards London Citizens on the basis of its base in London's faith communities, accusing it of being a 'front' for conservative faith. In so doing, Livingstone forced London Citizens' lay leaders to articulate the solidarity they felt for each other as this respondent describes:

[I] remember sitting in the office with the mayor and his senior cohorts and the mayor sort of accusing us of being a sort of new right-wing Christian political party. And it wasn't so much the Christians as the Communists present who really got really irate with him and said you've got the wrong end of the stick here, you've got to withdraw that ... This is not a right-wing Christian political party, I'm here because I'm a Communist and I'm a trades unionist and we're working together, you take that back! It was very, very powerful, and you could see this wasn't an *ad hoc* bunch of people who'd been shunted into a room and had no connection with each other, these were people who really understood the solidarity of what was going on and were prepared to articulate it.

(Representative from third sector community organisation, 28 April, 2005)

Through their shared experiences, people thus found themselves being able to forge civic relationships with people they would otherwise rarely encounter and likely contest. As this Marxist trade unionist put it when describing her developing relationship with the faith leaders involved in London Citizens:

> It's a working relationship, it's not a relationship outside of that, but I mean, it's a very solid working relationship. It's one of mutual respect and it's one about which I dare say they are surprised as I am! Coming from where they're coming from, [it's surprising] that we are able to have that degree of unanimity about objectives and about the process.
>
> (5 April 2005)

Participants reported finding it possible to respect and recognise those whom they might once have ignored and dismissed. As this Catholic sister from a church in membership of TELCO put it, London Citizens has 'enabled me to see trade unionists as being able to take on other dimensions, not just bang, bang, bang which was of course was what was happening for quite a lot of time with them' (9 February 2006). A number of participants similarly argued that making contact through London Citizens had facilitated a welcome respect for difference. As this ex-chair of trustees, Methodist Minister and ex-Chief Executive of a community organisation explained, his experiences of being together and acting together had profoundly transformative effects on his understanding and respect for Islam:

> It's almost like osmosis...I think you get the feel for the other person's culture and you get a sense of respect for it almost at an unconscious level. So the idea that a group of Muslims will go out in the middle of a meeting for prayer, and that can be brought into the way in which a meeting is organised, doesn't make me...think twice now, whereas at one time I'd have thought what on earth's going on? But you now recognise, well they've got to pray five times a day and if the prayer happens to fall in the middle of a meeting, obviously you've got to organise around that. So there's a sort of sense of what the other has to do to meet their needs [that] becomes part of your own thinking in a way that you wouldn't have dreamed. If I'd have set a meeting up ten years ago I wouldn't have asked the question 'is this going to hit the prayer time for the Muslims and should we allow some space for them', whereas now I would think about it.
>
> (28 April 2005)

Although London Citizens has fostered a productive politics of diversity on the basis of 'mutual differentiation' ('unity across difference'), it has simultaneously contributed to the emergence of a super-ordinate – enlarged – identity as members of London Citizens. Echoing the words of Hewstone and his colleagues (2002, 590), the alliance has replaced 'subordinate (us and them) with super-ordinate (we) categorizations.' Over time, leaders from faith, trade union, school or community organisations have come to refer to themselves as members of London Citizens, expressing pride, commitment and belief in the larger identification. This identity is fostered through practice and experience rather than talk. Illustrated by these comments made by a Methodist minister contrasting her experience of working in London Citizens to the multi-faith working groups of which she is part, unity was created through action:

> [In London Citizens] 'there's a feeling of solidarity there, through the working together. I think it's the sort of solidarity you would never experience with people from other faiths otherwise because... things like the inter-faith groups that boroughs put on... you know, yes it's nice and polite but unless you're actually working on something together you don't get a working relationship with people.
>
> (24 November 2005)

An effective organisation

As outlined above, London Citizens has found a way to enable very different participant groups to belong. While this has been a product of efforts to reflect, respect and recognise difference, it has also been facilitated by having the power to act. In this section I briefly explore the importance of effectivity – and its impact on affectivity – in sustaining the organisation. Over time, the alliance has secured sufficient membership to enable change in the city and this has further enhanced its support. In addition, however, the experience of collective action has an affective dimension which also fosters continued support. Being both effective and affective, London Citizens has developed a set of leaders who are committed to working with each other over common concerns.

Without economic resources, the alliance has relied upon 'turnout' to generate political capital. Each local alliance will have at least one annual public assembly to which several hundred supporters are expected to come. These meetings are scheduled many months in advance and the key 'targets' of any campaigns (politicians, business leaders, local officials, media, etc.) will be invited along. Leaders from each member organisation will then devote considerable effort to getting their people along on the night. Similar attention is given to the agenda, as well as the representation and line up of the evening itself. Once people are in the room, the emphasis is on respectful recognition of the groups and people involved alongside efforts to 'do business' with the key power-brokers invited along. These evenings are politics as theatre performed in real time. Individuals *within* the crowd are encouraged to feel solidarity with each other in making their demands on those from *outside*.

When backed up with ongoing relationship building, mobilisation and engagement beyond these set-piece events, this form of politics is both effective and affecting. Over more than a decade, London Citizens has developed the capacity and moral authority to demand significant changes in material life – such as calls for living wages, social housing, safer streets and rights to citizenship. Campaigns like that for a living wage have demonstrated the power of the alliance to challenge the market, enforce corporate responsibility and empower low paid migrant workers (see Wills, 2004, 2008, 2009). Participants regularly cite the example of the living wage as a campaign that has achieved the impossible and this 'pays back' by reinforcing an urge to belong. As this representative from a Methodist Church in Stratford, East London explains,

> The changes in people's lives and some of the things TELCO has done is what gives me satisfaction, to be able to enable and empower people, to be able to see joy and to see progress in people's lives, that's my main motivation and that keeps me going, to know that I can make a difference to people's lives irrespective of who they are.
>
> (15 December 2005)

In addition, however, the experience of collective action can itself fuel a desire for further involvement. Social psychologists have been investigating the importance of past experiences of empowerment in fuelling further political action. As Drury and Reicher (2005: 51; see also Drury *et al.* 2005) explain,

> Empowerment (i.e. confidence in one's ability to challenge existing relations of domination, typically accompanied by positive affect) is an outcome of collective action if and when such action serves to realize participants' social identity (and hence their definition of legitimate practice) over [and] against the power of dominant out-groups.

In what they call 'collective self-realization' individuals are argued to realise their 'social identity against the power of dominant forces' and this creates a feeling of empowerment during and after events (Drury *et al.*, 2005: 309). Thus in joining London Citizens, participants have been able to challenge individualisation, foster community, recalibrate the market for contract cleaning and demand the respect of politicians, business leaders and policy-makers. In engaging the powerful through the drama of assemblies and campaigns, in securing concrete gains over the living wage (amongst other campaigns) and in working together, participants have experienced 'collective self-realization.' In the language used in London Citizens' training courses, participants have challenged the 'world as it is' and in some instances, made small steps to realising the 'world as it should be' (see also Drury *et al.*, 2005). In so doing, participants have become the subject rather than the object of politics and this feeling of collective power has long-lasting effects (for more on the importance of re-subjectification, see Gibson-Graham, 2006).

Without these experiences of individual and collective empowerment, which are themselves products – to some extent – of political success, London Citizens would not have the glue to hold people together. While the organisation depends upon being open to difference and enabling participation, it is also fuelled by the outcomes of its campaigns. Political victories are the fuel which sustains the organisation and have undoubtedly helped it to grow. It is thus no surprise that London Citizens' organisers and leaders consciously monitor both the internal and the external health of the organisation. The organisation needs both people and power if it is to survive, grow and prosper.

Concluding remarks

This short overview of the work of London Citizens has implications for Government policy in relation to democratic engagement and community cohesion. Indeed, the chapter has argued that the two sets of policies overlap very closely as people are exhorted to find new ways of working together and reconnect with political life. The experience of London Citizens suggests that the former can be achieved by doing the latter, and both depend upon identity-making through the practice of collection action itself. In so doing, however, London Citizens has created sets of relatively shallow civic relationships that reflect but do not depend upon the articulation of difference. As such, the work of London

Citizens chimes with the arguments made by Vertovec (2007a: 29) in his contribution to the community cohesion debate:

[D]esirable as these might be toward promoting better relations, 'sustained encounters' and 'deep and meaningful' interactions are simply not going to occur amongst most people in British cities today, whether ethnic majority, minority or new immigrant. Apart from a few contexts such as work or school, most urban encounters are fleeting or monetary, although importantly they might be regular... Ephemeral interactions comprise the bulk of social relations in libraries, parks and playgrounds, apartment buildings and housing estates, street markets, shops and shopping centres, hospitals and health clinics, hair salons and other commonplace sites... We would do well to think about how to conceive, appreciate and foster positive relations – if not common senses of belonging – amid the fleeting and superficial kinds of contact that are the daily stuff of urban existence.

London Citizens has been successful because it enables these safe civic relationships to develop. As such, it practices a form of identity politics that allows for mutual differentiation alongside the creation of a meaningful super-ordinate identity at the urban-wide scale.

Political action has always depended upon this process of 'up-scaling' identifications across difference, using language that travels to secure a broad coalition for change. The early trade union movement was successful in using the vehicle of the Labour Party to connect the particular experiences of work with the impact of class relations in the wider society (Hobsbawm, 1996; Wills and Simms, 2004). So too, groups organising around the particular experiences of sexism or homophobia have successfully used the language of civil rights to argue for equality, winning support from those not directly affected. Without an appeal to the wider society, most political movements remain trapped in their particular identifications, unable to appeal at the scale required to win (Reicher and Hopkins, 1996; Hopkins and Reicher, 1997; Wilchins, 1997).

In addition, however, such 'upscaling' clearly has limits and there is a danger that once successful, the grassroots becomes disconnected from the wider organisation and that face-to-face relations get lost. London Citizens is necessarily grounded in locality, in geographically 'vested' institutions and as long as it depends upon mobilisation for its political strength, it can not stay very far from the ground. In so doing, it is able to remake individual and collective identities through collective action for change.

Acknowledgements

I am very grateful to everyone who took part in this research. The cross-disciplinary cross-fertilisation of the programme has been extremely stimulating and the involvement of social psychologists – not least programme director Professor Margaret Wetherell – is evident here.

Notes

1. For more information, see http://www.geog.qmul.ac.uk/livingwage/index. html
2. Of course, in practice, no organisation will ever simply represent a single identity category as identity is necessarily multiple. Any collection of individuals will include differences of gender, age, time in the country, immigration status and heritage among other things.
3. This strap-line appears on London Citizens' publicity material including leaflets, reports and the website. It highlights the core activity of the organisation and the ease of entry for different groups.
4. As might be expected, however, the organisations involved in London Citizens have often found a remarkable degree of commonality in their beliefs and values too. As this Anglican Priest put it when talking about contact across the faith traditions: '[W]hen we all engage with what we *do* believe, there turns out to be a remarkable degree of common practice' (17.03.05).

References

Amin, A. (2002) Ethnicity and the Multi-Cultural City: Living with Diversity. *Environment and Planning A*. 34, 959–80.

Amin, A. (2006) The Good City. *Urban Studies* 43, (5/6) 1009–23.

Bach, R. (1993) *Changing Relations: Newcomers and Established Residents in US Communities*. New York: Ford Foundation.

Bauman, Z. (2001) *Community: Seeking Safety in an Insecure World*. Cambridge: Polity.

Brewer, J. B. and Gaertner, S. L. (2001) Toward Reduction of Prejudice: Intergroup Contact and Social Categorization. In R. Brown and S. L. Gaertner (eds.) *Blackwell Handbook of Social Psychology: Inter-Group Processes*. Oxford: Blackwell.

Commission on Integration and Cohesion (2007) *Our Shared Future*. Wetherby, West Yorkshire: Commission on Integration and Cohesion.

Dench, G., Gavron, K. and Young, M. (2006) *The New East End: Kinship, Race and Conflict*. London: Basic Books.

Dixon, J. and Durrheim, K. (2003) Contact and the Ecology of Racial Division: Some Variations of Informal Segregation. *British Journal of Social Psychology* 42, 1–23.

Drury, J., Cocking, C., Beale, J., Hanson, C. and Rapley, F. (2005) The Phenomenology of Empowerment in Collective Action. *British Journal of Social Psychology* 44, 309–28.

Drury, J. and Reicher, S. (2005) Explaining Enduring Empowerment: A Comparative Study of Collective Action and Psychological Outcomes. *European Journal of Social Psychology* 35, 35–58.

Drury, J., Reicher, S. and Scott, C. (2003) Transforming the Boundaries of Collective Identity: From the 'Local' Anti-Road Campaign to 'Global' Resistance? *Social Movement Studies* 2(2), 191–212.

Gaertner, S. L., Rust, M. C., Dovidio, J. F., Bachman, B. A. and Anastasio, P. A. (1994) The Contact Hypothesis: The Role of Common Ingroup Identity in Reducing Intergroup Bias. *Small Group Research* 25, 244–9.

Gibson-Graham, J. K. (2006) *A Post-Capitalist Politics*. Minneapolis: University of Minnesota Press.

Hewstone, M. (1996) Contact and Categorization: Social Psychological Interventions to Change Inter-Group Relations. In C. N. Macrae, C. Stangor and M. Hewstone (eds.) *Stereotypes and Stereotyping*. London: Guilford.

Hewstone, M., Rubin, M. and Willis, H. (2002) Intergroup Bias. *Annual Review of Psychology* 53, 575–604.

Hobsbawm, E. (1996) Identity Politics and the Left. *New Left Review* 217, 38–47.

Hopkins, N. and Reicher, S. (1997) Social Movement Rhetoric and the Social Psychology of Collective Action: A Case Study of Anti-Abortion Mobilization. *Human Relations* 50(3), 261–86.

Li, Y., Savage, M. and Pickles, A. (2005) Capital and Social Trust in Britain Journal. *European Sociological Review* 21(2), 109–23.

Jamoul, L. and Wills, J. (2008) Faith in Politics. *Urban Studies* 45, 2035–56.

London School of Economics (LSE) (2007) *The Impact of Recent Immigration on the London Economy*. London: City of London Corporation.

Massey, D. (2005) *For Space*. London: Sage.

Muir, R. (2007) *The New Identity Politics*. London: Institute for Public Policy Research.

Osterman, P. (2003) *Gathering Power: The Future of Progressive Politics in America*. New York: Beacon Press.

Pattie, C., Seyd, P. and Whiteley, P. (2004) *Citizenship in Britain: Values, Participation and Democracy*. Cambridge: Cambridge University Press.

Phillips, T. (2005) After 7/7: Sleepwalking to Segregation. Speech given at event organized by the Manchester Council for Community Relations, Manchester Town Hall, Thursday 22 September 2005. Accessible from: http://83.137.212.42/sitearchive/cre/Default.aspx.LocID-0hgnew07r.RefLocID-0hg00900c001001.Lang-EN.htm (accessed 9.10.08).

Power Enquiry (2006) *Power to the People: The Report of Power: An Independent Inquiry into Britain's Democracy*. The POWER Inquiry, York.

Putnam, R. (2007) E Pluribus Unum: Diversity and Community in the Twenty-First Century. The 2006 Johan Skytte Prize Lecture. *Scandinavian Political Studies* 30(2), 137–74.

Reicher, S. and Hopkins, N. (1996) Self-Category Constructions in Political Rhetoric: An Analysis of Thatcher's and Kinnock's Speeches Concerning the British Miners' Strike (1984–5). *European Journal of Social Psychology* 26, 353–71.

176   *Communities, Cities and Nations*

Robinson, D. (2005) The Search for Community Cohesion: Key Theories and Dominant Concepts for the Public Policy Agenda. *Urban Studies* 42(8), 1411–27.

Sandercock, L. (2003) *Cosmopolis II: Mongrel Cities of the Twenty-first Century.* London: Continuum.

Sennett, R. (1977) *The Fall of Public Man.* Cambridge: Cambridge University Press.

Valentine, G. (2008) Living with Difference: Reflections on Geographies of Encounter. *Progress in Human Geography* 32(3), 323–37.

Vertovec, S. (2007a) *New Complexities of Cohesion in Britain: Super-Diversity, Transnationalism and Civil-Integration.* London: Commission on Integration and Cohesion.

Vertovec, S. (2007b) Superdiversity and Its Implications. *Ethnic and Racial Studies* 30(6), 1024–54.

Voss, K. and Sherman, R. (2000) Breaking the Iron Law of Oligarchy. *American Journal of Sociology* 106(2), 303–49.

Wilchins, R. A. (1997) *Read My Lips: Sexual Subversion and the End of Gender.* Ithaca, NY: Firebrand Books.

Wills J. (2004) Campaigning for Low Paid Workers: The East London Communities Organisation (TELCO) Living Wage Campaign. In W. Brown, G. Healy, E. Heery and P. Taylor (eds.) *The Future of Worker Representation.* Oxford: Oxford University Press.

Wills, J. (2008) Making Class Politics Possible: Organizing Contract Cleaners in London. *International Journal of Urban and Regional Research* 32(2), 205–23.

Wills, J. (2009) Subcontracted Employment and Its Challenge to Labor. *Labor Studies Journal 34.*

Wills, J. and Simms, M. (2004) Building Reciprocal Community Unionism in the UK. *Capital and Class* 82, 59–84.

Young, I. M. (2000) *Inclusion and Democracy.* Oxford: Oxford University Press.

9
Residential Segregation and Intergroup Contact: Consequences for Intergroup Relations, Social Capital and Social Identity

Katharina Schmid, Miles Hewstone, Joanne Hughes, Richard Jenkins and Ed Cairns

This chapter examines the relationship between social context, inter-group contact, and social identity and intergroup processes in Northern Ireland. We do so by focusing explicitly on the consequences of residential segregation in this context, a feature typical of societies entrenched in intergroup conflict. Considerable attention has been devoted to understanding the implications of residential segregation for intergroup processes, although whether living in more or less segregated social environments has positive or negative consequences remains subject to contentious debate. So what are the effects of such separation on patterns of identification, attitudes to those defined as 'other', and group conflict? What kinds of intra- and intergroup relations do contexts of segregation or mixing encourage? What processes and variables mediate the effects of living in segregated versus mixed contexts?

Our primary aim in this chapter is to explore how the patterns of contact between groups living in segregated and mixed neighbourhoods are related with social identity processes and intergroup attitudes. We evaluate the differential effects for intergroup relations, social capital and social identity processes of sharing one's social environment with fellow ingroup members only or sharing a space with both ingroup and outgroup members. By focusing centrally on one context of intergroup conflict, Northern Ireland, we highlight, in an exemplary manner, the critical role of intergroup contact, and argue that the link between social environment and group-based processes should not be examined in isolation from intergroup contact. In an attempt to untangle the contested nature of the effects of segregation, we draw extensively on research evidence that has emerged from our own recent research programme, involving a comparison between segregated and mixed neighbourhoods in Northern Ireland.

This chapter is organized into three main parts. First, we discuss the consequences of segregation and intergroup contact for intergroup relations. Here we start by reviewing how the study of intergroup contact has advanced understanding of intergroup relations, before moving to a discussion of the consequences of segregation and contact for intergroup relations. Second, we discuss the consequences of segregation and intergroup contact for social capital and social trust. Here we provide a brief overview of the concept of social capital; we then address current debates on the relationship between diversity and social trust and present some data that shed light on the combined effects of context and contact on social capital. Third, we consider the consequences of segregation and contact for social identity processes. We present evidence that more diverse social environments and social experiences often prompt more complex and differentiated identity structures, and highlight, by drawing on some of our recent data, that segregation and contact may have profound consequences for emergent, superordinate forms of categorization, as well as for social identity complexity. We end by highlighting how taking account of the critical role of intergroup contact has advanced understanding of the consequences of segregation for group-based processes.

Segregation, contact and intergroup relations

Segregation and intergroup contact

Despite gradually moving towards a resolution of its conflict (see Hewstone *et al.*, 2005; Jenkins, 2008, for brief historical outlines of the conflict), Northern Ireland remains deeply segregated along ethno-religious lines. Segregation takes place at many levels and in many different domains, with the most noticeable types of segregation being residential segregation, personal and marital segregation, segregation in primary- and secondary-level education, and segregation in sport, work or leisure (see Hewstone *et al.*, 2005). The pervasiveness of segregation in Northern Irish society has been recognized as one of the main factors perpetuating conflict, in that segregation reinforces existing group boundaries, fosters mutual ignorance and suspicion, and maintains prejudice and negative stereotypes (Gallagher, 1995). Thus, considerable efforts by policy makers have been made to encourage cross-community contact (Hughes, 1999), a strategy based on theoretical and empirical foundations from over 50 years of research of social-science research on intergroup contact (e.g., Allport, 1954; Brown and Hewstone, 2005).

In its simplest form the 'contact hypothesis' (Allport, 1954) postulates that interaction with outgroup members can, under positive conditions, reduce prejudice and improve intergroup relations, and extensive empirical evidence backs up this claim (for a meta-analytic review, see Pettigrew and Tropp, 2006). Moreover, Pettigrew and Tropp's (2006) comprehensive meta-analysis has shown that contact can exert such positive effects even if not all of the optimal conditions proposed by Allport (1954) are met.

In Northern Ireland, research has shown that direct intergroup contact, especially in the form of cross-group friendship, is associated with reduced ingroup bias (Paolini *et al.*, 2004; Hewstone *et al.*, 2005; Tausch, Hewstone, Kenworthy, Cairns and Christ, 2007a; Tausch, Tam, Hewstone, Kenworthy and Cairns, 2007b) and increased intergroup trust and forgiveness (Hewstone *et al.*, 2008). Contact has also been found to exert positive effects on behavioural tendencies towards outgroup members. For example, research based on samples of students at desegregated universities and among a general population sample of Northern Irish adults has found that positive intergroup contact, especially in the form of cross-group friendships, is associated with less negative action tendencies towards outgroup members (respondents reported less willingness to verbally insult or intimidate outgroup members; see Paolini *et al.*, 2007; Schmid *et al.*, 2008). Prior contact can also affect individuals' attitudes towards or willingness to engage in future contact with outgroup members (Hewstone *et al.*, 2006). Moreover, the positive effects of so-called 'indirect' or 'extended' contact, that is the mere knowledge that an ingroup member has an outgroup friend (see Wright *et al.*, 1997), have also been confirmed in this context, even after controlling for direct contact (Paolini *et al.*, 2004). While most of these previous studies rely on cross-sectional data, we have recently also confirmed the relationship between contact and improved intergroup attitudes in longitudinal research (Tausch *et al.*, 2009).

Research on intergroup contact in this and other contexts has also made significant advances with regard to understanding the intervening, mediating mechanisms that determine how, as well as understanding the facilitating conditions that determine when, contact exerts positive effects on intergroup relations (see Brown and Hewstone, 2005, for a detailed review of mediators and moderators). Studies in Northern

Ireland have shown, for example, that contact works by reducing both individual-level (i.e. intergroup anxiety) and group-level (i.e. realistic and symbolic threat) threats (Tausch *et al.*, 2007; see also Stephan *et al.*, 2000), or by fostering positive intergroup emotions (Tam *et al.*, 2007). Consistent with the wider literature on moderators of contact effects, we have also observed that contact exerts stronger positive effects on intergroup perception when category salience is high than when it is low (Schmid *et al.*, 2009b; see also Voci and Hewstone, 2003). Contact effects tend to be more pronounced for members of majority or high status groups (Tropp and Pettigrew, 2005), a finding we also observed in the Northern Irish context. Specifically, we carried out multigroup comparisons to compare differences in the strength of the relationships between contact and attitudes for Catholics and Protestants, as well as for respondents who self-reported their ingroup to hold higher relative ingroup status contact, whether Catholic or Protestant. Our results showed that in both analyses, the positive effects of contact were more pronounced for Protestants (traditionally perceived to hold higher relative status than Catholics), as well as for respondents who self-reported higher relative ingroup status (Schmid *et al.*, 2009b).

Perhaps one of the most interesting findings, and one that could indicate the most far-reaching potential effects of intergroup contact, pertains to the generalization of contact effects from a target outgroup to other outgroups (Pettigrew, 1997), most recently termed the 'secondary-transfer effect' (Pettigrew, 2009). In his analysis of over 3800 majority group respondents in France, Germany, Great Britain and the Netherlands, Pettigrew (1997) found that cross-group friendship tended not only to reduce prejudice towards a target outgroup, but also had secondary effects on prejudice towards other non-target outgroups that were not directly involved in the contact.

We tested some of the claims concerning secondary-transfer effects of contact by considering two different routes for attitude generalization in a single model. Specifically, we tested whether direct contact leads to attitude generalization to a non-target outgroup via the attitude to the target outgroup, or whether it occurs via a re-appraisal of the ingroup, that is a process of 'deprovincialization' which results in a less glorified view of the ingroup (see Pettigrew, 1997). Using general population data collected in Northern Ireland, we showed that contact with the ethno-religious outgroup was predictive not only of attitudes towards that group, but also had 'knock-on' effects for attitudes towards ethnic minorities in Northern Ireland, an effect that was primarily mediated through attitudes towards the ethno-religious outgroup. This effect occurred even after controlling for direct contact with ethnic minorities. We replicated this effect in a number of different intergroup settings, including Greek- and Turkish-Cypriots in Cyprus, and with both cross-sectional and longitudinal data in Northern Ireland (Tausch *et al.*, under review). Overall, we found attitude generalization to be mediated by changed attitudes to the target outgroup, and not a re-appraisal of the ingroup. Such generalization effects are of particular merit in contexts where prejudice and discrimination are not targeted at a single outgroup, as is the case in Northern Ireland where racially motivated attacks occur frequently. This occurrence reflects, perhaps, an unfortunate displacement of conflict as Northern Ireland moves towards a resolution of its ethno-religiously rooted conflict.

The consequences for intergroup relations of between-group segregation: Threat vs contact theory

What are the consequences of living in more diverse social environments, as opposed to areas where space is shared solely with members of one's own ethnic, racial or religious group for intergroup relations? Some have argued that diverse, desegregated social environments foster group-based threat perceptions and, as a consequence, should co-vary negatively with intergroup attitudes and behaviour. In principle, this argument reflects the theoretical underpinnings of threat or conflict theory (Blalock, 1967), an approach that initially emerged to explain a dominant majority's prejudice towards minority groups (Blumer, 1958; Bobo, 1999). In short, advocates of threat theory predict a direct linear relationship between the percentage of minority group members in the majority's social environment and increased levels of prejudice towards the minority, a relationship that has been supported by some (e.g., Fossett and Kiecolt, 1989), but not other (e.g., Citrin *et al.*, 1990) research studies.

A more optimistic perspective on the relationship between diversity and intergroup relations is rooted in intergroup contact theory (Allport, 1954; Hewstone and Brown, 1986). As mentioned above, contact theory rests upon the assumption that frequent and positive interaction with outgroup members has positive implications for intergroup relations. Important then for a discussion of the nature of the relationship between social environment and intergroup relations is the consistent finding in intergroup contact research that the *opportunity* for contact tends to be a strong predictor of *actual* contact (e.g., Wagner *et al.*, 1989). One may thus argue that more diverse social environments, by virtue of affording more opportunities for engaging in outgroup interaction, should also be predictive of actual contact, a consequence of which should then be (if contact is positive) a reduction of intergroup tensions (see Wagner *et al.*, 2006; Schmid *et al.*, 2008). In other words, we argue that contact should mediate the effects of context on attitudes; thus living in more diverse areas should exert a positive, indirect effect on outgroup attitudes via contact, and particularly contact that takes place in the immediate social environment. And indeed, research evidence generally supports a positive relationship between living in more diverse environments and a higher degree of intergroup contact (Bledsoe *et al.*, 1995; Stein *et al.*, 2000; Wagner *et al.*, 2003). For example, Wagner *et al.* (2006), using data from a German probability sample, found a higher percentage of foreigners in a population district to be predictive of more frequent and positive contact with ethnic minorities, which in turn had a positive effect on perceptions of foreigners.

In sum, threat and contact theory make diverging theoretical predictions concerning the consequences of diverse, desegregated social environments for intergroup relations. According to threat theory, diversity inevitably holds negative consequences for intergroup relations. We contend, first, that threat theory contains conceptual flaws and, second, that it fails to account for a crucial intervening variable. The most notable flaws in the theory are that it equates the actual proportion with the perceived proportion of outgroup members in a social environment, that it equates the proportion of outgroup members living in the social environment with intergroup contact (which are two quite distinct things), and that it equates context with threat (see Semyonov *et al.*, 2004; Schmid *et al.*, 2008). The overlooked intervening variable in the relationship between context and intergroup attitudes is the degree and quality of intergroup contact itself. Yet although contact theory postulates a positive relationship between positive intergroup interaction and attitudes, we do not wish to argue the converse of threat theory, that diversity is positively associated with intergroup perception and behaviour. We agree that diversity in the absence of meaningful, positive contact may indeed be associated negatively with intergroup relations, particularly if one's social environment is dominated by a high outgroup-to-ingroup ratio (although whether diversity actually *causes* these negative effects remains questionable). However, we do argue that more diverse, desegregated areas may have positive, or at least less negative, implications for intergroup relations, if diversity is experienced positively, and if it coincides with positive and meaningful intergroup contact experiences.

Neighbourhood and contact effects on intergroup relations

Notwithstanding other types of segregation, perhaps the most conspicuous and enduring is the extent to which Northern Ireland remains residentially segregated. According to a report on the 2001 census, approximately 44 per cent of Catholics live in predominantly Catholic census output areas (where Catholics make up 90 per cent or more of the residents), and 30 per cent of Protestants live in predominantly Protestant census output areas (where Protestants make up 90 per cent or more of the residents) (Office of the First Minister and the Deputy First Minister, 2007). This feature of Northern Irish society makes it not only particularly conducive, but also vital, to examining some of the predictions made by threat and contact theories, respectively. For this reason we have recently conducted two large-scale studies comparing segregated and mixed neighbourhoods in Belfast and several smaller Northern Irish towns. We attempted to study specifically the consequences of segregation, in particular residential segregation, on intergroup perception and behavioural intentions. Importantly, this allowed us to examine not only the impact of context and contact on attitudes, in isolation from each other, but also made it possible to consider the combined effects of both. Although we tried as far as possible to match neighbourhoods on various criteria, some differences remained; thus this investigation of mixed vs. segregated neighbourhoods controlled for age, gender, education and income in all analyses that we refer to in this chapter.

As mentioned above, contact tends to exert positive effects on outgroup orientations and behavioural tendencies in Northern Ireland, but what are the consequences of living in segregated or mixed neighbourhoods? Our recent data show that respondents living in mixed neighbourhoods generally report more positive behavioural intentions towards outgroup members, such as a greater willingness for future contact, less negative action tendencies towards outgroup members and less support for violence (Hewstone *et al.*, 2008; Schmid *et al.*, 2008). However, when we considered the effects of context on attitude variables our data showed mixed results. In one of our studies involving neighbourhoods in Belfast, living in mixed areas was associated with more positive outgroup attitudes (Schmid *et al.*, 2008), while in our second study comprising six Northern Irish towns mixing was associated with more negative attitudes (Schmid *et al.*, 2009b). While the former findings appear to refute threat theory assumptions, the latter seemingly support them. Yet, when we considered contact as an intervening, mediating variable in the relationship between context and attitudes we found three interesting effects. First, living in mixed neighbourhoods was also associated with more positive intergroup contact experiences. Second, contact positively predicted attitudes. And third, direct contact in the neighbourhood positively mediated the effects of segregation versus mixing on intergroup attitudes, so that context exerted positive *indirect* effects on attitudes. Thus, these findings highlight the importance of considering the combined effects of context and contact on intergroup attitudes, rather than focusing on context effects only.

To extend this analysis further, one may also think of contact as a moderator of context effects, that is that context may have positive effects for intergroup relations only for those individuals who have contact with outgroup members (Schmid *et al.*, 2009c). To elaborate, it may be that living in more heterogeneous environments in the absence of positive contact experiences has negative effects for intergroup relations, yet such negative effects should not be witnessed for individuals living in more diverse areas who generally have positive intergroup contact experiences. Importantly, contact may act as a moderator of context effects even if contact takes place outside one's immediate residential environment, for example in the form of direct contact in work or educational settings outside one's neighbourhood, or through extended contact via family or friends who do not live in one's neighbourhood. In order to test some of these claims we examined the moderating effects of contact, in the form of cross-group friendship (a measure that was not limited to friendships in the neighbourhood), on the relationship between living in segregated versus mixed neighbourhoods and ingroup bias. This analysis showed that living in mixed areas was only negatively related with various measures of outgroup perception for respondents who had no or few outgroup friends; once contact in the form of cross-group friendships was accounted for, these negative effects were no longer witnessed (Schmid *et al.*, 2009c).

A clear implication of these findings is that it does not suffice to simply relate aggregate-level variables, such as the mere number of outgroup members in one's immediate residential environment, with outgroup orientations. Rather, one needs to also take account of the nature and quality of individuals' social experiences, that is how individuals living in more diverse social contexts interact with individuals who do not belong to their own group. It is only by considering the combined effects of macro- and individual-level variables that a more accurate approximation of the effects of living in segregated versus mixed environments becomes attainable.

Segregation, contact and social capital

Social capital theory

Although rooted in earlier works by Granovetter (1973), Coleman (1988), Bourdieu (1986) and, much earlier, by Wirth (1938), the concept of social capital in its most current definition and use, albeit at times somewhat inconsistent and fragmented, was largely popularized by Robert Putnam (2000). According to Putnam (2007), social capital refers to the connections among individuals, which include social networks, norms of reciprocity and trustworthiness. Indeed, social trust is a key variable typically measured in social capital research, alongside other variables such as participation and civic engagement (see e.g., Putnam, 2007). These connections among individuals are said to constitute valuable assets for individuals, and may promote mutual support, educational attainment, or psychological health. Moreover, it has been argued that social capital can have positive manifestations even beyond such individual-level effects, that is for communities or for societies at large. It is perhaps for this reason that the concept has increasingly entered the political sphere, being commonly regarded as prerequisite for the creation of meaningful and successful modern communities.

However, it is also known that social capital may have negative effects, particularly so when social capital links individuals only within, not between, networks and communities. For example, in the context of residential segregation the quality of individuals' social networks may be particularly strong within one's own community, yet this may go hand in hand with own-group favouritism, discrimination or corruption. Therefore, theoretically, a distinction has been made between 'bonding' and 'bridging' forms of social capital (Putnam, 2000), recognizing that positive effects should be maximized between, and not only within, communities (for a discussion of 'bridging' and 'bonding' social capital in the Northern Irish context, see Leonard, 2004). Bonding social capital, while important for the creation of valuable social networks, can be exclusive, inward-looking and tends to reinforce exclusive identities and homogeneous groups in the context of ethnically homogeneous or segregated societies. By creating strong ingroup loyalties, it may also create outgroup antagonism. Bridging social capital on the other hand is more inclusive, having the potential to generate broader identities and reciprocity between groups. In fact, the 'weak ties' that link between networks (Granovetter, 1973) are believed to be particularly strong and important precisely because they link networks.

Segregation and social capital: The role of intergroup contact

What are the consequences of living in homogeneous as opposed to more diverse social environments for social capital and social cohesion? In order to address this question we wish to reprise the discussion on threat versus contact theory at this point, yet extend it further to include a third theoretical perspective, constrict theory (see Putnam, 2007). This recently advanced perspective is rooted in findings stemming from the 'Social Capital Community Benchmark Survey' in the United States (see Putnam, 2007), which seem to suggest that living in more racially or ethnically heterogeneous social environments and neighbourhoods not only has negative consequences for intergroup trust (in line with threat theory), but also reduces intragroup trust, as well as social trust in general. Specifically, the results of this study revealed a consistent positive linear relationship between the percentage of census tract ethnic homogeneity and intergroup, intragroup and neighbourhood trust, and vice versa.

Naturally, these findings seem bleak at first, as they seem to suggest that ethnic, racial or religious diversity prompts individuals to retreat into social isolation. However, recent research evidence shows that the effects of socio-economic disadvantage or deprivation tend to outweigh the effects of diversity on social trust and social cohesion (e.g., Laurence and Heath, 2008; Letki, 2008). Moreover, the pessimism surrounding the implications of Putnam's findings about the consequences of diversity has since been partly defused by findings showing that diversity may only be problematic for social trust in the absence of positive social interactions with those diverse others that make up one's diverse residential environment (Stolle *et al.*, 2008). Thus, at the risk of sounding repetitive, we again argue that the effects of context on social trust should not be examined in isolation from individuals' contact experiences with those comparative others that co-inhabit one's diverse social environment. Hence, just as threat theory may be missing a crucial link regarding the quality of individuals' interethnic, interracial or interreligious interactions in the relationship between context and intergroup relations, so may constrict theory be missing that same link in the relationship between context and social trust. And similar to the conjecture on the relationship between context and attitudes, we argue that one needs to consider the combined effects of diverse residential contexts and intergroup contact experiences when aiming to disentangle the effects of diversity on social capital and cohesion.

In an attempt at testing some of these claims, and similar to aforementioned analyses examining threat versus contact theory assumptions, we examined the consequences of living in segregated versus mixed areas and experiencing different amounts and types of intergroup contact using data collected through our recent surveys in Northern Ireland, yet this time using neighbourhood trust as the outcome variable (Schmid *et al.*, 2009c). Although our survey did not include items measuring ingroup or intragroup trust, it did include a number of items measuring the extent to which respondents felt they could trust people in their neighbourhood, as well as their feeling of belonging in the neighbourhood.

Our results revealed that both neighbourhood (segregated versus mixed) and contact exerted direct, independent effects on the extent to which individuals felt they could trust others in their neighbourhood, as well as the extent to which they rated their feeling of belonging in the neighbourhood. However, while contact, in the form of direct neighbourhood contact and cross-group friendship, typically exerted positive effects on both trust and belonging, neighbourhood effects were in the opposite direction. Respondents living in mixed neighbourhoods felt they could trust their neighbours less and reported less belonging in the neighbourhood than did respondents living in segregated areas. However, when we considered the combined effects of neighbourhood and contact, by treating contact as a potential moderator, our results revealed that living in mixed neighbourhoods only exerted negative effects on trust and belonging in the absence of contact (see also Stolle *et al.*, 2008). Importantly, and extending Stolle *et al.*'s (2008) findings, we observed this effect for different types of contact, including direct contact in the form of contact with neighbours, but also cross-group friends, as well as extended contact via family and friends. For individuals who had contact, particularly those who reported having many cross-group friends, the negative effects of context on neighbourhood trust and belonging disappeared. And similar to aforementioned analyses of the effects of context on attitudes we found that living in mixed as opposed to segregated neighbourhoods also exerted an indirect effect on feelings of belonging and neighbourhood trust (Schmid *et al.*, 2009c). Specifically, we observed that respondents living in mixed neighbourhoods reported a greater sense of belonging and more neighbourhood trust, the more positive contact they had, and particularly so via direct contact with outgroup members in their immediate neighbourhood. These findings thus confirm our assumption that contact plays a key role in the relationship between social environment and social trust, both as mediator and as moderator of context effects.

Of course we need to keep in mind that our data were gathered in a context of relative racial homogeneity (albeit in a society that has witnessed extreme ethnic intergroup conflict), thus we should be cautious in generalizing our findings across other contexts involving different types and degrees of ethnic diversity. Also, our studies included a limited number of sites; in order to test the effects of context more stringently it will be advantageous to use more sampling points allowing us to model the hierarchical nature of such data. Nonetheless, the fact that our findings, albeit preliminary at this stage, have been replicated in two different neighbourhood surveys in Northern Ireland gives us reason to take a somewhat more optimistic view of the consequences of ethnic or racial diversity. At the very least, the results of our research allow us to suggest that there may be scope, via intergroup contact, for counteracting any potential negative effects of neighbourhood diversity on trust and intergroup relations.

Segregation, contact and social identity

It is a well-established fact that individuals typically belong to many social groups and thus hold multiple social identities (see, e.g., Crisp and Hewstone, 2007), even in societies that are as polarized as Northern Ireland (see Jenkins, 2008; Schmid *et al.*, in press). It has also been argued that more complex societies, where group boundaries are less clearly defined and individuals rely less on a single ingroup identity for meeting the psychological needs of 'belonging', hold reduced potential for intergroup conflict (see Brewer and Gaertner, 2001). Despite this, the consequences of living in more or less diverse social environments, or indeed of intergroup contact, for complex or emergent forms of social identity remain largely unexplored. In our recent studies in Northern Ireland we have begun to study the relationship between context, contact and such complex and emergent forms of self-description, as well as the consequences of these for intergroup relations. Specifically, we were interested in examining the extent to which respondents living in mixed areas would be more likely to self-categorize in terms of and identify with superordinate, common ingroup categories as opposed to more exclusive subgroup identities, as well as to find out whether social environment and social experiences tend to co-vary with the complexity of individuals' identity structure (Roccas and Brewer, 2002).

Subgroup versus superordinate identification

Although it is generally assumed that most individuals in Northern Ireland self-categorize as, and identify with, either Catholic or Protestant, there are other identities relevant to the conflict that are also commonly endorsed as important and self-descriptive, including national or neighbourhood identities (see Schmid *et al.*, in press). Although Catholic and Irish identities, on the one hand, and Protestant and British identities, on the other, overlap to a large extent, there is also a significant minority of the population that cross-cuts this divide, choosing combinations such as Catholic-and-British or Protestant-and-Irish. Interestingly, such cross-cutting category combinations are significantly more likely to be found among individuals living in mixed than in segregated neighbourhoods (see Schmid *et al.*, in press). Increasingly, an emergent form of national self-description is being claimed, a 'Northern Irish' identity. Many regard this 'Northern Irish' identity as a superordinate, common ingroup identity (see also Gaertner *et al.*, 1993), given that approximately one-third of both Catholics and Protestants consistently, and almost equally, endorse it. Again, our data show respondents living in mixed areas to be more likely to do so (see Schmid *et al.*, in press).

Informed by the common ingroup identity model of recategorization (Gaertner *et al.*, 1993; Gaertner and Dovidio, 2000), we further examined the extent to which this emergent form of self-description may have positive consequences for intergroup perception in this context. The recategorization perspective argues that exclusive subordinate categorizations ('us' and 'them') can be replaced with more inclusive superordinate categorizations ('we'), a consequence of which should be the perception of outgroup members in more favourable terms. Applied to the Northern Irish case one may therefore expect respondents who self-categorize as 'Northern Irish' to report more positive outgroup attitudes than do respondents who self-categorize in subgroup terms (e.g., as Catholic or Protestant, or British or Irish), a hypothesis supported by our recent findings (see Schmid *et al.*, in press). It has also been argued, however, that in many instances the common ingroup model may be an unrealistic possibility, given that it risks depriving individuals of valued, powerful and long-established social categories. Noteworthy here is that our respondents reported significantly lower levels of identification with the superordinate than the subgroup categories, a perhaps unsurprising finding given the relative novelty of the, as yet less well defined, superordinate category.

It has been argued that a dual identity model (Gaertner and Dovidio, 2000), whereby individuals may endorse both the subgroup and the superordinate identity as equally valued and shared identities, may be more likely to yield positive intergroup effects than is endorsement of the superordinate identity alone. In an attempt to test some of these predictions, we examined the combined effects of both subgroup and superordinate identities on the relationship between contact and outgroup attitudes. Our results revealed that contact, in the form of extended contact, was a particularly strong predictor of positive outgroup attitudes for individuals who reported both high levels of subgroup and high levels of superordinate identification, whereas contact exerted only a weak effect on attitudes for individuals highly identified with the superordinate category only (Schmid *et al.*, 2009b). We also considered the combined effects of living in segregated versus mixed neighbourhoods, subgroup identification and common ingroup identification on ingroup bias, and found that living in mixed neighbourhoods was associated with a reduction in bias for dual identifiers, yet we did not witness a difference in bias between respondents living in segregated and mixed neighbourhoods for high common ingroup identifiers. Considered together, these findings appear to support the predictions of the dual identity model over those of the recategorization model, a set of analyses we aim to follow up on in future research.

Although we do not have space for a detailed discussion of the consequences of threat perceptions for attitudes in this chapter (but see Stephan and Stephan, 2002; Tausch *et al.*, in press), we do however wish to report one additional finding that we find particularly interesting. Informed by research showing that perceived threat exerts negative effects on intergroup relations, and that threat typically exerts stronger effects for individuals highly identified with the threatened group (e.g., Tausch *et al.*, 2007), we examined the moderating properties of subgroup – and superordinate group identification on the relationship between threat perceptions and ingroup bias in Northern Ireland (Schmid *et al.*, 2009b). Although both subgroup and superordinate identification emerged as statistically significant moderators, there were marked differences in the nature of effects. While threat perceptions were particularly predictive of negative attitudes for high subgroup identifiers, supporting previous research in this area, a reverse, 'mirror image' effect was observed for superordinate identifiers. Here threat perceptions were particularly predictive of negative attitudes for those who reported low levels of identification with the superordinate category. All in all, this general set of findings allows for some optimism surrounding the implications of this novel identity category, Northern Irish, for intergroup relations.

Social identity complexity

Social identity complexity (Roccas and Brewer, 2002) refers to the fact that individuals tend to organize and perceive their multiple ingroup identities in more or less exclusive terms, and defines an individual's subjective representation of the interrelationships among his or her multiple identities (Roccas and Brewer, 2002). Thus an individual's identity structure may be relatively simplified, to the extent that individuals may perceive their range of ingroup identities as largely overlapping, whereby only individuals who share membership of all important ingroup categories are perceived as fellow ingroup members. Conversely, individuals who recognize that not all of their respective ingroups converge and overlap, that is that some people will be ingroup members on some, but outgroup members on other categories, are said to hold a relatively more complex, less exclusive identity structure. In order to have a complex, differentiated identity structure, individuals need to be aware of their multiple ingroup category memberships, and need to recognize that others' various ingroup memberships typically are different from their own multiple ingroup memberships (Roccas and Brewer, 2002). Complexity may refer to an individuals' perceived overlap between multiple categories (overlap complexity), or the degree to which an individual perceives different categories as similar in terms of the perceived prototypical attributes surrounding the categories (similarity complexity). To illustrate, an individual may perceive all members of one ingroup (e.g., 'Catholics') to simultaneously share membership of another ingroup category (e.g., 'Republican'), indicating low overlap complexity. Similarly, an individual may perceive all members of their different ingroup categories to be highly similar to each other (e.g., perceiving that being a 'Protestant' means the same as being a 'Unionist', and vice versa), exemplifying low similarity complexity.

It has been argued that living in more diverse social environments and being subjected to more diverse social experiences, such as engaging in contact with outgroup members, should predispose people to a more inclusive and complex identity structure. Moreover, social identity complexity is known to co-vary positively with outgroup attitudes, for example greater outgroup tolerance, as well as more general attitude variables, such as support for affirmative action and multicultural policies (Roccas and Brewer, 2002; Brewer and Pierce, 2005). We have recently begun to examine the role of social identity complexity in the relationship between context, contact and outgroup attitudes in

Northern Ireland, focusing explicitly on the religious and national categories as these are the most central to the study of intergroup relations in this context. Specifically, we asked people to rate the extent to which they perceived the religious and national identities to overlap, as well as how much similarity they perceived between the two categories, thereby assessing both conceptual types of social identity complexity, similarity and overlap complexity. Our results showed that more positive contact experiences exerted a positive effect on both types of complexity. Being high in similarity and overlap complexity also predicted more favourable outgroup perceptions, such as less ingroup bias and more outgroup tolerance. Importantly, social identity complexity, in the form of similarity complexity, also emerged as a significant mediator of contact effects on attitudes (Schmid *et al.*, 2009a). In a further analysis, we explored the nature of neighbourhood effects on social identity complexity. In line with Brewer and Pierce's (2005) predictions on the effects of living in more diverse social environments on social identity complexity, we found that respondents living in mixed neighbourhoods reported higher degrees of both overlap and similarity complexity.

In a separate analysis, we also considered the extent to which social identity complexity may act as a mediator of the 'secondary transfer effect' (Pettigrew, 2009) already referred to above. Earlier we reported that attitude generalization effects did not occur via re-appraisal of the ingroup (Tausch *et al.*, 2009); we now considered the hypothesis that attitude generalization may occur via increases in social identity complexity rather than through changes in ingroup attitude (arguably, accepting a wider, more inclusive notion of the ingroup is a key aspect of 'de-provincialization'). Using one of our general population samples (Schmid *et al.*, 2009d), we examined the relationship between the number of ethno-religious outgroup friends and attitudes towards four non-target outgroups not included in the contact, including, for example, immigrants and homosexuals. Extending our previous studies, we included three mediators, that is not only attitudes towards the ethno-religious outgroup and the ingroup, but also social identity complexity in the form of similarity complexity. Results of this analysis revealed that both attitude to the ethno-religious target outgroup and social identity complexity, but not ingroup evaluation, acted as intervening mechanisms in the generalization of attitudes to the four non-target outgroups, even after controlling for direct contact with each of them. Thus it seems that part of the generalization effect of contact can be explained by variations in cognitive re-structuring of one's social identity, that is, social identity complexity.

Conclusion

In this short contribution we have evaluated the consequences of segregation versus diversity for three different group-based processes: intergroup relations or outgroup attitudes, social capital and social trust, and social identity processes. We have argued that diversity does not inevitably have negative implications for both intergroup and intra-group relations, as seems to be the, rather gloomy, implication of some recent academic and political debate on this topic. Instead, we have argued that diversity should not be examined in isolation, but rather in combination with intergroup contact, as an indication of how individuals actually experience diversity. Our discussion, underlined by some of our recent research evidence, has illustrated that living in more diverse, desegregated environments offers individuals the opportunity for contact which, if taken up, can positively mediate the effects of diversity on both intergroup attitudes and social trust. Moreover, contact may also moderate the effects of living in mixed social environments, to the extent that negative effects of diversity only occur in the absence of positive intergroup contact. Additionally, this chapter has addressed a previously unexplored feature of segregation versus diversity, namely the extent to which greater diversity affects social identity processes. We have shown that diversity and desegregation, as well as intergroup contact, have consequences for less exclusive, more differentiated self-descriptions, a phenomenon that also has positive implications for outgroup perceptions.

As societies are growing ever more diverse, and intergroup conflicts tend to prevail in many parts of the world, the need to disentangle the nature of effects is becoming ever more urgent. Although we have tried to address some unanswered research questions and conceptual considerations, there still lies a long road ahead to understanding the exact consequences of residential context and growing diversity on intergroup relations, social trust and social identity processes. Nonetheless, we believe we have paved the way to understanding, at least in part, how social identification processes can affect social perception and social action. We also hope to have aided understanding, again in part, of the consequences of segregation, by offering an original way of thinking about diversity that combines theoretical conjectures of threat and constrict theory with the theoretical underpinnings of contact theory.

References

Allport, G. W. (1954) *The Nature of Prejudice*. Reading, MA: Addison-Wesley.

Blalock, H. M. (1967) Percent Non-White and Discrimination in the South. *American Sociological Review*, 22, 677–82.

Bledsoe, T., Welch, S., Sigelman, L. and Combs, M. (1995) Residential Context and Racial Solidarity among African Americans. *American Journal of Political Science*, 39, 434–58.

Blumer, H. (1958) Racial Prejudice as a Sense of Group Position. *Pacific Sociological Review*, 23, 3–7.

Brewer, M. and Gaertner, S. L. (2001) Toward Reduction of Prejudice: Intergroup Contact and Social Categorization. In R. Brown and S. L. Gaertner (eds.) *Blackwell Handbook of Social Psychology: Intergroup Processes*. Oxford: Blackwell.

Brewer, M. B., and Pierce, K. P. (2005) Social Identity Complexity and Outgroup Tolerance. *Personality and Social Psychology Bulletin*, 31, 428–37.

Brown, R. J. and Hewstone, M. (2005) An Integrative Theory of Intergroup Contact. In M. Zanna (ed.) *Advances in Experimental Social Psychology* (Vol. 37). San Diego, CA: Academic Press.

Bobo, L. (1999) Prejudice as Group Position: Microfoundations of a Sociological Approach to Racism and Race Relations. *Journal of Social Issues*, 55, 445–72.

Bourdieu, P. (1986) The Forms of Capital. In J. C. Richards (ed.) *Handbook of Theory and Research for the Sociology of Education*. New York: Greenwood Press.

Citrin, J., Reingold, B. and Green, D. P. (1990) American Identity and the Politics of Ethnic Change. *Journal of Politics*, 52, 1124–54.

Coleman, J. C. (1988) Social Capital in the Creation of Human Capital. *American Journal of Sociology*, 94, 95–120.

Crisp, R. J. and Hewstone, M. (2007) Multiple Social Categorization. In M. Zanna (ed.) *Advances in Experimental Social Psychology* (Vol. 39). San Diego, CA: Academic Press.

Fossett, A. M. and Kiecolt, K. J. (1989) The Relative Size of Minority Populations and White Racial Attitudes. *Social Science Quarterly*, 70, 820–35.

Gaertner, S. L. and Dovidio, J. F. (2000) *Reducing Intergroup Bias: The Common-Ingroup Identity Model*. Hove: Psychology Press.

Gaertner, S. L., Dovidio, J. F., Anastasio, P. A., Bachman, B. A. and Rust, M. C. (1993) The Common Ingroup Identity Model: Recategorization and the Reduction of Intergroup Bias. In W. Stroebe and M. Hewstone (eds.) *European Review of Social Psychology* (Vol. 4). Chichester, UK: Wiley.

Gallagher, A. M. (1995) The Approach of Government: Community Relations and Equity. In S. Dunn (ed.) *Facets of the Conflict in Northern Ireland*. New York: St. Martin's Press.

Granovetter, M. (1973) Strength of Weak Ties. *American Journal of Sociology*, 78, 1360–80.

Hewstone, M. and Brown, R. (1986) Contact Is Not Enough: An Intergroup Perspective on the Contact Hypothesis. In M. Hewstone and R. Brown (eds.) *Contact and Conflict in Intergroup Encounters*. Oxford: Basil Blackwell.

Hewstone, M., Cairns, E., Voci, A., Hamberger, J. and Niens, U. (2006) Intergroup Contact, Forgiveness and Experience of 'The Troubles' in Northern Ireland. *Journal of Social Issues*, 62, 99–120.

Hewstone, M., Cairns, E., Voci, A., Paolini, S., McLernon, F., Crisp, R. J., Niens, U. and Craig, J. (2005) Intergroup Contact in a Divided Society: Challenging Segregation in Northern Ireland. In D. Abrams, J. M. Marques and M. A. Hogg (eds.) *The Social Psychology of Inclusion and Exclusion*. Philadelphia, PA: Psychology Press.

Hewstone, M., Tausch, N., Hughes, J. and Cairns, E. (2008) *Direct and Indirect Cross-Community Contact and Tolerance in Mixed and Segregated Areas of Belfast: Quantitative Analysis*. Research Report: Central Community Relations Council, Northern Ireland.

Hewstone, M., Cairns, E., Kenworthy, J., Hughes, J., Tausch, N., Voci, A., von Hecker, U., Tam, T. and Pinder, C. (2008) Stepping Stones to Reconciliation in Northern Ireland: Intergroup Contact, Forgiveness and Trust. In A. Nadler, T. Malloy and J. D. Fisher (eds.) *The Social Psychology of Inter-Group Reconciliation*. New York, NY: Oxford University Press.

Hughes, J. (1999) *Bridging the Gap: Community Relations Policy in Northern Ireland*. Ulster (Papers in Public Policy and Management, No. 87). Belfast: University of Ulster.

Jenkins, R. (2008) *Rethinking Ethnicity: Arguments and Explorations* (Second edition). London: Sage.

Laurence, J. and Heath, A. (2008) Predictors of Community Cohesion: Multi-Level Modelling of the 2005 Citizenship Survey. Unpublished manuscript, Oxford University.

Leonard, M. (2004) Bonding and Bridging Social Capital: Reflections from Belfast. *Sociology*, 38, 927–44.

Letki, N. (2008) Does Diversity Erode Social Cohesion? Social Capital and Race in British Neighbourhoods. *Political Studies*, 56, 99–126.

Office of the First Minister and Deputy First Minister (2007) *A Shared Future and Racial Equality Strategy*. Accessed at http://www.ofmdfmni.gov.uk/good-relations-report.pdf [accessed on 1 October 2008].

Paolini, S., Hewstone, M. and Cairns, E. (2007) Direct and Indirect Friendship Effects: Testing the Moderating Role of the Affective-Cognitive Bases of Prejudice. *Personality and Social Psychology Bulletin*, 33, 1406–20.

Paolini, S., Hewstone, M., Cairns, E. and Voci, A. (2004) Effects of Direct and Indirect Cross-Group Friendships on Judgments of Catholics and Protestants in Northern Ireland: The Mediating Role of an Anxiety-Reduction Mechanism. *Personality and Social Psychology Bulletin*, 30, 770–6.

Pettigrew, T. F. (1997) Generalized Intergroup Contact Effects on Prejudice. *Personality and Social Psychology Bulletin*, 23, 173–85.

Pettigrew, T. F. (1998) Intergroup Contact Theory. *Annual Review of Psychology*, 49, 65–85.

Pettigrew, T. F. (2009) Secondary Transfer Effect of Contact: Do Intergroup Contact Effects Spread to Noncontacted Outgroups? *Social Psychology*, 40, 55–65.

Pettigrew, T. F. and Tropp, L. T. (2006) A Meta-Analytic Test of Intergroup Contact Theory. *Journal of Personality and Social Psychology*, 90, 751–83.

Putnam, R. (2000) *Bowling Alone: The Collapse and Revival of American Community*. New York: Simon & Schuster.

Putnam, R. (2007) E Pluribus Unum: Diversity and Community in the Twenty-First Century. The 2006 Jonathan Skytte prize lecture. *Scandinavian Political Studies*, 30, 137–74.

Roccas, S. and Brewer, M. B. (2002) Social Identity Complexity. *Personality and Social Psychology Review*, 6, 88–106.

Schmid, K., Tausch, N., Hewstone, M., Hughes, J. and Cairns, E. (2008) The Effects of Living in Segregated vs. Mixed Areas in Northern Ireland: A Simultaneous Analysis of Contact and Threat Effects in the Context of Micro-Level Neighbourhoods. *International Journal of Conflict and Violence*, 2, 56–71.

Schmid, K., Hewstone, M., Tausch, N., Cairns, E. and Hughes, J. (2009a) Antecedents and Consequences of Social Identity Complexity: Intergroup Contact, Distinctiveness Threat and Outgroup Attitudes. *Personality and Social Psychology Bulletin*, 35, 1085–98.

Schmid, K., Hewstone, M., Tausch, N., Cairns, E. and Hughes, J. (2009b) Neighbourhood and Contact Effects on Threat and Attitudes: Moderation by Salience, Identification and Status. *Manuscript in preparation*.

Schmid, K., Hewstone, M., Tausch, N., Cairns, E. and Hughes, J. (2009c) The Consequences of Residential Segregation for Intergroup Relations and Social Capital: Examining the Mediating and Moderating Properties of Intergroup Contact. *Manuscript in preparation*.

Schmid, K., Hewstone, M., Tausch, N., Cairns, E. and Hughes, J. (2009d) Mediators of Generalized Contact Effects to Non-Target Outgroups: Social Identity Complexity or Generalized Attitude Effects? *Manuscript in preparation*.

Schmid, K., Hewstone, M., Tausch, N., Jenkins, R., Hughes, J. and Cairns, E. (in press) Identities, Groups and Communities: The Case of Northern Ireland. In M. Wetherell and C. T. Mohanty (eds.) *The Sage Handbook of Identities*. London: Sage.

Semyonov, M., Raijman, R., Tov, A. Y. and Schmidt, P. (2004) Population Size, Perceived Threat and Exclusion: A Multiple Indicator Analysis of Attitudes Toward Foreigners in Germany. *Social Science Research*, 33, 681–701.

Stein, R. M., Post, S. S. and Rinden, A. L. (2000) Reconciling Context and Contact Effects on Racial Attitudes. *Political Research Quarterly*, 53, 285–303.

Stephan, W. G. and Stephan, C. W. (2000) An Integrated Threat Theory of Prejudice. In S. Oskamp (ed.) *Reducing Prejudice and Discrimination*. Hillsdale, NJ: Erlbaum.

Stephan, W. G., Diaz-Loving, R. and Duran, A. (2000) Integrated Threat Theory and Intercultural Attitudes. Mexico and the United States. *Journal of Cross-Cultural Psychology*, 31, 240–9.

Stolle, D., Soroka, S. and Johnston, R. (2008) When Does Diversity Erode Trust? Neighbourhood Diversity, Interpersonal Trust and the Mediating Effect of Social Interactions. *Political Studies*, 56, 57–75.

Tam, T., Hewstone, M., Cairns, E., Tausch, N., Maio, G. and Kenworthy, J. B. (2007) The Impact of Intergroup Emotions on Forgiveness in Northern Ireland. *Group Processes and Intergroup Relations*, 10, 119–35.

Tausch, N., Hewstone, M., Kenworthy, J., Cairns, E. and Christ, O. (2007a) Cross-Community Contact, Perceived Status Differences and Intergroup Attitudes in Northern Ireland: The Mediating Roles of Individual-Level vs. Group Level Threats and the Moderating Role of Social Identification. *Political Psychology*, 28, 53–68.

Tausch, N., Tam, T., Hewstone, M., Kenworthy, J. and Cairns, E. (2007b) Individual-Level and Group-Level Mediators of Contact Effects in Northern

Ireland: The Moderating Role of Social Identification. *British Journal of Social Psychology,* 46, 541–56.

Tausch, N., Hewstone, M., Kenworthy, J., Psaltis, C., Schmid, K., R. Popan, J., Cairns, E. and Hughes, J. (2009). 'Secondary Transfer' Effects of Intergroup Contact: Alternative Accounts and Underlying Processes. *Manuscript under review.*

Tausch, N., Schmid, K. and Hewstone, M. (in press) The Social Psychology of Intergroup Relations. In G. Salomon and E. Cairns (eds.) *Handbook of Peace Education.* Mahwah, NJ: Lawrence Erlbaum.

Tropp, L. and Pettigrew, T. F. (2005) Relationships Between Intergroup Contact and Prejudice among Minority and Majority Status Groups. *Psychological Science,* 16, 951–7.

Voci, A. and Hewstone, M. (2003) Intergroup Contact and Prejudice toward Immigrants in Italy: The Meditational Role of Anxiety and the Moderating Role of Group Salience. *Group Processes and Intergroup Relations,* 6, 37–54.

Wagner, U., Christ, O., Pettigrew, T. F., Stellmacher, J. and Wolf, C. (2006) Prejudice and Minority Proportion: Contact Instead of Threat Effects. *Social Psychology Quarterly,* 69, 380–90.

Wagner, U., Hewstone, M. and Machleit, U. (1989) Contact and Prejudice between Germans and Turks: A Correlational Study. *Human Relations,* 42, 561–74.

Wagner, U., van Dick, R., Pettigrew, T. F. and Christ, O. (2003) Ethnic Prejudice in East and West Germany: The Explanatory Power of Intergroup Contact. *Group Processes and Intergroup Relations,* 6, 22–36.

Wirth, L. (1938) Urbanism as a Way of Life. *American Journal of Sociology,* 44, 1–24.

Wright, S. C., Aron, A., McLaughlin-Volpe, T. and Ropp, S. A. (1997) The Extended Contact Effect: Knowledge of Cross-Group Friendships and Prejudice. *Journal of Personality and Social Psychology,* 73, 73–90.

10
Crossing Thresholds: Acculturation and Social Capital in British Asian Children

Charles Watters, Rosa Hossain, Rupert Brown and Adam Rutland

This chapter draws on a longitudinal study of identity transitions among young children from migrant and host society backgrounds in schools in England. The research included a quantitative study of involving just fewer than 400 schoolchildren aged between 5 and 11 and a qualitative study based on interviews with 32 children who participated in the main study. We outline below some of the key reasons for studying issues of identity and social action among young children from migrant backgrounds and salient theoretical issues and orientations. The chapter includes a brief description of the research project and an examination of the key findings from the quantitative and qualitative studies. We conclude with reflections on the implications of the research for the formulation of educational policies and for developing further theoretical frameworks for work in this area.

The study was conducted in a context of widespread debate about migration and integration in the wake of the 9/11 and 7/7 attacks. Within the United Kingdom, these events have been seen as evidence of a general failure of multiculturalism and have heralded calls for an increasing emphasis to be placed on restrictions on immigration and the 'integration' of migrants into British society (e.g. Goodhart, 2004). These calls were not confined to the United Kingdom and were reflected widely across Europe, North America and Australia. Commentators confronted the public with a spectre of migrant communities turning in upon themselves and maintaining and developing identities and affiliations often antagonistic to those predominant in host societies. Multicultural policies were, in this context, often seen as, at best, naïve and at worst as contributing significantly to a breakdown in social cohesion (e.g. Liddle, 2004). As a consequence of this reaction multicultural policies and orientations were often revised with renewed emphasis placed on the contribution of public programmes towards the 'integration' of society. In practical terms this resulted in the scrapping or significant revision of programmes that were seen as catering exclusively for specific ethnic minority groups and these had to demonstrate how they were actively promoting the integration of society. A further component was an emphasis on the articulation, and allegiance of migrant populations to, 'British values'.

While much recent political and policy debates have focussed on individuals and groups deemed to pose a threat to social cohesion, there has been relatively little attention paid to the ordinary, day-to-day ways in which the vast majority of migrants interact in host societies. Specifically, the tenor of public debate in recent years has tended towards viewing migrants implicitly as having fixed, immutable identities and strong affiliations towards heritage cultures and religions. Somewhat paradoxically, this often overriding perception arises in the wake of extensive research in the social sciences demonstrating that, far from being fixed, 'identity' and 'culture' are dynamic; changing and evolving in iterative interaction between migrants and host societies (e.g. Hall, 1992; Sen, 2006).

A further complexity here relates to the scale and diversity of contemporary migration. While the past centuries have witnessed major movements of people owing to war, famine or persecution, contemporary times have seen a differentiation in the reasons for migrating and in its socio-political contexts of migration. There are, for example, contracted labour migrants who have left their countries of origin to search for employment elsewhere, processes of family unification whereby typically women and children have joined husbands and fathers in a new country, as well as forced migrants, fleeing their countries owing to war and persecution and in most cases reaching only the borders of neighbouring states (Castles and Miller, 2003).

The migration of children in the past century has reflected this diversification. Many migrant children have not themselves moved but are the sons and daughters, or grandchildren of earlier migrants and are fully citizens of receiving countries. The country of reception is their home and they may not have known any other. Others may have moved much more recently with their parents or alone and have experienced childhoods spanning more than one country or continent. For those children who are second- and third-generation migrant backgrounds much academic literature focussed initially on stresses between parents and children who were viewed as caught 'between two cultures'

(Watson, 1977). The hypothesis here was that parents would seek to maintain their background cultures and to pass these on to their children. Children, by contrast would become increasingly assimilated to the values and norms of host societies and this would introduce tensions into parent–child relationships. Research focussed on issues such as teenagers 'rebellion' against practices such as arranged marriages or prohibitions against alcohol and pressures towards religious conformity.

An underlying assumption was that parents were predominantly conservative and sought to cling to often idealised identities, images and practices from their cultural heritages. Children by contrast were represented as finding the cultures of their parents increasingly stultifying and as desiring an ability to exercise a sense of freedom compatible with that perceived as experienced by their peers from the host society. Within this framework, children's identities were seen as caught between the making of painful choices between accepting and rejecting parental cultures, values and aspirations.

Despite its wide ranging impact in social sciences and the arts (with a number of British books and films exploring the tensions in the lives of second-generation South Asian families in particular), this approach has a number of serious limitations. First, the view that first-generation immigrant families are fundamentally traditional in outlook and idealise the homeland is clearly too much of a generalisation. There are differences between first-generation families in the extent to which they may seek to identify with or reject the cultures of host societies. Acceptance or rejection is, again, rarely wholesale and a family may very happily engage with elements in the host society, for example, interest in football, while rejecting others, for example, drinking alcohol.

Furthermore, engagement may be severely circumscribed owing to exclusionary and racist attitudes within the host society. These may place particular groups in cultural 'exclusion zones' through what Sen has described as processes of 'plural monoculturalism' whereby groups are designated fixed identities that are systematically reinforced by the practices of public and private institutions. Rather than promoting multiculturalism, these processes rather generate specific social, political and economic spaces that inhibit cultural fluidity. A further weakness of this approach is that it presupposed that children and young people would generally find the cultures of the host society more attractive than their heritage cultures. Empirical research has challenged this view, often showing that young people have a strong engagement with the cultures of their parents, and, in some instances, exceeding them in terms of their fervour for aspects of the heritage culture (e.g. Shaw, 1994).

More fundamentally, the study of migrant children's identities has been inhibited by a general positioning of children at the margins of social theory within which they appear largely within the context of studies of processes of socialisation. Here there has been a preoccupation with studying the ways in which children reach the status of adulthood by the definitions of particular cultures or societies. However, in the past two decades there has been a discernible shift towards studies that examine children's agency and specifically the way in which children make sense of their own lives. This, according to James *et al.*, 'represents a definitive move away from the more or less inescapable implication of the concept of socialisation: that children are to be seen as a defective form of adult, social only in their future potential but not in their present being' (James *et al.*, 2005: 6). Recent times have seen the emergence of a new paradigm in which children 'are now seen as individuals, whose autonomy should be safeguarded and fostered and whose being can no longer be nested into the family or institution' (ibid.).

Despite this growth of studies that engage with the ways in which children make sense of their own lives, questions of identity remain often influenced primarily by the differentiation that takes place between children and adults. As James *et al.* contend, 'Children learn who they are through interaction with (usually) the adult other' (ibid., p. 203). For the children of migrant families this process of identity formation should be seen within a wider context of the family and community. Here questions of identity and social action relate to the historical and political contexts of migration. To take an example, migrants of Gujarati origin in the United Kingdom may have defined themselves as Gujarati Muslims or Hindus in India, as 'Asians' when large numbers settled in the East African countries of Uganda and Tanzania and subsequently as 'Asian' or 'Indian' in the United Kingdom. These latter identities were ascribed in a very generalised way to groups from highly diverse, cultural, linguistic and religious backgrounds on the basis of assumed cultural homogeneity and phenotypical characteristics. While the weakness of the generalisations that gave rise to these ascribed identities can be easily demonstrated, it should be noted that they created a discursive space that could be utilised by migrants themselves. Thus numerous grassroots organisations in the United Kingdom for migrants from India, Pakistan and Bangladesh adopted the designation 'Asian' in their tile and Gujarati migrants who arrived in the United Kingdom from East Africa in the early 1970s founded the 'Asian Times'. These generic ascribed identities thus formed part of the self-identification of migrant groups and these relatively recently acquired designations were subsequently internalised by children.

Thus, as indicated above, identity and social action suggests an iterative interplay in which identity is ascribed, incorporated and used strategically within specific social political and economic contexts. Consciousness of specific identities may arise within conditions in which a group feels threatened such as in the reinforcement of Muslim identities in the wake of the response to the 9/11 attacks. Conversely, identities may be asserted to distinguish a section of the population from a stigmatised group such as has been observed in relations between Hindu and Muslim communities in the United States following 9/11 (Mohammad-Arif, 2007).

Group identification may be further reinforced in response to the bureaucratic categories operated within host societies. The census categories adopted, for example in the United States and United Kingdom, serve to generate groupings and disseminate resources in accordance with categorisations that would otherwise have little relationship to the actual formation of communities and solidarities (Hollinger, 2000). Indeed, groups of migrant children may be constituted as occupying a particular 'problem-space' that distinguishes them from their peers and give rise to programmes that help generate a sense of solidarity among disparate groups. An example here is the case of refugee children who are the subjects of a range of programmes in host societies aimed at promoting a sense of common identity between children from a wide range of countries and backgrounds. Within these contexts refugee children are encouraged to view themselves as having a set of common experiences and needs, the recognition of which elicits social support from the host society (Watters, 2008).

As indicated above, a preoccupation with the relationship between children and adults has resulted in a dearth of research examining processes of socialisation and identity formation outside of the home. This is surprising as children as young as 4 or 5 routinely spend much of their time in schools interacting with teachers and peers. The formation of identity within this context arises in the institutional settings of classrooms and playgrounds. Within these contexts acculturation theory presents a potentially valuable framework for examining processes of identity formation and social action among children from migrant and host families. In the study described here we sought to examine the acculturation strategies developed by cohorts of migrant and host society children aged between 5 and 11.

Theoretical orientations – acculturation, developmental theories and social capital

The interaction between identity and social action has been examined from a range of theoretical standpoints within the social sciences with social and developmental psychology offering some particularly influential theoretical frameworks. Within social psychology, a prominent approach in considering the socio-psychological dynamics of host-immigrant relationships is Berry's acculturation framework (e.g. Berry, 2001). This identifies four acculturation strategies, formed from the combination of two orientations: a desire to maintain (or relinquish) ethnic identity, and a desire to interact with other groups (or not). People can be classified as 'high' or 'low' on each orientation, resulting in the strategies of 'integration' (high on both), 'assimilation' (low, high), 'separation' (high, low) and 'marginalisation' (low, low). Within the research tradition inspired by Berry's framework the majority of studies have focused on the implications of adopting one or other of these acculturation strategies for psychological well-being and mental health. To date, there is some consensus that the first strategy (integration) is usually associated with the most favourable outcomes and the fourth with the least favourable (Berry, 1997; Liebkind, 2001).

Acculturation orientations have typically only been assessed in adult or adolescent samples, with the result that we know little about how young immigrant children view the challenges of maintaining or relinquishing their heritage cultures as they interact with members of the host society (for exceptions, see Knight, Kagan, Nelson and Gumbiner, 1978; Pawliuk *et al.*, 1996; Costigan and Su, 2004). This is surprising since research suggests that children soon develop an understanding of social categories which becomes more sophisticated and ceases to rely solely on physical cues (e.g., skin colour). This also coincides with the onset of ethnic constancy in which children understand that ethnic group membership is typically stable and does not depend on superficial transformations in clothing or context (Rutland *et al.*, 2005).

Nonetheless, the developmental literature on ethnic identity development is potentially relevant here. This has shown that the development of a 'mature' and 'secure' ethnic identity in childhood and adolescence, which involves confidence in one's own group membership and a greater openness to other ethnic groups, is related to more positive intergroup attitudes (Cross, 1991; Phinney and Ferguson, 1997; Marks *et al.*, 2007; Phinney *et al.*, 2007). There are parallels between Berry's 'integration' acculturation strategy and 'secure' and 'mature' ethnic identification, since both entail adopting, or being open to, multiple identities.

At a more conceptual level, the principal focus in the acculturation literature has been on the psychosocial outcomes of adopting one or other acculturation strategy and much less attention has been paid to the implications of such strategies for intergroup attitudes and to the dynamics of the acculturation process – that is, the interplay between one group's preferred acculturation orientation and that of another group. Yet, these are important issues. Bourhis *et al.* (1997) proposed an 'interactive acculturation model' in which they suggested that the 'fit' between one group's acculturation orientation and another's would be predictive of subsequent intergroup relations between them. Some research has borne out these ideas (Zagefka and Brown, 2002; Pfafferott and Brown, 2006; Zagefka, Brown, Broquard and Leventoglu Martin, 2007). Typically, we find that where 'own' and (perceived) 'other' orientations coincide, particularly if these are 'integrationist', intergroup attitudes are more positive than if the orientations are discrepant. Finally, given that ethnic identity is such a central concept in Berry's acculturation framework, it is surprising that individual variations in the strength of ethnic identification have been little studied. From the by now large Social Identity Theory research literature, it is clear that such individual differences can play an important role (Brown, 2000).

A further significant body of social research concerns the increasingly influential concept of social capital, as articulated, for example, by Putnam and Coleman in the United States and Halpern in the United Kingdom (Coleman, 1988; Putnam, 2002; Halpern, 2005). Robert Putnam, the most influential contemporary exponent of social capital theory and research describes it in the following terms, 'We describe social networks and the associated forms of reciprocity as social capital, because like physical and human capital (tools and training), social networks create value, both individual and collective, and because we can "invest" in networking' (Putnam, 2002: 4). Social capital is here not only a useful concept for the examination and analysis of societies and social processes but is seen here as a 'social good' that should be encouraged by politicians and policy makers as it enhances the social well-being of countries. Thus high levels of social capital are associated with the trust people feel towards institutions, lower crime figures and higher educational achievements.

However, drawing on a major study of social capital in the United States, Putnam suggests that ethnic diversity has a negative impact on social capital:

> It appears that ethnic heterogeneity and high rates of immigration are part of the story. If so, then the rapid increase in ethnic immigration in most OECD countries in recent decades may pose important challenges to both the quality and social distribution of social capital in all our countries.
>
> (Putnam, 2002: 415)

Putnam describes the presence of ethnic diversity as resulting in processes of 'hunkering down' in which people limit social contact tend to associate solely with people from the same ethnic group. It is perhaps here of critical importance that (at the time of writing) Putnam bases this conclusion on research carried out exclusively in cities across the United States which have their own particular histories of ethnic and racial segmentation and stark economic disparities. These findings, if replicated internationally, would have potentially highly significant impact on issues of identity and social action. In the present study, for example, it would suggest that in schools with highly diverse student populations students would experience higher levels of mistrust and be oriented towards social networking that largely confined them to a single ethnic group. In wider policy terms it may further indicate that students would experience educational and social advantages through being sent to schools that catered for largely homogeneous populations.

Putnam's conceptualisation of 'bridging' and 'bonding' is influential in differentiating between the bonding happening between 'like' individuals and the bridging taking place between members of 'separate' social groups. Indeed there are parallels here with Berry's concept of integration as close interaction with 'like' individuals is seen here as complementary, rather than antagonistic to a subsequent development of 'bridging' social capital that generates social networks across disparate groups. These concepts have been influential in the development of programmes for migrant groups in the United Kingdom, not least as elements of the National Strategy for Refugee Integration (Ager and Strang, 2004; Home Office, 2004). However, while operationalised within policy literature, the concepts of 'bridging' and 'bonding' often remain ill-defined and it is hard to relate them clearly to aspects of social interaction.

Arguably, a distinction between 'bridges' and 'doors', based on Simmel's (1997) classic essay on the symbolic meanings of these two objects, suggests a more holistic and, simultaneously, dynamic way of looking at the relations between social action and identity. The bridge, to Simmel, is an object that connects two essentially connected, if separate, landscapes: in other words, the bridge emphasises a sense of unity. The door, in contrast, emphasises differentiation by its arbitrary reference to an 'inside' and 'outside'; however, the door also reminds us that 'separating and connecting are only two sides of precisely the same act' (p. 172), in the sense that doors are built to be locked, but also to be knocked on. Simmel's symbols of bridge and door seem particularly appropriate in the context of domestic borders and territories relevant to the social integration of settled ethnic minorities. In this context, the positive function of social capital processes is both to build bridges across separate spheres of social life and to enable movement between social spaces constructed around a notion of difference.

With respect to children, a growing body of qualitative research is emerging with much of it engaging with adolescents or young adults. Social capital research with a focus on ethnic minority youth has examined the role of social and 'ethnic' capital in educational settlings and employment (Bankston and Zhou, 2002; Modood, 2004; Crozier and Davies, 2006). The focus on youth is partly due to the preoccupation in much of social capital literature on social assets, such as employment status, educational outcomes and political participation, which may seem less relevant in the case of young children. Younger children may also receive less attention due to their dependence on the family. From a developmental perspective, it is often concluded that young children are less independent in their patterns of socialising, and rely primarily on family resources rather than neighbourhood and community social capital (Harpham, 2002; Offer and Schneider, 2007). It is also widely held that children's psychological well-being largely centres on their families. For instance, Leonard (2005) suggests that children may accord a higher value than adults to the 'immediate use value' of social capital, referring to forms of emotional satisfaction stemming from family relations.

While younger children's social worlds may indeed be more circumscribed than those of older children, schools also constitute an important setting for social interaction for the younger children. The 5- to 11-year olds who were the focus of this study were pupils in primary schools in England undertaking the component of the National Curriculum known as Key Stage 2. They typically attend school for five days a week during term time between the hours of 9 to 3.30. In other words, for much of the year the children interact primarily with teachers and their peers for more than six hours per day, five days a week. In England the estimated proportion of ethnic minority pupils in primary schools rose from a fifth in 1997 to a third in 2005. There are significant disparities in terms of school performance with higher than average levels of achievement recorded for pupils of Chinese and Indian origins and pupils from mixed Asian and White backgrounds. By contrast boys in particular from Black Caribbean and pupils from Roma backgrounds performed generally poorly in national examinations (DfES, 2006). The children included in our study were largely second generation and from Indian backgrounds, a group normally associated with higher than average achievement.

Findings from the quantitative study

In our study we set out to examine the mutual acculturation orientations of White British and South Asian British children. Doing so necessitated the development of some new psychometrically adequate and age-appropriate measures not only of acculturation orientations but also of measures of well-being, identification, intergroup attitudes and social exclusion. We also used a longitudinal design to allow us some insight into the causal direction of the effects we observed. Finally, we adopted a multi-method approach which drew on not just quantitative self-report ratings from the children, but also in-depth accounts that they themselves provided and teacher ratings of the children's behaviour.

For the main study, there were nearly 400 children, tested three times over the space of a year. The children ranged from 5 to 11 years roughly divided into Younger (5–7 years) and Older groups (8–11 years). Their ethnic backgrounds were: 180 white British; 218 ethnic minority, of whom the majority were of Indian origin (41 per cent); other cultural groups were Pakistani (4 per cent), Bangladeshi (6 per cent), Sri Lankan (2 per cent), Nepali (1 per cent) and mixed ethnicity (2 per cent). The majority of the ethnic minority children were second generation, with a small number of first generation (N = 40).

Ethnic identification was measured by asking children how much they considered themselves a member of the group in question, how proud they were to belong to the group, how important it was to them to be a member, and how they felt about being a member. The former three questions were answered on a four-point scale ('not at all', 'a little bit', 'quite', 'very') represented by an image of balloons of increasing sizes. The last question required a response on a five-point scale represented by schematic 'smiley faces' showing a big frown, a moderate frown, a neutral expression, a moderate smile and a big smile. Perceived discrimination was measured by showing two pictures in which a child was excluded from a playground game because of his/her ethnicity and asking the child how often something similar had happened to them. And we were able to obtain teachers' ratings of every child on such aspects as 'emotional symptoms' (e.g., 'has fears, easily scared'), 'peer problems'. In the event, most of these measures had satisfactory internal reliability (Nigbur *et al.*, 2008) and, as we shall see, had predictive validity also.

Drawing on the findings for ethnic minority children, we can note that a vast majority of the minority children favoured an 'integrationist' orientation. Depending on the children's age, anywhere between 60 and 83 per cent of the children preferred a simultaneously high level of ethnic cultural maintenance and degree of participation with the majority culture. This was most evident in the older age group. There was much less interest in the other three Berry strategies although the younger children were more inclined to favour the 'separatist' orientation than their older peers (21 per cent vs 3 per cent).

A key aspect of our research design was its longitudinal nature. This allowed us for the first time to examine whether the adoption of a particular acculturation orientation at one point in time had consequences for well-being and social relations later on. It was evident that it did. On several measures, we found longitudinal effects in which prior acculturation attitudes predicted later outcomes. These results told a mixed story. On the one hand, there were some clearly favourable outcomes associated with 'integration': those adopting this strategy subsequently had higher self-esteem and felt more accepted by their peers. On the other hand, there were some costs associated with this strategy as well. Examination of the teachers' ratings of the children indicated that those with a more integrationist orientation also manifested slightly more emotional symptoms than those adopting a more 'separatist' outlook. It is easy to see how this 'two edged' consequence of integration could come about. Insofar as 'integrationist' children were more interested in participating fully in the culture of the majority (as well as maintaining their own heritage culture), they also ran the risk of experiencing more rebuffs from the other children. Thus, although they benefited (higher self-esteem and peer acceptance), they may have had to work harder to achieve these benefits (more emotional symptoms noticed by teachers).

Overall the findings from the quantitative component of the study can be summarised as follows:

(1) Greater ethnic diversity in schools was associated overall increases in self-esteem and pro-sociality, more balanced cross-group friendships, and reductions in emotional symptoms, peer problems, perceived acculturation discrepancies and experiences of discrimination. Minority children, especially first generation, reported less peer acceptance, self-esteem and in group bias, and more peer problems and discrimination experiences. There were relatively few age effects, the most notable being in group bias (younger children showing more) and in acculturation orientations of minority children (older children being more 'integrationist').

(2) The pattern of longitudinal relationships indicated a mixed story. Minority children's initial 'integrationist' orientations were predictive of later higher social acceptance and self-esteem. But those same integrationist orientations were also longitudinally associated with more emotional symptoms and increased perceived ethnic discrimination. Perhaps their desire to want to 'join in' with the majority children's activities led to a higher chance of their occasional rejection and subsequent negative side effects.

There are three main implications to be drawn from our findings. First, minority children as young as five years seem to have well-developed ideas about their preferred acculturation orientation. Most opt for the 'integrationist' strategy, although this preference becomes more marked with age. Moreover, this acculturation orientation predicts subsequent outcomes such as self-esteem, peer acceptance and (negatively) emotional symptoms and perceived discrimination. Second, although the general picture of intergroup relationships in the schools we studied was a positive one, minority children (especially first generation) showed some 'decrements' (e.g., lower self-esteem and peer acceptance, and more peer problems). Third, the effects of school diversity were consistent, most evidently on social relations: higher self-esteem, fewer peer problems and more cross-group friendships. Such findings show that school ethnic composition can significantly affect the promotion of positive intergroup attitudes.

Findings from the qualitative studies

Our qualitative studies yielded several examples of the nuanced nature of children's responses. For example, questions of racism were considered within the context of the 'Big Brother'[1] race row and the 7/7 bomb attacks in London. Some children held a belief that there was greater caring and understanding within their own ethnic group, while others gave illustrations of key trusting relationships from outside their ethnic group. The examples given by children indicated the important ways in which social capital was being maintained within contexts of social change. Cultural traditions, such as visiting the Gudwara, were often framed in terms of their enjoyment in playing with friends and meeting relatives. Issues of trans-national links were also present among the sample of children interviewed.

One factor that our interviews demonstrated was that the family was indeed very important to the young ethnic minority children in our study. However, our findings go beyond this observation, first, by extending the concept of family to reflect the frequent availability of extended and often transnational family networks to the majority of our respondents. These included adults who were considered 'like family'. Secondly, the family (in its enlarged definition) acted, to the children, as a 'bridge' to the wider social world and central aspects of their social existence, contributing to their emotional resilience and sense of self. Further, our data illustrated the fact that children were adept at crossing social boundaries and passing through the 'doors' that exist in the social spaces inhabited by both adults and children, thus actively contributing both to their own and to family/community social capital.

Most of our respondents seemed to have secure and strong attachments to a variety of both immediate and extended family members who supported them in difficulties and helped them in various direct and indirect ways to reinforce positive self-conceptions and feelings of self-worth. At school, support from both adults and other children was usually available for dealing, to varying degrees of success, with problems such as discrimination or lack of friends. Earlier research has discovered that many British Asian children chose to share their school experiences with siblings and friends, rather than their parents, both as a means to retain a degree of independence from and as a means to 'protect' their adult family members from any embarrassment or abuse they may have experienced at school (Crozier and Davies, 2006). In other words, other children can be an important source of social solidarity and emotional support, which challenges Coleman's (1988) view that a large number of children reduce a family's levels of social capital. Conversely, children with no trusted friends or siblings may be more vulnerable to the impacts of negative experiences, even if they have good relations with their parents.

To refer to our earlier metaphor, children's social spaces contained various 'doors', that is distinctions based on binaries, for example 'girls'/'boys', 'adult'/'child' or 'Indian'/'English' (although the boundaries between the latter pair of categories may be less fixed), that could be used either to connect and/or to separate, depending on time and context. Simmel's theorising around the symbolic connotations of 'doors' and 'bridges' also draws attention to the concrete, physical markers of unity and distinction. Our findings illustrated the importance of such, through the ways in which children and adults related to these markers.

In the example below a child of Indian background describes the very close relations she and her family have with their next door neighbours:

What kind of things do you do after school?
Sometimes I got to my next-door neighbours. [...] And sometimes I stay at home.
Who are your next-door neighbours?
Doris and...Mike....Sometimes when Mike's not feeling very well sometimes I go visit him.
...
How old are they?
They're both 80.
How do you know Doris and Mike?
Since I was a baby. Sometimes my dad used to give me next door to Mike and Doris....
Over the fence.

In this case, the fence – usually built high enough to protect privacy, yet low enough not to create a sense of isolation as a wall would – enabled social interaction between a young Indian and older English couple, perhaps precisely through its dual function of protecting from/ inviting neighbourly interaction. Compared to a door, a fence provides opportunities to contact more casual than a formal visit through a gate and a door. However, only a baby is light enough to make a complete passage in this way. The handing over of a baby over a fence to a neighbour can be seen as a deeply trusting and generous act; at the same time, it is somewhat ambiguous, since it is only the child who passes on to the other side. From the same respondent:

> How often do you go and see them?
> Sometimes
> Every week?
> Nearly. When I'm back from holiday I give them a present so some-times when I...mum's opened the suitcase and after I've got their presents I go round.
> So when you go and visit Mike and Doris after school what do you do?
> I sit and talk with them.
> What kind of things do they talk with you about?
> What I've been learning at school. Have I finished all my food.
> (Girl, British Indian, eight)

According to her own account, the respondent usually visited her cherished neighbours on her own; however, her parents also participated in this exchange indirectly, through the initial 'lending' of the baby and later, through the gifts, presumably acquired by the parents. In return, the neighbours gifted their care and attention to the child, much as grandparents might. This example serves to amplify the way in which an 'integrationist' orientation may work in practice on a day-to-day level. As indicated above, it is also illustrative of the role the family may play as a 'bridge' to the wider society, extending the child's social network to include adults from the host society, while children, perhaps partly due to the cultural meanings attached to childhood, may cross both physical and symbolic thresholds with relative ease.

'Playing the Game'

In a number of examples children gave accounts of interactions with white English children consisting of calling round on their houses to play games. Girls, in particular, reported less structured games, which more frequently highlighted the requirement of having access to cultural capital – quite literally, 'knowing the game'. At the same time, this 'knowledge' appeared closely related to the power to define the rules of the game. To the uninitiated, the rules could seem arbitrary. The imbalance of power is evident in the fact that although rules of a game may be 'made up' by the person(s) in power, those with less power are not in a similar position to make up their responses; as suggested below, they have to learn or be explained the rules from those in power.

...'miss said I'll help you find someone to play. Found Sarah and Louise and then they ran off with Laura and Josie and Ellie and they started playing but I didn't know them so I thought no and plus I don't know any games they play'
What kind of games do they play?

Um polar bears...never heard of it. They make it up like so you say polar bears or this game where you have to * little penguins. That's all I know so far.

[...] my cousin she really likes playing Barbies and I'm not really good at that. She plays like in some games I really don't know and she calls them English games...
(Girl, British Pakistani, eight)

I've been to India before and I like playing with people there because they all know each other and they all know each other and if someone...they're really nice there so if you're going to play with a child they would probably tell you like in England if you play with a child they will probably say like let's go here and let's go there and but in India they normally just sort of do what you want probably because maybe you came in the country or something and that.

OK. So, it's easier to play with them?

No. I think um...is it easier to play? I think both the same. I think they're just...everyone's people so I think it's just the same to make friends in England and in India. They're both easy.

[later in the interview] What do you like about going to India?

My cousins and stuff. I'm free because I'm sort of free because in England at home I just normally stay at home and read stuff and in India I just walk around anywhere I want. And if you get lost people would probably tell you and there's like a sweet shop right near the house. Its only about three or four meters away. It's really near.

So why do you think you're more free in India?

I don't know probably because...I know in England loads of people play but in India everyone knows you and then they can even...like if they're playing they would like um like go somewhere that they know that you know probably not somewhere that you don't know and in England if you had friends um they would probably go somewhere like you have never been like sometimes you could be scared of that place and you didn't tell them. They'd probably go there and in India they probably just go in normal places where they think that you would know because you're from another country so they don't want you to get lost.

(Girl, British Indian, eight)

In the above, distinctions are drawn between 'English' games and the ways that 'children in England' play, although there are important differences between the two examples. In fact, many of our respondents told us about games that could be described as 'traditional English' games, and presumably most children would learn such games at school. The reason for the game being described as 'English' in the first example is not clear, but in the second example, 'English' children's play seemed to be less emotionally containing. It seems that the cultural label referred more to ways of negotiating or communicating rules and expectations, rather than the rules themselves. In 'normal' places and 'normal' schools, people behaved in expected and emotionally supportive ways.

Bullying and discrimination

As noted in the more general findings, there was evidence that some children who pursued an integrationist approach may experience more exclusion and discrimination. An example is given here of a boy who contrasted his experiences in Pakistan and in England.

Why do you think you get bullied [in England but not in Pakistan]?
Well it's because I go to a normal school in Pakistan there's not that much bullies. They don't have bullies there.

The above respondent reasoned he was not bullied because of his ethnic background. However, our survey revealed that over half of all children (majority and minority) in the sample thought that there occurred some level of racist discrimination, such as name calling, in their school playground. Among ethnic minority children, a third reported to have personally experienced racial discrimination, but extreme cases of bullying appeared rare. Some children ultimately felt more secure among members of their own ethnic group, even in a relatively unfamiliar environment. Visiting India, they knew they could trust on being helped and cared for, precisely because of being 'guests'. In such contexts, the children often talked about non-verbalised emotions, possibly expressed in physical gestures or expressions.

> If I speak to English children then I speak with them about, like friends, and if you go here, can you come with me there. If you speak with... Indian children, they'll care about you more, maybe....
> How can you tell they care more?
> Cause...you might see it in their face, all their feelings.
> (Girl, British Indian, nine)

None of the children talked about differences in values, norms and so on, which are commonly seen as core elements of ethnic identity, for example in social capital literature. Instead, in passages such as above, they chose to verbalise the subtler, embodied markers of a shared identity. Of course, these may be related to particular cultural norms around expected forms of behaviour and interaction. The perceived distinctions that occurred along such lines did not seem to prevent inter-ethnic friendships, but may have rendered some of such friendships feeling more shallow, artificial or emotionally demanding.

Conclusion

The results from the 32 interviews in the qualitative part of the study broadly supported the general finding that children were primarily oriented towards 'integration' in Berry's sense. What the qualitative study did was to explore in some depth the more subtle and nuanced aspects of an 'integrationist' orientation. As noted, one interesting feature was the examples of the role that adult family members may play in fostering this orientation by making 'bridges' between the children and wider society. In this respect the findings challenge a prevailing view of migrants and ethnic minority communities turning in on themselves. There were many examples of the maintenance of a 'heritage' culture through participation in religious activities and through the links maintained with families in countries of origin. However, these relationships, while highly valued, were generally part of children's wider social and cultural repertoire that encompassed also individuals and aspects from the country of settlement.

However, a concerning aspect of the findings was the apparent emotional labour involved in seeking an integrationist approach with the suggestion here that children may experience degrees of rejection. The benefits of higher self-esteem and peer acceptance may in some cases only be won through working through experiences of bullying and discrimination. An implication of this may be that teachers and parents need to be particularly vigilant in promoting integration (in Berry's sense) as a routine aspect of schools activities.

At a more theoretical level, the findings of our study challenge some of the implications drawn from Putnam's work on social capital. One significant feature here is the correlation drawn between social homogeneity, trust and social capital. As indicated above, in some of Putnam's recent work, findings indicating a high correlation between homogeneity and social capital are matched by a negative correlation linking ethnic diversity with low social capital. More precisely, according to Hallberg and Lund, 'what Putnam has been perceiving for some time is the negative correlation between ethnic diversity, on the one hand, and community cohesion and social trust, on the other' (ibid., 2005: 58). It is too early to assess fully the impact of Putman's diversity hypothesis, but it is reasonable to suggest that it strengthens the position of policy makers sceptical of multiculturalism. As indicated above, a weakness in this hypothesis is that Putnam's conclusions derive from research conducted in localities in the United States, and requires considerable caution in terms of assessing general validity. Bourdieu pointed to an unfortunate tendency to generalise from findings derived from the sociohistorical particularities of the United States (Bourdieu and Wacquant, 1999). As Watters notes, emerging findings from the United Kingdom, for example, suggest that a negative correlation between social capital and ethnic diversity cannot be easily drawn and the picture is complex. Consistent with the findings in our research, recent evidence has pointed to closer demographic integration of ethnic groups, a comparatively high level of mixed marriages and relationships, improving social attitudes to diversity and marked improvements in school performance of some ethnic groups (Rutter, 2006; Watters, 2008).

A central implication of the study for policy makers is that ethnically mixed schools are generally good for children. This finding challenges the view that ethnic diversity necessarily results in diminishing social trust and social cohesion. As we have indicated, diversity has a range of potential educational, social and personal advantages for children and wider society.

Note

1. The 'Big Brother' row centred on the racist abuse of an Indian contestant in the reality TV show.

References

Ager, A. and Strang, A. (2004) *Indicators of Integration*. Final Report. London: Home Office.

Bankston III., C. L. and Min Zhou (2002) Social Capital as Process: The Meanings and Problems of a Theoretical Metaphor. *Sociological Inquiry* 72(2), 285–317.

Berry, J. W. (1997) Immigration, Acculturation, and Adaptation. *Applied Psychology: An International Review* 46(1), 5–68.

Berry, J. W. (2001) A Psychology of Immigration. *Journal of Social Issues* 57(3), 615–31.

Bourdieu, P. and Wacquant, L. (1999) On the Cunning of Imperialist Reason. *Theory, Culture & Society* 16(1), 41–58.

Bourhis, R. Y., Moise, L. C., Perreault, S. and Senecal, S. (1997) Towards an Interactive Acculturation Model: A Social Psychological Approach. *International Journal of Psychology* 32(6), 369–89.

Brown, R. (2000) Social Identity Theory: Past Achievements, Current Problems and Future Challenges. *European Journal of Social Psychology* 30(6), 745–78.

Castles, S. and Miller, M. (2003) *The Age of Migration 3rd Edition*. Basingstoke: Macmillan.

Costigan, C. L. and Su, T. F. (2004) Orthogonal Versus Linear Models of Acculturation among Immigrant Chinese Canadians: A Comparison of Mothers, Fathers and Children. *International Journal of Behavioural Development* 28, 518–27.

Cross, W. E. (1991) *Shades of Black: Diversity in African American Identity*. Madison, WI: University of Wisconsin Press.

Crozier, G. and Davies, J. (2006) Family Matters: A Discussion of the Bangladeshi and Pakistani Extended Family and Community in Supporting the Children's Education. *Sociological Review* 54(4), 678–95.

Coleman, J. (1988) Social Capital in the Creation of Human Capital. *The American Journal of Sociology* 94(Supplement), S95–S120.

Department for Education and Skills (DfES) (2006) Ethnicity and Education: The Evidence on Minority Ethnic Pupils Aged 5–16. DfES, London.

Goodhart, D. (2004) Too Diverse? *Prospect*. London: Prospect Publishing Limited.

Hall, S. (1992) New Ethnicities. In J. Donald and A. Rattansi (eds) *A 'Race', Culture and Difference*. London: Open University Press.

Halpern, D. (2005) *Social Capital*. Cambridge: Polity Press.

Harpham, T. (2002) *Measuring the Social Capital of Children*. Young Lives.

Hollinger, D. (2000) *Postethnic America*. New York: Basic Books.

Home Office (2004) *Integration Matters: A National Strategy for Refugee Integration*. London: Home Office.

James, A., Jenks, C. and Prout, A. (2005) *Theorising Childhood*. Cambridge: Polity Press.

Knight, G. P., Kagan, S., Nelson, W. and Gumbiner, J. (1978) Acculturation of Second- and Third-Generation Mexican American Children: Filed Independence, Locus of Control, Self-Esteem and School Achievement. *Journal of Cross-Cultural Psychology* 9, 87–97.

Leonard, M. (2005) Children, Childhood and Social Capital: Exploring the Links. *Sociology* 39(4), 605–22.

Liddle, R. (2004) How Islam Has Killed Multiculturalism. *The Spectator*. London: The Spectator Limited.

Liebkind, K. and McAlister, A. (1999) Extended Contact through Peer Modeling to Promote Tolerance in Finland. *European Journal of Social Psychology* 29, 765–80.

Marks, A. K., Szalacha, L. A., Lamarre, M., Boyd, M. J. and Garcia Coll, C. (2007) Emerging Ethnic Identity and Interethnic Group Social Preferences in Middle Childhood: Findings from the Children of Immigrants Development in Context (CIDC) study. *International Journal of Behavioral Development* 31, 501–13.

Modood, T. (2004) Capitals, Ethnic Identity and Educational Qualifications. *Cultural Trends* 13(50), 87–105.

Mohammad-Arif, A. (2007) The Paradox of Religion: The (re)Construction of Hindu and Muslim Identities amongst South Asian Diasporas in the United States. *South Asia Multidisciplinary Academic Journal, Migration and Constructions of the Other* [Online], http://samaj.revues.org/index55.html [accessed on 15 March 2009].

Nigbur, D., Brown, R., Cameron, L., Hossain, R., Landau, A. and Le Touze, D. (2008) Acculturation, Well-being and Classroom Behaviour among White British and British Asian Primary-School Children in the South-East of England: Validating a Child-Friendly Measure of Acculturation Attitudes. *International Journal of Intercultural Relations* 32, 493–504.

Offer, S. and Scheider, B. (2007) Children's Role in Generating Social Capital. *Social Forces* 85(3), 1125–42.

Pawliuk, N., Grizennko, N., Chan Yip, A., Gantous, P., Mathew, J. and Nguyen, D. (1996) Acculturation Style and Psychological Functioning in Children of Immigrants. *American Journal of Orthopsychiatry* 66, 111–21.

Pfafferott, I. and Brown, R. (2006) Acculturation Preferences of Majority and Minority Adolescents in Germany in the Context of Society and Family. *International Journal of Intercultural Relations* 30, 703–17.

Phinney, J. S. and Ferguson, D. L. (1997) Intergroup Attitudes Among Ethnic Minority Adolescents: A Causal Model. *Child Development* 68(5), 955.

Phinney, J. S., Jacoby, B. and Silva, C. (2007) Positive Intergroup Attitudes: The Role of Ethnic Identity. *International Journal of Behavioral Development* 31(5), 478–90.

Putnam, R. (2002) *Democracies in Flux: The Evolution of Social Capital in Contemporary Society*. Oxford: Oxford University Press.

Rutland, A., Cameron, L., Bennett, L. and Ferrell, J. M. (2005) Interracial Contact and Racial Constancy: A Multi-Site Study of Racial Intergroup Bias in 3–5 year old Anglo-British Children. *Journal of Applied Developmental Psychology* 26(6), 699–713.

Rutter, J. (2006) *Refugee Children in the UK*. Milton Keynes: Open University Press.

Sen, A. (2006) *Identity and Violence: The Illusion of Destiny*. London: Allen Lane.

Shaw, A. (1994) The Pakistani Community in Oxford in Ballard. In D. Pardesh (ed.) *The South Asian Presence in Britain.* London: Hurst.

Simmel, G. (1997) Bridge and Door. In D. Frisby and M. Featherstone (eds.) *Simmel on Culture: Selected Writing.* London: Sage.

Watson, J. (ed.) (1977) *Between Two Cultures: Migrants and Minorities in Britain.* Oxford: Blackwell.

Watters, C. (2008) *Refugee Children: Towards the Next Horizon.* London: Routledge.

Zagefka, H. and Brown, R. (2002) The Relationship between Acculturation Strategies, Relative Fit and Intergroup Relations: Immigrant-Majority Relations in Germany. *European Journal of Social Psychology* 32, 171–88.

Zagefka, H., Brown, R., Broquard, M. and Leventoglu Martin, S. (2007) Predictors and Consequences of Negative Attitudes towards Immigrants in Belgium and Turkey: The Role of Acculturation Preferences and Economic Competition. *British Journal of Social Psychology* 46, 153–69.

11
Identity, Social Action and Public Space: Defining Civic Space in Belfast

Dominic Bryan and Sean Connolly

Belfast has been the location of the most long lasting, and most violently destructive, communal conflict within the modern United Kingdom. In this conflict public displays of identity – parades, demonstrations, the use of flags and emblems – have consistently played a prominent part. Belfast's first recorded sectarian riot, in 1813, arose from a Protestant commemoration of 12 July. Today negotiations over emblems and marches remain central to attempts to consolidate a precarious political settlement (Baker, 1973; Bryan, 2000; Farrell, 2000; Hirst, 2002). Commentators and policy makers have for the most part taken the claims of competing practices at face value, as reflecting 'identities', Nationalist and Unionist, legitimised by their roots in a distant past. In Ireland as elsewhere, however, the work of Hobsbawm and Ranger (1983) has encouraged historians to look more sceptically at the claims of 'tradition'. 'Irishness', 'nationalism' and 'unionism' now appear, not as fixed entities, but as fluid categories repeatedly redefined in response to changing circumstances (Connolly, 1997; Comerford, 2003). Against this background, a reassessment of the identity practices lying at the heart of Belfast's long-standing troubles is overdue.

The starting point for the present attempt at such a reassessment is the close association, in an urban context, between identity politics, the idea of the civic, and the use of public space. Identity can be defined as a relationship between the individual and the collective, representing a process of internal and external definition (Jenkins, 2004: 24). In this process collective practices play a crucial role (Hopkins and Reicher, 1997). In political terms identity is most commonly defined in terms of the relationship to the nation-state (Faulks, 2000: 29–45), and it is in these terms, as an opposition between Irish nationalism and British unionism, that Belfast's conflicts have most frequently been interpreted. But the rapidly expanding and economically dynamic industrial cities of the nineteenth century, of which Belfast was one, also developed their own civic culture. Liberated from aristocratic control, and empowered by municipal reform, urban elites created an increasingly elaborate body of ceremonial and display designed to create in the wider urban population a sense of corporate identity (Gunn, 2000). Against this background, participation in the rituals of urban civic life became part of a process of recognition within the polity, allowing people to participate in, or witness, expressions of their identity, in other words their sense of self, within the public sphere.

Such participation, however, depended on another characteristic feature of the new urban environment: differential access to public space. Greatly expanded in size, and now largely non-residential as inhabitants moved to outlying districts, the new town centre became a different type of space and posed both a challenge and a threat. It was a site in which civic pride could find expression, and the urban community could be defined, through the erection of monuments and signature buildings, the laying out of boulevards, squares and parks, and the staging of public ceremonies and processions. But it was also a place in which behaviour had to be policed and regulated, and which was to be made available only to those identity practices defined as falling within the civic. If admission to public space, and to participation in the identity practices enacted there, conferred membership of the urban community, exclusion was in effect a denial of citizenship.

To illustrate the relevance of these points, this chapter will look briefly at three significant episodes in the development of Belfast's civic culture: the visit of Queen Victoria in 1849, the contested centenary of the rebellion of 1798, and the changing character of street protest in the 1960s. It will conclude by examining recent developments in the staging of two major civic events, the Lord Mayor's show and the celebration of St Patrick's Day. Each section deals with a complex episode, to be studied elsewhere at greater length.[1] But taken together these four case studies illuminate the complex history that lies behind current identity practices in Belfast and the conflicts to which they give rise.

Queen Victoria visits Belfast, August 1849

The brief visit of Queen Victoria, during a tour of Ireland in August 1849, came at a significant moment. At a time when other urban centres had entered on a long decline, and when the country as a whole was suffering a devastating famine, Belfast was Ireland's only economic success story. The successful mechanisation first of cotton then of linen spinning had given the town a firm industrial base. Its population had risen from 20,000 at the beginning of the century to 98,000 by 1851, displacing Cork as Ireland's second largest urban centre. Its political structures had also been transformed. From 1842 the oligarchic corporation controlled by the local landed magnate, Lord Donegall, had been replaced by an elected body, while the current marquis's financial irresponsibility had forced him to surrender the economic control his family had formerly exercised as ground landlords (Beckett, *et al.*, 1983; Maguire, 1993; Gillespie and Royle, 2003–7).

The response of this newly empowered civic elite to the challenge of the queen's visit reveals a town only just becoming aware of its own enhanced importance. The whole event lasted just five hours, in a tour of 11 days. However, there was no indication that civic leaders felt slighted by the brevity of the visit. Instead what can be detected is an undercurrent of worry that Belfast, with its lack of substantial public buildings and historic sites, would have too little to show the royal party. In the event, the civic authorities rose impressively to the occasion. The 40 members of the town council appeared in elaborate robes, scarlet gowns trimmed with ermine over dress suits. The queen's party, disembarking from the royal yacht at a newly constructed quay, made its way up the main thoroughfare under a succession of arches, past galleries holding 4,000 spectators. Its subsequent route encompassed the key landmarks of the emerging industrial giant: the White Linen Hall, centre of Belfast's staple manufacture, the new railway terminus, the Queen's College, and Mulholland's spinning mill, Belfast's largest industrial premises. Time, as one newspaper regretted, prevented the inclusion of another characteristic landmark of the early Victorian city, the new prison and courthouse just completed on the Crumlin Road. Overall the visit, commemorated for some years afterwards by an annual fete, represented a huge boost to Belfast's self-esteem.

The Belfast Queen Victoria visited in 1849 was already a religiously and politically divided town. There had been further outbreaks of sectarian fighting since 1813, most notably in 1832 and 1835. The reformed corporation, since its establishment in 1842, had been firmly in the hands of a Conservative party that identified itself with explicitly Protestant interests. The rise elsewhere in Ireland of a nationalist movement seeking the repeal of the act of union had added a political dimension to sectarian divisions. Support for repeal was strong among the town's Catholic minority. But Protestants, whether Liberal or Conservative in their politics, remained almost unanimously opposed, and when the repeal leader Daniel O'Connell attempted to hold a meeting in Belfast in 1843 he was forced to retreat ignominiously in the face of a hostile and potentially violent crowd (McComb, 2003).

Against this background what was remarkable was the successful exclusion from the ceremonial surrounding the royal visit of any hint of sectarian or political division. The committee set up to manage the arrangements included the Catholic bishop of the diocese, given his title as 'the Right Reverend Doctor Denvir', as well as Presbyterian and Anglican churchmen. An attempt by the Rev. Thomas Drew to assert the superior status of the established Church of Ireland by calling for the inclusion in addition of the archbishop of Armagh was firmly rebuffed (*BNL*, 27 July 1849). In all of this the civic authorities were following a clear lead from the government, which had decreed that the queen's visit was to be kept free of all taint of religious or political partisanship. But their willingness to comply with the injunction to neutrality, in comparison to the intransigent exclusiveness of later decades, remains striking. When Drew went on to object to the inclusion in the queen's itinerary of the newly opened non-denominational university college, on the grounds that it was a 'godless' institution, he was shouted down by a hostile audience (*BNL*, 27 July 1849). Nor was it only Belfast Protestants who responded to the call for a display of civic unity. When the queen arrived, Bishop Denvir appeared at the head of the Catholic clergy to present a loyal address, and it was noted that the inhabitants of the predominantly Catholic Hercules Street had joined in erecting banners and arches in honour of the occasion (*NW*, 14 Aug. 1849).

The Queen's visit by its nature also made necessary a display of the symbolism of identity. And here what was striking was the willingness of the town's inhabitants to herald the monarch, not just through the iconography of British loyalism, but also through the language and imagery of Irish patriotism. The decorations erected along the route of the royal party's progress included the royal arms, the union jack, the cross of St George, and banners proclaiming 'God Save the Queen'. But there were also numerous harps. One house in High Street ostentatiously invoked the suspension of traditional animosities by displaying a union jack and harp mounted against a green background, alongside a crown in orange. There were also no less than four displays of the Irish greeting *Céad Mile Fáilte*, one of them from a window of offices belonging to the firmly Protestant *Belfast Newsletter*. Other accounts referred to 'the emerald isle' and improbably presented the Anglophone and predominantly Protestant crowd as hailing the queen with the words 'cushla machree' (*cúisle mo chroí*, beat of my heart). Protestant Belfast had by this time firmly identified its interests with the maintenance of the union of Ireland and Great Britain. In time this rejection was to be expressed in terms of a claim to be British rather than Irish. But in 1849 those concerned had not yet ceased to think of themselves as living in an Irish city.

The 1798 commemoration, June 1898

Half a century after the queen's visit, the nationalists of Belfast organised an elaborate ceremonial to mark the hundredth anniversary of the rebellion of 1798. On 6 June 1898 a procession estimated at some 2,000 persons set off from near Smithfield Market. Many were dressed in green and a large number carried replica pikes. They were accompanied by banners, and marshalled by a mounted man in period costume. Several bands accompanied the procession, most playing nationalist airs, although a hostile newspaper claimed that some 'had resort to the music hall for catchy march tunes' (*BNL*, 7 June 1898). There were some brief skirmishes as the procession passed near Protestant parts of the working-class residential district to the west of the city centre, including one revolver shot. Otherwise the day passed without incident. Assembled in a muddy field at Hannahstown on the rising hills to the west of the town, the crowd heard a succession of rousing speeches recalling the glories of a century earlier and denouncing the continued British misgovernment of Ireland. As they marched back to the city, the rear of the procession sustained a more determined assault from Protestant counter-demonstrators. The main violence, however, came after the marchers had dispersed. Angry crowds from Protestant districts engaged in a sustained attack on the police, eventually forcing them to withdraw from the area and leave troops to take control. The crowds wrecked pubs and other premises belonging to Catholics. In addition, following a pattern already seen in earlier outbreaks of violence, several hundred Catholics were expelled from places of work, while others were forcibly evicted from dwellings in mainly Protestant streets.

The contrasting reaction of Belfast's two religious groups to the centenary of the insurrection reflected the dramatic changes that had taken place over the preceding century in the politics of the town and surrounding region. In the 1790s the Protestants of Belfast and the surrounding countryside, inspired by the ideas of the American and French revolutions, had joined with parts of the mainly Catholic south in an armed insurrection aimed at creating an independent Irish republic.

After 1800, on the other hand, Belfast Protestants, like their coreligionists elsewhere on the island, came to see continued union with Great Britain as their only protection against an increasingly assertive Catholic majority. Support for reform politics did not die away overnight. But by the mid-1880s, Protestants of all classes and denominations were united in their resistance to any extension of Irish political autonomy (Budge and O'Leary, 1973; Wright, 1996).

What is remarkable about this complex historical background is how comprehensively it was ignored by both parties during the disputed centenary celebrations. Protestant opponents of the commemoration condemned the rebellion of their late eighteenth-century ancestors as a wholly unjustifiable act of treason, while remaining conveniently vague as to the identity of those responsible. Catholics, for the most part descended from migrants drawn into the town well after 1798, appropriated to themselves the memory of an episode in which their coreligionists of a century earlier had played at most a peripheral role. In doing so, however, they relied on an iconography derived from the predominantly Catholic insurrection that had taken place in southern counties, in particular Wexford, rather than from events closer to home. Overall there could hardly be a clearer demonstration of the mutability of historical memory, or of the part played in identity formation by acts of imaginative identification on the one hand and of selective amnesia on the other.

The 1898 disturbances continued a dispute over access to public space that had been in progress for over two decades. The refusal of militant Protestants to accept the legitimacy of Catholic or nationalist meetings or processions can be traced back to the forcible silencing of O'Connell in 1843. However, conflict was for long muted by central government legislation, the Party Processions Acts, that had sought to preserve the public peace by outlawing all displays of religious or political emblems. In 1872 Belfast Catholics attempted to take advantage of the recent repeal of this legislation by organising a Lady Day procession, ostensibly a religious celebration but in fact with strong political overtones, only to come under attack at what proved to be the beginning of a week of fighting (CSORP, 1873/1022). Thereafter Catholic processions confined themselves to the mainly Catholic districts, while Protestant Twelfth of July parades routinely took over the entire central area. The organisers of the 1898 commemoration initially planned to begin their march from the city centre. However, magistrates insisted that they should confine themselves to the usual route for Catholic processions, from Smithfield Market on the edge of the city centre through Catholic west Belfast to

Hannahstown. In the event even this rerouting was not sufficient to prevent sustained violence.

The dominant image communicated by the events of 1898 is thus of an urban population starkly divided along lines of religion and political allegiance. Yet it would be wrong to think in terms of two undifferentiated ethnic or religious groups. On the Catholic side the self-assertion of the centenary celebrations masked a deep division. The natural heirs to the United Irishmen of 1798, in political if not in denominational terms, were the members of the Irish Revolutionary Brotherhood or IRB, recently returning to life after a long moribund period and still theoretically committed to armed insurrection as a means of ending British rule in Ireland. The centenary celebrations, however, were organised by the leaders of the numerically much stronger constitutional nationalist movement, with the explicit aim of ensuring that the anniversary should not be exploited by their more militant rivals. The martial symbolism of the gathering at Hannahstown, with its uniforms, pikes and rhetoric of past military glories, was thus an elaborate charade, disdainfully boycotted by Belfast's small circle of genuine republican militants (Hepburn, 2008: 78–80).

On the Protestant side, the divisions were along lines of class rather than ideology. Despite their alarm at the rising threat of nationalism, the Protestant propertied elite of Belfast had long kept their distance from the confrontational traditions of plebeian loyalism. By the 1890s the electoral success of nationalism in the rest of Ireland had created new pressures for a united front. But concern about plebeian disorder remained. In the run up to the commemoration the Grand Master and Secretary of the Orange Order published an appeal for calm, insisting that 'the very genius of Protestantism is to allow to all others as full a liberty as we claim for ourselves'. The *Belfast Newsletter*, organ of conservative Protestantism, took a similar line, calling on the loyal inhabitants to 'attend with double diligence to their business' on the anniversary, 'and let the procession alone' (*BNL*, 2 June 1898). When these appeals were ignored both Order and newspaper found themselves torn between their fear of disorder and the imperatives of political and sectarian solidarity. The *Newsletter* deplored what had taken place, but laid the blame for the disturbances firmly on the 'annoying and provoking' demeanour of the processionists, who had allegedly taunted their antagonists from the safety of a police cordon. Faced with the unpalatable fact that Protestant violence had been directed mainly against the police, rather than against the nationalist demonstrators, the paper even went so far as to suggest that the constabulary had laid themselves open to popular hostility by unnecessary harassment of Orange bandsmen (*BNL*, 7 June 1898). In the same way the Orange Grand Master, while condemning the rioting, warned against subjecting those arrested to 'punishment of a vindictive nature' that took no account of the provocation to which they had been subjected (*BNL*, 9 June 1898).

There remains the problem of accounting for the behaviour of the Protestant crowd. The obvious answer would be that they gave violent expression to their hostility towards any manifestation of Irish nationalism. In doing so, however, they blatantly ignored the advice of their political and religious leaders. The display of nationalist regalia and music may well have irritated. But the procession had already been prevented from challenging the Protestant monopoly of the city centre, and the violence in any case continued long after it had dispersed. This would suggest that, once the confrontation had begun, crowd behaviour had its own dynamic. The violence that took place was undoubtedly ugly: one policeman was killed and others seriously injured, while hundreds of families suffered through eviction from their homes or the expulsion from a workplace of the main breadwinner. Yet this does not preclude the existence of a recreational element in the initial skirmishing, seen for example in the reports of blanks fired from revolvers. The subsequent escalation, including the workplace expulsions and clearing of streets, represented a falling into what was by this time a well-established pattern. Furthermore it could be argued that participation in such a highly charged sequence of events did not merely reflect a collective identity, but helped to constitute it. The Catholics who processed from Smithfield to Hannahstown, and the Protestants who turned out to oppose them, were both motivated by existing political and religious loyalties. But the confrontations that followed must have played their own part in telling them who and what they were.

Demonstrations in Belfast in the early 1960s

To turn from these nineteenth-century episodes to the period after 1920 is at first sight to move to a more straightforward pattern of hegemony and suppression. Belfast was now the capital of a politically separate Northern Ireland, menaced both from without, by an irredentist southern Irish state and, from within, by a disaffected Catholic minority. Belfast nationalism remained divided between competing revolutionary and constitutionalist wings. But the triumph of republicanism in what was now a separate southern state meant that the public ceremonial even of the latter included elements, such as the Tricolour and an annual

commemoration of the Dublin rising of 1916, that could be easily presented as a threat to public order and to the state. Hastily introduced
legislation, in the form of the Civil Authorities (Special Powers) Act
of 1922, gave the newly formed, and predominantly Protestant, Royal
Ulster Constabulary (RUC) sweeping powers to prescribe organisations
and ban or reroute parades. Their use ensured that overt demonstrations
of Irish republican allegiance never appeared in the centre of Belfast. Policy towards nationalist events in predominantly Catholic areas varied.
In 1933, 5,000 people were reported to have knelt on the Falls Road,
in the predominantly Catholic west of the city, and recited the Rosary
when the RUC attempted to ban a march to Milltown Cemetery. Bans
were enforced in the years following leading, in 1937, to serious rioting
on the Falls Road. In 1939, however, the same event continued unhin-
dered although police asked those participating to remove Easter lilies,
a symbol of Irish Republicanism.

Demonstrations based on class presented greater difficulties. Belfast,
as Ireland's only major centre of manufacturing industry, had a strong
tradition of labour organisation. It also badly affected by the decline
of heavy industry in the interwar period, affecting its two core sec-
tors of textiles and shipbuilding. The strong trade union loyalties of
Protestant workers made it difficult to deny legitimacy to class-based
demonstrations, such as the May Day parades that became a regular
event from 1921. Social protest, on the other hand, was deeply alarm-
ing to a socially conservative Unionist administration. In 1925 a large
demonstration to protest at the conditions of the poor in Belfast was
banned. Protests in 1932 produced a striking if short-lived display of
unity across sectarian boundaries, as Catholic and Protestant activists
joined in demonstrations against the meagre level of unemployment
relief offered by the Belfast Board of Guardians. In response the government again invoked the Special Powers Act. In addition ministers, in
what appears to have been a conscious manipulation of sectarian tensions, appealed for Protestant solidarity against what they presented as
a covert nationalist attempt to destabilise Northern Ireland.

Strict control of the use of public space continued into the post-war
period. There was a new Public Order Act in 1951, while the increased
potency of the Tricolour following the declaration of a republic in the
southern state in 1948 provoked a Flags and Emblems (Display) Act in
1954. But the dichotomy between a hegemonic unionism and a sup-
pressed nationalism no longer monopolised the public arena. Instead
evidence from the early 1960s reveals a relatively vibrant political space.
There were protests by the Campaign for Nuclear Disarmament (CND);

socialists held rallies against US military intervention in Vietnam; tenants of Belfast housing corporation, from both unionist and nationalist areas, protested against rent rises; and mothers angry at the lack of road safety also held demonstrations (Nagle, 2008). In some cases adaptation to this new environment allowed nationalist organisations to gain an access to public space they would otherwise have been unable to secure, as when members of the Republican Party demonstrated against the proposed sale of the locally owned Northern Bank to the 'British owned' Midland Bank (*IN*, April 1965).

Two examples provide a not untypical picture. On 2 August 1965, 400 Corporation tenants, mostly women, part of the Amalgamated Corporation Tenant's Association, demonstrated in front of Belfast's City Hall against an increase in rents. A not so snappy placard from the Ballymurphy estate in west Belfast read, 'Higher rents, higher fares, higher food prices – why not just change the name of Belfast to Belsen' (*IN*, 3 Aug. 1965). The following month a sit-down protest by CND at the American Consulate in Queen Street clashed with the police. Later that day another sit-down protest was organised on Chichester Street near City Hall (*BNL*, 20 Sept. 1965).

These apparently minor events are significant for two reasons. First, they reflect political activity in public space by groups drawn from a wide range of backgrounds. The Amalgamated Committee of the Belfast Corporation Tenants Association, formed in 1961, contained representatives from across the city. It mobilised nine Councillors in August 1961 to march on City Hall (*IN*, 2 Aug. 1961). Nationalists from Ballymurphy, Turf Lodge and Andersonstown were active protestors on issues, such as housing, that would become part of the civil rights protests that start in earnest in 1967 (Nagle, 2008: 53–54). Indeed Nagle identifies a central weakness of the People's Democracy arm of this later civil rights movement, based as it was in political activism at Queen's University, as lying in its failure to connect with the tenants' groups already active in the city (Nagle, 2008: 55). Northern Ireland CND was formed in 1958, and initiated a regular Easter parade from May 1960. Over the years that followed, its campaigns concentrated on the US consulate in the city. Membership incorporated Protestant clergymen and Quakers as well as trade unionists and a range of left-wing activists. It is also interesting to note that, although the movement was organised on a Northern Ireland basis, the Republic's branch participated in the 1962 demonstration (*BTel*, 21 April 1962). Its demonstrations were initially commended as highly law abiding (*BNL*, 9 Oct. 1961), but by the mid-1960s forms of direct action, such as the sit down protests noted above, became more common. This more confrontational approach reflected the increased involvement of a number of radical organisations and individuals that would later become part of the civil rights movement (Nagle, 2008: 49).

Second, these events suggest that the rules governing access to public space in Belfast were more complex than the dichotomy of privileged Orangeism and prescribed nationalism would suggest. Displays of the Irish Tricolour were still routinely prevented (Jarman and Bryan, 1997: 41–50). But radical politics reflecting more complex constructions of identity were permitted to occupy public space, including the area in front of the City Hall. This raises the question of why, a few years later, the Civil Rights Movement, involving many of the same individuals, focussing on the many of the same issues, and using the same tactics, was not permitted the same access. Widespread commemoration by nationalists north and south of the 50th anniversary of the rising of 1916 may have helped to reawaken Unionist fears (Daly and O'Callaghan, 2007). But the most likely explanation is divisions within unionism, as the reformist Prime Minister Terence O'Neill came under attack from upholders of the traditional policy of sectarian exclusiveness.

The Lord Mayor's show and St Patrick's day

The annual Twelfth Orange parades, despite their privileged access to public space, were not official events. Government ministers frequently took a leading part, in their capacity as leading members of the Orange Order. But there was no direct funding. Instead the civic life of the city found expression in such events as the turning on of the Christmas tree lights in the grounds of City Hall and, of particular importance in the post-war period, the Lord Mayor's Show, organised by the Junior Chamber of Commerce. Reports from the 1960s indicate that participants came from a broad spectrum of civic life, including charities and major local companies. Themes included 'Ulster Entering the Sixties' (*IN*, 23 May 1960), 'Ulster in Action' (*BNL*, 19 May 1962), 'Buy Ulster Goods' (*IN*, 6 May 1963), 'Pride in Progress' (*BNL*, 22 May 1964) and 'Enterprise 65' (*BNL*, 15 May 1965). The event was ostensibly non-political: in 1966 the *News Letter* reported that six of the floats were from the Irish Republic. But it nevertheless had a strong establishment flavour and represented an essentially sectional understanding of what constituted the civic. In 1964 a visit from Princess Margaret coincided with the show (*BNL*, 20 May 1964), while the armed services made a regular appearance. In 1962, for example, the Army had five floats, including a Centurion tank.

Such displays of ostensible civic harmony were always vulnerable to disruption. In 1968 protestors against the Vietnam war threw themselves in front of a contingent of sailors, from the American warship *USS Keppler*, taking part in the show (*BTel*, 2 Aug. 1968). But the damage inflicted by the communal violence of the 1970s and 1980s was on a wholly different scale. By 1980 the President of the Chamber of Commerce was appealing for the big employers, who had not recently taken part in the Lord Mayor's Show, to return (*IN*, 4 Dec. 1980). In the event, however, what took place was not a revival but a slightly strange reinvention. By the late 1990s the floats sponsored by business firms and corporate bodies had been replaced by exhibits from community groups and performers drawn from a variety of ethnic backgrounds. In 1998, for example, the event, now explicitly described as a 'carnival', included Chinese dragons and a float from the more renowned Notting Hill Carnival in London. The transition created new occasions for conflict. In 1995 the Republican Prisoners group *Saoirse* demonstrated a few hundred yards from City Hall to protest at not having been allowed to participate (*IN*, 5 May 1995). In 1998 the parade, led for the first time by a nationalist Mayor, had to be diverted to avoid a blockade by loyalists protesting at the inclusion of a float entered by the Ormeau Residents Action Group, conspicuous for their opposition to Orange parades through their neighbourhood (*BNL*, 25 May 1998). But such events served only to encourage the process of redefinition. By 2008 the former Lord Mayor's Show has become the Belfast Carnival, notable for its colourful floats and costumes while containing almost nothing in terms of either local traditions or sponsorship. Belfast's major civic event now seeks to display the artistic, the multi-cultural and the exotic at the expense of local and more conflict-ridden identities.

This reinvention can be compared with the different evolution of another civic event. On 17 March 2006, a St Patrick's day celebration was organised through the centre of the city. The main part of this parade also took the form of a multi-ethnic 'carnival', with images of St Patrick being provided by a number of the community groups involved. Under the Council's guidelines for events, no political flags, which in theory included both the Union flag and Tricolour, were to be carried in the carnival parade or at the staged event in Custom House Square. Indeed, to avoid the potentially contentious use of the colour green, which some unionists had complained about, children attending were handed multi-coloured shamrocks by Council workers. In the event a few Tricolours were carried by people walking along with the parade, and approximately 100 were waved by the 4,000 spectators in Custom House Square, making the attempt at creating a neutral event a qualified success.

The spectacle of Belfast Council, a former stronghold of Unionism, organising the celebration of a day normally associated with Irish nationalism was the culmination of a series of rapid developments in relation to the use of public space. The long-standing ban on republican parades and demonstrations in the city centre had continued after 1969. In August 1993, however, despite protests from unionist councillors, a parade commemorating the internment of republican activists in 1971 was allowed into the city centre and the president of Sinn Féin, Gerry Adams, gave a speech in front of the statue of Queen Victoria at City Hall. In March 1998 the first St Patrick's Day event took place in the city. Organisers came from the West Belfast Festival, Féile an Phobail, an event which had itself been born out of the internment commemorations in the west of the city, but which had succeeded in attracting public funding. The organisers were thus alert to the possibility that St Patrick's Day too could obtain support, and from 1997 onwards a debate began over the role that Belfast City Council might play.

The debate was all the more interesting because Patrick, as the saint who supposedly brought Christianity to Ireland, had long been recognised and celebrated both in Ireland and in Irish emigrant communities (Cronin and Adair, 2002), and by Protestants as well as Catholics, so that there was from the start the possibility of a cross-community, 'inclusive' event. In fact St Patrick's day parades in the nearby towns of Armagh and Downpatrick already drew such cross community support. In Belfast, however, the early parades included the same Republican prisoner support groups that had attempted to enter the Lord Mayor's Show in 1995, and were characterised by a variety of nationalist symbols. One Republican commentator, writing in the *Andersonstown News*, made clear that for some at least the event was indeed about nationalists making claim to the city.

> The tens of thousands who turned Belfast city centre black with green on Tuesday were doing more than scribbling footnotes, more than even contributing chapters to our history. They were shredding the pages of past wrongs, binning the Belfast of the pogroms and second-class citizenship, erasing the painful memory of too many Twelfths on the wrong side of the swagger stick … and proudly painting their own prologue: we've arrived.
>
> ('Glorious Green Gridlock', *Andersonstown News*, 21 March 1998)

The evolution of St Patrick's Day as a civic event thus involved significant changes in outlook on both sides. City Council debates on the merits of funding the day were contentious, and initial claims by the organisers that the event was now 'inclusive' were not readily accepted. In 2002, for example, Unionist newspapers reacted badly to what was intended as a humorous display of men in black berets and dark glasses driving a white car with 'Garda' on the side (*BNL*, 18 March 2002).

By this time, however, the political and policy environment was changing rapidly. The 1998 multi-party Agreement cleared the way for the institution of a devolved government in which nationalists and republicans shared ministerial office with the two unionist parties, while Belfast City Council was now a hung Council with the non-denominational Alliance Party holding the balance of power. In addition the Northern Ireland Act (1998) had imposed upon public authorities a legal duty to promote equality and 'to have regard to the desirability of promoting good relations between persons of different religious belief, political opinion, and racial group' (Section 75). In 2004 Belfast City Council adopted a good relations strategy which, amongst other aims, looked to celebrate diversity (Belfast City Council, 2004). In 2005 the Office of the First and Deputy First Minister issued a policy document, *A Shared Future*, calling for 'support for cultural projects which highlight the complexity and overlapping nature of identities and their wider global connections' (1.2.2). Against this background, the City Council finally agreed, in 2005, that it should take the lead in organising the following year's St Patrick's Day. The resulting attempt to stage an officially sponsored and 'inclusive' open air event, with improbably multicoloured shamrocks replacing Tricolours, and council T-shirts being offered to wearers of Celtic football tops, has proved to be largely a success. In 2006 stewards employed by the Council were visibly apprehensive as they asked people to put Tricolours away at the entrance to Custom House Square. By the 2008 St Patrick's Day Carnival event they were much more confident, and spectators asked to 'please put the flag away as this is a cross-community event' were generally willing to comply. Belfast's own particular version of St Patrick's Day, described as a carnival, had joined the list of official council civic events.

Conclusion

The changing pattern of social action and the use of public space outlined in these four case studies can be properly understood only within its broader context. The second half of the nineteenth century was the golden age of the British city (Briggs, 1968; Gunn, 2000; Hunt, 2004). Liberated from aristocratic dominance, and entrusted through a series of reform acts with control of their own internal affairs, urban elites in Leeds, Manchester, Birmingham and elsewhere developed an assertive and forward looking public culture, reflected in investment in ambitious schemes of urban improvement and in the development of elaborate new forms of civic pageantry. The Belfast that Queen Victoria visited in 1849 showed every sign of sharing this new optimism about the potential of urban living. There was the same eager interest in development projects, and the same successful assumption by elected corporate bodies of a role as representatives of an imagined urban community. Neither development, however, was sustained. Urban political life, poisoned by a conflict over sovereignty whose origins and dynamic lay far beyond the city boundaries, lost much of its initial creativity and dynamism. In place of the symbolic enactment of community seen elsewhere, public displays of identity became either celebrations of sectional triumph or trials of strength between opposing forces. Behind the increasingly violent sectarian clashes of the late nineteenth and twentieth centuries it is thus possible to discern a deeper history: the stifled birth, in the mid-nineteenth century, of a culture of civic pride and municipal progress. By the same token recent attempts to promote more inclusive forms of pageantry, as in the case of St Patrick's day, can be seen as an attempt to recover something of that lost tradition.

Contests over rights of access to public space are a recurring theme in the history of nineteenth- and twentieth-century Belfast. For much of the period control of what was to be defined as a legitimate part of the civic lay with a dominant unionist and Protestant elite. Yet even at points where this elite appeared at its most dominant, the centre of the city offered challenges. The political value of plebeian loyalist culture, with its potential for violence and riotous celebration, had to be balanced against the affront to new standards of public decorum. The tensions evident in the response to the United Irish commemoration of 1898, between the imperatives of sectarian and political solidarity on the one hand and a concern for respectability and public order on the other, were a permanent part of the history of Belfast Orangeism (Bryan, 2000). Where nationalist demonstrations could be excluded from the city centre as threats to the civic order itself, trade union and socialist events, drawing support from Protestant as well as Catholic workers, demanded a more cautious response. The lively culture of demonstrations and street protests visible in the early and mid-1960s likewise used public space to challenge the existing political order in ways that could not readily be excluded from the civic.

From the 1990s onwards the rules governing the use of public space in Belfast have been radically rewritten. During that period the Irish Tricolour gained access to the city centre, marking its acceptance within a broad notion of what was now acceptable in Belfast's central civic space. But when St Patrick's Day became part of the more narrowly defined notion of 'shared space' now sponsored by the Council, the Tricolour was asked to leave again. If unionists had been required to cede exclusive control of space they had formerly monopolised, nationalists had to revise their identity practices in conformity with a new idea of the civic. Their willingness to do so has meant that what began as a distinctly republican event is now a recognised part of Belfast's civic calendar, while the Twelfth of July, which long enjoyed a privileged monopoly of public space, still struggles to rebuild a civic reputation. All this has taken place within the context of a policy of respect for diversity, and the creation of 'shared space', adopted by central and local government as part of the 1998 political settlement. The implementation of the new policy has at times been contentious. But despite a lack of support, particularly from Sinn Féin and the Democratic Unionist Party, the perceived need to promote civic activity in the city has led to the adoption of new social practices of shared, if somewhat neutralised, public space.

Studies of levels of segregation in the residential districts surrounding the city point to a further deepening of communal divisions in the period since 1998 (Shirlow and Murtagh, 2006). However, social activity within the centre of the city tells a more nuanced story. In the case of St Patrick's Day and the Lord Mayor's Show a degree of mutual accommodation has been developing, achieved both through the negotiated redefinition of long-standing identity practices and through the emergence of new ones. What is perhaps revealing is that in both cases the outcome has been a form of 'carnival', not an indigenous tradition, in which symbolic representation of a distinctively local political or ethnic identity have given way to a generalised representation of cultural and ethnic diversity. In this particular case of a divided city seeking a new vision of the civic, carnival, so often an occasion on which the established order is subverted or opposed, has become the acceptable space for civic representation.

Two main conclusions emerge from this case study of identity practices in Belfast since the nineteenth century. The first is to confirm the need, even in this seemingly most immutable of conflicts, to look critically at claims for continuity and historical legitimacy. Expressions of identity through rituals and collective symbolic activity are revealed, not as a fixed inheritance, but as negotiated practices. In their changing forms they provide evidence of the variety of identities that have existed within the urban population, and of the potential for development and adaptation often concealed by appeals to 'tradition'. The second conclusion concerns the central importance of the notion of public space, and of the definition of the civic. For most of the period reviewed, access to Belfast city centre was disproportionately controlled by expressions of a Protestant and unionist identity. But the forms which that control took, and the nature of both permitted and excluded identity practices, were repeatedly reshaped and modified in response to developments in the broader economic and political context, and also to changes in the specific character of urban living. The city centre emerges, not as the site for straightforward processes of domination and exclusion, but as a complex and, once again, negotiated space. That process of negotiation, moreover, involved not just a policing of what was and was not to be permitted within the bounds of the civic, but a definition and redefinition over time of the nature of the civic itself. In this respect a case study of Belfast, as an urban environment beset with particularly acute conflicts of identity, points above all to the importance of understanding the complex relationship between ideas of identity, of citizenship and of public space.

Note

1. Unless otherwise stated, information on the four events discussed draws on material from the database of Irish public events compiled as part of the Imagining Belfast Project. Fuller accounts, with detailed documentation, will appear in due course.

Thanks are due to Dr John Nagle and Dr Gillian McIntosh, our collaborators on the project.

References

Baker, S.E. (1973) Orange and Green: Belfast 1832–1912. In H.J. Dyos and M. Wolff (eds.) *The Victorian City: Images and Realities*. London: Routledge & Kegan Paul.

Beckett, J.C. *et al.* (1983) *Belfast: The Making of the City*. Belfast: Appletree.

Belfast City Council (2004) *Belfast City Council Good Relations Strategy: Building Our Future Together*. Belfast: Good Relations Unit, Belfast City Council. http://www.belfastcity.gov.uk/publications/GoodRelationsStrategy.pdf.

BNL: *Belfast Newsletter.*
Briggs, A. (1968) *Victorian Cities.* Harmondsworth: Penguin.
Bryan, D. (2000) *Orange Parades: The Politics of Ritual, Tradition and Control.* London: Pluto.
BTel: *Belfast Telegraph.*
Budge, I. and O'Leary, C. (1973) *Belfast, Approach to Crisis: A Study of Belfast Politics 1613–1970.* London: Macmillan.
Comerford, R. (2003) *Inventing the Nation: Ireland.* London: Arnold.
Connolly, S.J. (1997) Culture, Identity and Tradition: Changing Definitions of Irishness. In B. Graham (ed.) *In Search of Ireland: A Cultural Geography.* London: Routledge.
Cronin, M. and Adair, D. (2002) *The Wearing of the Green: A History of St Patrick's Day.* London: Routledge.
CSORP. (1818–1924) Chief Secretary's Office Registered Papers, Dublin: National Archives.
Daly, M. and O'Callaghan, M. (eds.) (2007) *1916 in 1966: Commemorating the Easter Rising.* Dublin: Royal Irish Academy.
Farrell, S. (2000) *Rituals and Riots: Sectarian Violence and Political Culture in Ulster 1784–1886.* Lexington: University Press of Kentucky.
Faulks, K. (2000) *Citizenship.* London: Routledge.
Gillespie, R. and Royle, S. (2003–7) *Belfast: Irish Historic Towns Atlas.* Dublin: Royal Irish Academy.
Gunn, S. (2000) *The Public Culture of the Victorian Middle Class: Ritual and Authority in the English Industrial City 1840–1914.* Manchester: Manchester University Press.
Hepburn, A.C. (2008) *Catholic Belfast and Nationalist Ireland in the Era of Joe Devlin 1871–1934.* Oxford: Oxford University Press.
Hirst, C. (2002) *Religion, Politics and Violence in Nineteenth-Century Belfast: The Pound and Sandy Row.* Dublin: Four Courts Press.
Hobsbawm, E. and Ranger, T. (1983) *The Invention of Tradition.* Cambridge: CUP.
Hopkins, N. and Reicher, S. (1997) Social Movements Rhetoric and Social Psychology of Collective Action: A Case Study of Anti-abortion Mobilisation. *Human Relations* 50(3), 261–286.
Hunt, T. (2004) *Building Jerusalem: The Rise and Fall of the Victorian City*, London: Weidenfeld and Nicolson.
IN: *Irish News.*
Jarman, N. and Bryan, D. (1997) *From Riots to Rights: Nationalist Parades in the North of Ireland.* Coleraine: Centre for the Study of Conflict.
Jenkins, R. (2004) *Social Identity.* London: Routledge.
Maguire, W.A. (1993) *Belfast.* Keele: Ryburn.
McComb, W. (2003) *The Repealer Repulsed.* In P. Maume (ed.) Dublin: UCD Press.
Nagle, J. (2008) From 'Ban the Bomb' to 'Ban the Increase': 1960's Street Politics in Pre-Civil Rights Belfast. *Irish Political Studies* 23(1), 41–58.
NW: *Northern Whig.*
Shirlow, P. and Murtagh, B. (2006) *Belfast: Segregation, Violence and the City.* London: Pluto Press.
Wright, F. (1996) *Two Lands on One Soil: Ulster Politics Before Home Rule.* Dublin: Gill & Macmillan.

12
Defining Common Goals without Speaking the Same Language: Social Identity and Social Action in Wales

Andrew Livingstone, Russell Spears, Antony S. R. Manstead and Martin Bruder

Any consideration of the relationship between social identity and social action begs a rather basic question: what is *social* about social identity? What is implied by the epithet 'social' that differentiates it from personal, or non-social, aspects of identity? In the sense that we use the term, there are several aspects to the sociality of social identity. These follow from a basic definition of social identity as 'the individual's knowledge that he [or she] belongs to certain social groups together with some emotional and value significance to him [or her] of this group membership' (Tajfel, 1972: 32). As such, social (as opposed to personal) identity is the psychological basis of intergroup behaviour, so that rather than *subverting* identity (c.f. Le Bon, 1897; Zimbardo, 1969), acting in terms of one's membership of a social group entails acting in terms of a *different*, equally valid and meaningful aspect of one's self-concept.

The validity and meaning of social identities derives in turn from the wider social setting in which groups are seen to be located by their members. Rather than being cognitively 'fixed', the scope (i.e., who shares in) and content (i.e., the meaning) of social identities shift fluidly, defined in context through comparison with relevant outgroups (Turner, 1985; Turner *et al.*, 1987). The inherently comparative nature of social identities also provides a basis for understanding one's and one's group's position in *stratified* social systems, structured by differential status and power relations between groups, along with perceptions of the legitimacy and stability of these relations (Tajfel and Turner, 1979).

In one sense, then, social identity is (at least in part) a theory of social relations. One part of its link to action is therefore in providing a basis from which to appraise and act upon aspects of these social relations, by constituting an understanding of what is possible and proper (i.e., legitimate) given one's own and one's group's social position (Drury and Reicher, 2000). The scope and form of social action thus reflects and is tailored to these understandings, encompassing attempts to create, maintain, or change social reality (Scheepers *et al.*, 2006; Spears *et al.*, 2001, 2002).

While social identity provides a basis for social action, the impact of action on social relations also suggests that the identity–action relation is bidirectional. This is true in at least three senses. First, action (e.g., in the form of ingroup bias) can have the integrity of ingroup identity as its focus, either through establishing social identity at the group formation stage (Spears *et al.*, 2002; Tajfel *et al.*, 1971), or maintaining the distinctiveness of existing identities when they are seen to be undermined (e.g., Jetten and Spears 2004; Jetten *et al.*, 1996, 1997, 2001). Second, collective action and intergroup *inter*action (e.g., between protestors and police) can produce dynamics that change one's understanding of social relations through the process of acting on them – particularly where outgroups (e.g., police) have the power to *impose* their (different) understandings of social relations (Drury and Reicher, 1999, 2000; Stott *et al.*, 2007, 2008; Stott and Drury, 2000; Stott and Reicher, 1998). Third, action can take the form of rhetorical strategies aimed at defining the intergroup context, including the relevance, scope, and content of social categories, and the projects towards which they are mobilised (Billig, 1985, 1996; Edwards, 1991; Reicher *et al.*, 2005; Reicher and Hopkins, 1996a, 1996b, 2001; Reicher *et al.*, 1997; Wetherell and Potter, 1992).

The above aspects of the identity–action link constitute important assumptions in our research, and arguably highlight an important tension when it comes to examining the link between identity and social action in large-scale social categories. Specifically, it demands on the one hand a concern with broad patterns of identification, appraisals, and emotions among people who claim membership of the category, in a manner that arguably assumes a degree of sharedness or consensus – at least when it comes to mobilisation towards collective goals. On the other hand, it demands recognition of the variation and contestation among those who claim a category membership over the meaning, scope, and position of that category. In other words, the action–identity link also requires examination of how identity is argued over and reified.

With these concerns in mind, in this chapter we aim to illustrate our approach to the study of social identity and social action, drawing on our research on national identity in Wales. First and foremost, we aim to provide an overview of some of our findings relating to national identifications in Wales, particularly in terms of contestation over the meaning of the Welsh language, and how the perceived importance of the Welsh language can in turn have varied consequences for support for political goals such as national autonomy. Our initial focus here is on the value of qualitative enquiry into the different ways in which particular attributes, such as the Welsh language, are deployed strategically as identity management resources. We then turn to the findings of survey-based research about the consequences of defining identity in terms of particular attributes – and how these consequences differ across contexts. In turn, we focus on how these patterns of identification translate, through emotional experience, into support for intergroup action of various forms. In doing so, we hope to illustrate how our methodological approach was geared to meet these twin goals of studying the *process* of identity construction and reification – how group members seek to essentialise ingroup identity in terms of particular characteristics – and the potential *consequences* of identity reification for social action.

This dual concern with processes and consequences of identity reification led to a methodological strategy involving a combination of interviews and questionnaire-based surveys. Because of the relatively empowering nature of interview settings (at least relative to surveys) for interviewees, semi-structured interviews can provide an opportunity to examine the strategic construction and deployment of identity-defining attributes, rather than simply offering a fine-grained insight into 'what people think' (Reicher and Hopkins, 2001). Questions along the lines of 'how is the Welsh language characterised and deployed to manage identity, how is this justified, and to what end?' become the focus of analysis. In short, interview data can highlight the *contested* (as opposed to simply varied) nature of 'Welshness' and its defining features. Building on this analysis, survey findings provide an insight into the potential *consequences* of defining Welsh identity heavily in terms of the Welsh language – both in terms of the national affiliation of Welsh-speakers and non-Welsh-speakers and in terms of support for the possible goal of national autonomy for Wales.

National identity concerns in Wales

Our theoretical concerns are therefore quite broad, touching upon processes and dynamics that occur in a wide range of settings. What, then, makes Wales a particularly good setting in which to investigate these issues? One important factor here is the place of the Welsh language in national identity in Wales. This is a potent issue, historically and in the here and now (Davies, 1994). Although only approximately 20 per cent of the population of Wales can speak Welsh, it is commonly positioned as a defining dimension of Welsh identity for both Welsh-speaking and non-Welsh-speaking Welsh people alike (Welsh Language Board, 2003). A broad acceptance of the language's importance can clearly have important consequences for non-Welsh speakers, such as making them feel less Welsh (Bourhis *et al.*, 1973) and less culturally consistent (Giles *et al.*, 1977b).

However, despite its prominence, the importance of Welsh is far from a 'given'. For one thing, it is also possible to redefine the Welsh language as a *symbolic* resource (Coupland *et al.*, 2003), allowing non-Welsh speakers to incorporate it into a 'full' sense of Welshness. Moreover, it is possible to define Welsh identity using dimensions other than the language (Coupland *et al.*, 2005). The way in which the main Welsh nationalist party, Plaid Cymru, has consistently placed the Welsh language at the heart of its campaigns also testifies to the language's relevance (and utility) to intergroup concerns, both as a focus of outgroup threat and as a basis for resistance (see also Bowie, 1993). That is, the minority position of the Welsh language poses a potential threat to identity from the dominance of the English language within as well as without the ingroup, whereas it also forms a coping resource, and stakes a claim to identity, helping to face up to this threat. Meanwhile, this potential for threat is heightened further by the historical absence of social and political structures that define Wales in relation to England (Fitz, 2000). This means that Welsh national identity is not only heavily constituted in terms of 'ethno-linguistic vitality' (Giles *et al.*, 1977a, 1977b), but is also acutely vulnerable to threats to this vitality (Thompson and Day, 1999). Moreover, such threats are often seen as originating from the influence of English culture and the influx of English people into traditionally Welsh-speaking areas (Bowie, 1993; Cloke *et al.*, 1998; Trosset, 1986).

For those who claim 'Welshness', there is clearly much variation in – and argument over – the significance of the Welsh language. The conduct and consequences of these arguments are major issues for national identity in Wales, in terms of both the intergroup relationship between Wales and England, and who can claim a Welsh national identity in the first instance (Bourhis and Giles, 1977; Giles *et al.*, 1977a, 1977b). Importantly, these arguments and outcomes are structured by considerable differences in regional contexts across Wales, particularly in terms of Welsh language ability and how criterial the language is seen as being for

Welsh identity (Bowie, 1993; Osmond, 1985; Thompson and Day, 1999). This provided us with the opportunity to test specific hypotheses about the consequences of Welsh language ability for national identification, and for support for political goals.

Finally, the Welsh context provided an opportunity to investigate the *range* of intergroup orientations and forms of action that are open to members of minority groups. In the political sphere, national identity concerns can clearly translate into support for the project of national autonomy, as indicated by the vote in 1997 to establish a devolved Welsh Assembly. However, the range of identity concerns alluded to above is also reflected in alternative forms of action, including direct action campaigns by Welsh language organisations, and even a series of arson attacks – attributed to the group Meibion Glyndŵr – directed at empty, English-owned 'second homes' in Wales in the 1970s and 1980s. A concern with social action therefore meant that investigating the psychological basis of these different strategies, rather than action in a generic sense, was a priority in the Welsh context.

Arguments over the meaning of the Welsh language

The primary concern in the interview phase of the project was to explore how identity-defining attributes can be deployed in quite different ways by ingroup members (both in terms of importance and in terms of why and how they are important), and how these are given impetus by characterisations of the ingroup's intergroup position. To do so, we conducted a qualitative thematic analysis of two public speeches and 17 conversational interviews, focusing on how the Welsh language is deployed as an identity-defining attribute by self-defined Welsh people. We focused on how this deployment was located within respondents' characterisations of their own and others' social positions. This includes characterisations of intergroup power relations (between Wales and England in particular), the legitimacy and stability of these relations, and of the nature of intergroup threat that flows from them. It also includes characterisations of intra-group position, both as a justification for particular orientations towards the language and as an outcome of how the language is used to manage group boundaries and hierarchies. Finally, the analysis also focused on how characterisations of social position and of the Welsh language are used to generate *imperatives* for others who claim ingroup membership. In this way, we do not assume that these characterisations merely *reflect* understandings of social relations. Rather, we were interested in their role as *entrepreneurial* products by examining the ways in which they can implicitly or explicitly create impetus towards alternative social relations (Billig, 1985; Reicher and Hopkins, 2001).

Examples from interviews with two male Welsh-speakers help to illustrate this point. Both proclaimed themselves to be passionate about the Welsh language, but with quite different characterisations of the relationship between Wales and England – and of the importance of the Welsh language in these structural contexts. On the one hand, the interviewee in the extract below characterises Wales' relationship with England as being one of illegitimate low status/power through direct subordination. Moreover, this relationship is portrayed as stable and unlikely to change. This characterisation is used to imply an erosion of identity that leaves the Welsh language as the only available means by which to protect or assert Welsh distinctiveness:

> If you cut out the language, the language makes a heck of a difference because Anglo-Welsh culture or whatever it's called really isn't that distinctive. When you look at Welsh culture, Welsh, Welsh language culture, you've got a whole lot of things (...) the problem is when you get rid of the religion, the industry and stuff like that, and the language, there's not that much that sort of defines us as a people. (I5, male)

This characterisation is then used to generate an imperative on anyone who claims Welshness to learn and use the Welsh language:

> People who feel very Welsh, who are proud of being Welsh, I think they should, um, I think they should learn the language (...) it's such an important part of their identity (...) it's important that they speak Welsh, that they learn Welsh in order to keep their birthright alive. (I5, male)

This interviewee therefore deploys the Welsh language as an essential identity-defining attribute that is fundamental to the existence of the Welsh national category. Moreover, this attribute becomes fundamental to *membership* of the category.

Our second interviewee offers a quite different characterisation of the relationship between Wales and England. While the relationship has historically been one of Welsh subordination, this is explicitly characterised as a changeable and changing relationship. Importantly, this speaker emphasises change as an ongoing process involving not only the strengthening and consolidation of Welsh identity, but also the real-isation of political equality and ultimately separation from the United Kingdom. The broader project of Welsh identity is therefore explicitly bound up with a specific vision of the current and future political status of Wales. It is within this framework that he deploys the Welsh language:

> That's what's, what's brought about the big renaissance, say from 1950 onwards...the Welsh language, and people like Saunders Lewis kicked off, the students got hold of it, and it's, it became a political football at the time...you cannot divorce politics as well (...)

> This is what I call the silent revolution (...) you cannot, uh, divorce the language and compartment it, can't divorce the culture, you know, um, it's all part of the Welsh whole you see (...) they can exist on their own, but when they come in, together, that's when the Welsh identity is really good (...) So you put all the economies, the politics, the cultural and the language (...) Before you're very vulnerable to England walking over us. They don't walk over us any more. (I9, male, Plaid Cymru)

For this interviewee, the 'Welsh whole' thus requires a combination of cultural and political dimensions. As part of this construction, the Welsh language is deployed not only as a marker of cultural distinctiveness, but also as a means of political mobilisation and consciousness-raising. Its value is therefore in its potential to direct ingroup members towards particular political goals, as well as the extent to which it bestows distinctiveness on the ingroup. In turn, the entrepreneurial aspect of this construction becomes most evident in the associated prescription for the position of non-Welsh speakers in the national category:

> I don't mind it, because I think we need to take them on board, because you can't, you know, alienate, it's a bonus that you speak the language, I wouldn't think less of anybody because they don't speak the language. (I9, male, Plaid Cymru)

The cultural and political importance of the language is here balanced against the reality that the majority of Welsh people cannot speak the language. Defining the national category in terms of language ability could therefore potentially undermine the mobilisation potential of the category. Indeed, this construction couches the inclusion of non-Welsh speakers in the national category in overtly strategic terms. In particular, the rationale that 'we need to take them on board' still presumes a Welsh-speaking 'we', a non-Welsh-speaking 'they', and a specific political imperative for their inclusion in the national movement. While the deployment of the Welsh language as a means of collective mobilisation goes hand-in-hand with a particular characterisation of the Wales–England relationship, it is also constrained by other structural realities within Wales that may impede the goal of national mobilisation. This can be contrasted with first interviewee's emphasis on the identity-preservation role of Welsh. In particular, the lack of potential for political and structural change and the associated need to secure the ingroup's distinctiveness and cultural existence means that non-Welsh speakers risk being placed outside the national category (see also Morton *et al.*, 2007).

While these examples clearly illustrate the strategic elements of Welsh language characterisations, they only hint at the range and nuance of such characterisations. This is particularly so when it comes to non-Welsh speakers, for whom characterisations of the Welsh language were associated most strongly with their own need to negotiate a place within the national category, ranging from acceptance of the language's criterial importance right through to direct contestation of its importance. The unifying point to draw from these varied identity positions is the importance of locating analyses of the uses and importance of group-defining attributes within the social setting that gives them meaning. While an attribute such as ingroup language offers a range of identity management possibilities for low-power groups, how it is actually used to change social relations depends on how those social relations are understood and characterised.

The consequences of Welsh language ability for political action

Clearly, then, it is important to appreciate the contested nature of national identifications, including the definition, meaning, and social structural position of one's national ingroup. However, variation is only part of the story when it comes to social action. Identities are not just fleeting, ephemeral representations of one's social position; rather, they form the basis from which one can act to change that social position. Variation in what it means to be Welsh (for example) is therefore more than just a difference of opinion. Instead, it reflects a process of social influence in which attempts are made to generate consensus about the meaning of identities that are presumed to be shared with other ingroup members (Haslam *et al.*, 1998a, 1998b; Reicher *et al.*, 2005; Reicher *et al.*, 1997). This is often done with the goal of generating truly *collective* tendencies towards different forms of action (e.g., support for national autonomy). Appreciating the contested nature of social identities therefore needs to be balanced against the recognition that broad patterns of identification and social action can emerge from the mix, shaped and constrained by broader relations – defined by power, status, and legitimacy – between the ingroup and outgroups (Drury and Reicher, 1999, 2000; Stott and Reicher, 1998). In short, structural relations shape collective identity, and *vice versa*.

Our second research concern was to examine the consequences of language-contingent definitions of Welshness for national identification. Although the role of the Welsh language is contested strategically from a range of positions, there is a considerable degree of consensus about its criterial role in Welsh national identity. This places something of a reality constraint on attempts to contest its role, meaning that the argument as to whether or not the language is important has largely been conceded in favour of seeing it as a fundamental feature of Welsh national identity. Clearly, the historical hegemony of England has much to do with this. Our focus was on how differing views of Welshness impact on the potential to change relations with England. It was here that we turned to questionnaire and survey-based methods to explore the broad consequences of defining identity in terms of particular attributes.

The aim in this phase of the research was to examine (1) the role of context in shaping the identity consequences of having or not having identity-defining attributes such as the Welsh language, and (2) the implications of this for collective mobilisation towards group goals (national autonomy for Wales in this case). This analysis focuses on a potential dilemma faced by members of groups that experience not just low power, but also threats to their essence or existence. On the one hand, asserting the criterial importance of a particular attribute (the Welsh language) may provide a means of preserving the ingroup's existence. However, it may also undermine the potential of group members to mobilise towards particular group goals, such as national autonomy. This is because the identity criteria that define group membership may in turn affect group identification among ingroup members who do not possess the identity-defining attribute (i.e., non-Welsh speakers).

We tested these ideas in two questionnaire-based studies. In the first of these, we sampled 116 sixth-form students, aged 16 to 18, at a Welsh-medium school. These students had Welsh as their language of instruction, but their ability to speak Welsh outside school varied.

We took measures of the students' self-reported Welsh language ability; their degree of Welsh identification (using a scale adapted from Cameron, 2004); and their support for political autonomy for Wales. We found a positive association between Welsh language ability and support for Welsh political autonomy. Greater Welsh language ability was associated with greater support for autonomy – or put another way, *lower* ability was associated with *reduced* support for autonomy. The key findings, however, was that this relationship was fully mediated (explained) by Welsh national identification. In other words, Welsh language ability appears to impact on support for autonomy through its effect on Welsh identification.

Of course, pre-existing settings involve more than one category with which people can identify (Hornsey and Hogg, 2000a, 2000b; Mummendey and Wenzel, 1999; Turner *et al.*, 1987). This is certainly true in Wales, where other national identities available to people in Wales include 'English' (the main majority outgroup identity). Specifically, in contexts where being able to speak Welsh is seen as essential to being Welsh, those who cannot speak Welsh but would otherwise define themselves as Welsh can find themselves being defined as 'English' (Bowie, 1993; Trosset, 1986).

We therefore predicted that the consequences of having/not having the ingroup language for national identification would be evident not only in ingroup (Welsh) identification, but also in 'outgroup' (English) identification. Moreover, we expected that these effects would be more pronounced in contexts where the perceived importance of the language as an ingroup-defining attribute was highest. Finally, we hypothesised that having or not having the identity-defining attribute of language would also impact on group members' support for the group goals of greater national autonomy, and that this effect would be mediated by the effects on identification(s).

We tested these hypotheses in a survey that sampled from two regional contexts that differ in terms of how widely spoken Welsh is, and in its perceived importance for ingroup (Welsh) identity (see Balsom, 1985). We refer to these as Welsh-speaking regions (*Y Fro Gymraeg*, as defined by Balsom, 1985) and non-Welsh-speaking regions (incorporating British Wales and Welsh Wales, as defined by Balsom, 1985). In each of these regional contexts, we gauged ingroup language ability, ingroup (Welsh) and outgroup (English) identification, and desire for national autonomy. We expected that ingroup language ability would positively predict ingroup identification and negatively predict outgroup identification. In turn, we predicted that these effects would be stronger in the region(s) in which the ingroup language is most prominent. Finally, we expected that ingroup (Welsh) identification would positively predict support for the goal of national autonomy and that outgroup (English) identification would negatively predict support for the goal of national autonomy.

In this study, we surveyed 646 adults who identified themselves as Welsh. Of these, 190 were from Welsh-speaking regions, and 456 from non-Welsh-speaking regions. The study consisted of a telephone survey (available in Welsh if the respondent wished), in which measures were taken of self-reported Welsh language ability; national identification as Welsh and as English (using shorter versions of the scale used in the first study); and support for political autonomy for Wales.

As in the first study, Welsh language ability was associated with stronger Welsh identification in both regions. In addition, *low* Welsh language ability was associated with stronger *English* identification – but *only* in Welsh-speaking regions. This pattern is illustrated in Figure 12.1,

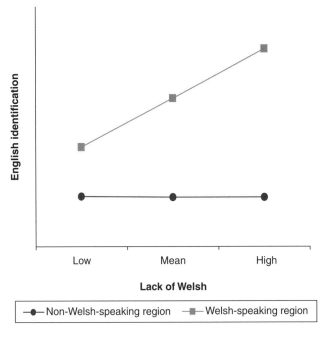

Figure 12.1 Association between Welsh language fluency and English identification among self-defined Welsh people in Welsh-speaking and non-Welsh-speaking regions

and suggests that non-Welsh speakers in Welsh-speaking contexts may not only find themselves positioned as 'English' (Bowie, 1993; Trosset, 1986), but can actually come to identify to some degree with 'English-ness', despite strong Welsh identification.

Turning to support for national autonomy, Welsh language ability was again positively associated with a more positive attitude to greater autonomy – an association that was explained by the effects of language ability on Welsh identification, and on English identification – but only in Welsh-speaking regions. Specifically, Welsh identification was associated with greater, and English identification with lesser, support for autonomy.

Together, the results of these studies suggest that there is an association between Welsh language ability and attitudes to political autonomy for Wales, and that this relationship is one that works 'through' national identification: Greater Welsh language ability predicts stronger Welsh identification, which predicts more positive attitudes to political autonomy. The flipside is that *lower* Welsh language ability can *lower* Welsh identification, which lowers support for autonomy. In Welsh-speaking regions, low Welsh language ability also predicts greater *English* identification among self-defined Welsh people. English identification, in turn, is associated with lower support for political autonomy – another way in which low Welsh language ability might undermine support for Welsh political autonomy. This suggests that in contexts where national identity is more strongly defined in terms of language, those who lack this 'criterial attribute' can start to see themselves as somewhat English (despite also feeling Welsh), making them less positive about greater autonomy for Wales. Thus, although defining Welsh identity largely in terms of language might help to distinguish Wales from England and Englishness, it might also undermine moves for greater political separation by marginalising non-speakers (c.f. Jetten *et al.*, 2006; Jetten *et al.*, 2003).

A broader point that these data make is that members of minority groups, and members of ethnolinguistic groups in particular, may face something of a dilemma when it comes to reacting to the identity threats faced by the ingroup. On the one hand, a distinct ingroup identity is necessary for the pursuit of ingroup goals, particularly when it comes to mobilisation towards goals such as political autonomy. On the other hand, establishing particular criteria or dimensions as identity-defining may in some circumstances undermine the mobilisation potential of ingroup identity and actually *strengthen* the identities which the 'exclusive' criteria are meant to undermine (e.g., Englishness in Welsh-speaking regions). The challenge faced by members of such groups is therefore to construct social identities that allow for meaningful differentiation between the ingroup and relevant outgroups but at the same time to define identity in terms broad and inclusive enough to provide a meaningful basis for mobilisation.

How identity threat, illegitimacy, and emotion shape support for different intergroup strategies

While the above example is indicative of the survey-based aspects of the project, it by no means covers all the factors that can shape social action, or the *range* of orientations, goals, and forms of action open to people in Wales. Our third concern was to examine how different intergroup orientations – for example, protecting ingroup identity by radical or non-radical means, or seeking social and political equality – are rooted in differing appraisals of the ingroup's social position, and the emotions they evoke (Mackie *et al.*, 2000; Smith, 1993; van Zomeren *et al.*, 2004). In particular, we examined the interaction between appraisals of threat to the existence of ingroup identity and of illegitimacy in the relationship between the ingroup and outgroup (England).

Our hypothesis here was that a sense of the illegitimacy of the ingroup–outgroup relationship focuses the consequences of perceived threat more on radical, or even violent identity protection orientations against the outgroup (e.g., sympathy for an arson campaign). Likewise, perceiving threat as well as illegitimacy should draw orientations towards identity protection rather than political change (e.g., support for national autonomy), because securing ingroup identity is a pre-requisite for engaging in identity-based social change strategies. In addition to support for greater national autonomy, we therefore used the survey to measure participants' willingness to sign a petition in support of efforts to strengthen Welsh identity (legal identity protection), and sympathy for the Meibion Glyndŵr arson campaign (radical/illegal identity protection).

Consistent with these ideas, the findings indicated that for people in both Welsh-speaking and non-Welsh-speaking regions, the perceived vulnerability of Welsh identity and the perceived unfairness of the relationship with England both (independently) predicted anger. Although anger, in turn, predicted support for all three types of political strategies, it most strongly predicted support for the radical identity protection strategy (sympathy for the arson campaign). Again, however, differences emerged between the Welsh-speaking and the non-Welsh-speaking

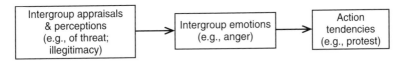

Figure 12.2 Sequence of intergroup appraisals, intergroup emotions and intergroup action tendencies, as proposed by intergroup emotion theory (Smith, 1993)

regions. Specifically, in the Welsh-speaking region only the *combination* and *interaction* of both (high) vulnerability and (greater) perceived unfairness predicted anger, over and above the separate (main) effects of these appraisals. Anger, in turn, became a stronger predictor of the radical identity protection strategy than was the case in the non-Welsh-speaking region.

These findings suggest that emotions such as anger play an important role mediating the relation between perceptions of illegitimacy of the relationship between the English and the Welsh, and perceptions of threats to Welsh identity, on the one hand, and political strategies and actions, on the other (Mackie *et al.*, 2000; Smith, 1993; van Zomeren *et al.*, 2004). This conceptual relationship is illustrated in Figure 12.2.

Given the range of strategies open to members of minority groups, understanding the conditions under which support might shift from constitutional means of furthering group interests to more radical means is an important issue. These survey data suggest that in Wales, support for more radical actions is most likely under a specific set of circumstances: when Welsh identity is perceived to be vulnerable and the relationship with England is seen as unfair by persons living in communities where identity is most defined in terms of the Welsh language.

Conclusions

As we argued in the introduction to this chapter, the two-way relation between identity and action serves to highlight the irreducibly *social* nature of social identities. As well as denoting a social position (out there as well as part of the self) such social identities encode a theory of surrounding intergroup relations, shaped by and through action, providing a basis from which to act in the future. Thus, as well as being *reflections* of one's social position, social identities are also achievements in themselves, and offer possibilities for changing the social realities that help to bring them about. In terms of our research project, the link between social identity and social action is one that required an examination of (1) how claims to, and the meaning of identities such as 'Welsh' are not only varied, but actively contested by those who claim that identity, and (2) how argumentation and difference over meaning are constrained by structural realities, providing a basis from which broad patterns of identification can emerge and collective action can take place. More generally, the examples we have provided illustrate our approach to the study of social identity and social action.

We suggest that the combination of interview and survey methods provides insight into how broad processes relating to Welsh language ability, national identity and social action play out (a wholly realist analysis, but in which identity is at the same time actively construed and constructed), while also recognising that these insights privilege one among many possible sets of alternative definitions, meanings, and outcomes. In sum, our approach has been guided by the assumptions that (1) recognising and examining the range of differing identity constructions does not preclude analyses of what happens when particular constructions become dominant (e.g., the essential, and essentialised nature of the Welsh language); while (2) the study of dominant identity constructions should always be qualified by the realisation that alternatives are always available. We conclude, then, by emphasising that the link between identity and action requires an appreciation not only of how action requires shared identity as a basis from which to appraise and act, but also of how identity often requires action as a means of shaping and protecting a shared sense of who 'we' are.

References

Balsom, D. (1985) The Three-Wales Model. In J. Osmond (ed.) *The National Question Again: Welsh Political Identity in the 1980s*. Llandysul, Wales: Gomer Press.

Billig, M. (1985) Prejudice, Categorization and Particularization: From a Perceptual to a Rhetorical Approach. *European Journal of Social Psychology* 15: 79–103.

Billig, M. (1996) *Arguing and Thinking: A Rhetorical Approach to Social Psychology, Revised Edition*. Cambridge: Cambridge University Press.

Bourhis, R. Y. and Giles, H. (1977) The Language of Intergroup Distinctiveness. In H. Giles (ed.) *Language, Ethnicity and Intergroup Relations*. London: Academic Press.

Bourhis, R. Y., Giles, H. and Tajfel, H. (1973) Language as a Determinant of Welsh Identity. *European Journal of Social Psychology* 3: 447–60.

Bowie, F. (1993) Wales from Within: Conflicting Interpretations of Welsh Identity. In S. Macdonald (ed.) *Inside European Identities*. Oxford: Berg.

Cloke, P., Goodwin, M. and Milbourne, P. (1998) Cultural Change and Conflict in Rural Wales: Competing Constructs of Identity. *Environment and Planning* 30: 463–80.

Coupland, N., Bishop, H. and Garrett, P. (2003) Home Truths: Globalisation and the Iconising of Welsh in a Welsh-American Newspaper. *Journal of Multilingual and Multicultural Development* 24: 153–77.

Coupland, N., Bishop, H., Williams, A., Evans, B. and Garrett, P. (2005) Affiliation, Engagement, Language Use and Vitality: Secondary School Students' Subjective Orientations to Welsh and Welshness. *The International Journal of Bilingual Education and Bilingualism* 8: 1–24.

Davies, J. (1994) *A History of Wales*. London: Penguin.

Drury, J. and Reicher, S. (1999) The Intergroup Dynamics of Collective Empowerment: Substantiating the Social Identity Model of Crowd Behaviour. *Group Process & Intergroup Relations* 2: 381–402.

Drury, J. and Reicher, S. (2000) Collective Action and Psychological Change: The Emergence of New Social Identities. *British Journal of Social Psychology* 39: 579–604.

Edwards, D. (1991) Categories Are for Talking: On the Cognitive and Discursive Bases of Categorization. *Theory and Psychology* 1: 515–42.

Fitz, J. (2000) Local Identity and National Systems: The Case of Wales. In K. Shimahara and I. Holowinsky (eds.) *Ethnicity, Race and Nationality in Education: A Global Perspective*. Hillsdale, NJ: Erlbaum.

Giles, H., Bourhis, R. and Taylor, D. M. (1977a) Towards a Theory of Language in Ethnic Group Relations. In H. Giles (ed.) *Language, Ethnicity and Intergroup Relations*. London: Academic Press.

Giles, H., Taylor, D. M. and Bourhis, R. Y. (1977b) Dimensions of Welsh Identity. *European Journal of Social Psychology* 7: 165–74.

Haslam, S. A., Turner, J. C., Oakes, P. J., McGarty, C. and Reynolds, K. J. (1998a) The Group as a Basis for Emergent Stereotype Consensus. *European Review of Social Psychology* 9: 203–39.

Haslam, S. A., Turner, J. C., Oakes, P. J., Reynolds, K. J., Eggins, R. A., Nolan, M. and Tweedie, J. (1998b) When do Stereotypes become Really Consensual? Investigating the Group-Based Dynamics of the Consensualisation Process. *European Journal of Social Psychology* 28: 755–76.

Hornsey, M. J. and Hogg, M. A. (2000a) Assimilation and Diversity: An Integrative Model of Subgroup Relations. *Personality and Social Psychology Review* 4: 143–56.

Hornsey, M. J. and Hogg, M. A. (2000b) Subgroup Relations: A Comparison of the Mutual Intergroup Differentiation and Common Ingroup Identity Models of Prejudice Reduction. *Personality and Social Psychology Bulletin* 26: 242–56.

Jetten, J., Branscombe, N. R. and Spears, R. (2006) Living on the Edge: Dynamics of Intragroup and Intergroup Rejection Experiences. In R. Brown and D. Capozza (eds.) *Social Identities: Motivational, Emotional and Cultural Influences*. London: Sage.

Jetten, J., Branscombe, N. R., Spears, R. and McKimmie, B. M. (2003) Predicting the Paths of Peripherals: The Interaction of Identification and Future Possibilities. *Personality and Social Psychology Bulletin* 29: 130–40.

Jetten, J. and Spears, R. (2004) The Divisive Potential of Differences and Similarities: The Role of Intergroup Distinctiveness in Intergroup Differentiation. *European Review of Social Psychology* 14: 203–41.

Jetten, J., Spears, R. and Manstead, A. S. R. (1996) Intergroup Norms and Intergroup Discrimination: Distinctive Self-Categorisation and Social Identity Effects. *Journal of Personality and Social Psychology* 71: 1222–33.

Jetten, J., Spears, R. and Manstead, A. S. R. (1997) Strength of Identification and Intergroup Differentiation: The Influence of Group Norms. *European Journal of Social Psychology* 27: 603–9.

Jetten, J., Spears, R. and Manstead, A. S. R. (2001) Similarity as a Source of Discrimination: The Role of Group Identification. *European Journal of Social Psychology* 31: 621–40.

Le Bon, G. (1897) *The Crowd: A Study of the Popular Mind* (2nd edition). London: T. Fisher Unwin.

Mackie, D. M., Devos, T. and Smith, E. R. (2000) Intergroup Emotions: Explaining Offensive Action Tendencies in an Intergroup Context. *Journal of Personality and Social Psychology* 79: 602–16.

Morton, T. A., Postmes, T. and Jetten, J. (2007) Playing the Game: When Group Success is More Important than Downgrading Deviants. *European Journal of Social Psychology* 37: 599–616.

Mummendey, A. and Wenzel, M. (1999) Social Discrimination and Tolerance in Intergroup Relations: Reactions to Intergroup Difference. *Personality and Social Psychology Review* 3: 158–74.

Osmond, J. (ed.) (1985) *The National Question Again: Welsh Political Identity in the 1980s.* Llandysul, Wales: Gomer Press.

Reicher, S., Haslam, S. A. and Hopkins, N. (2005) Social Identity and the Dynamics of Leadership: Leaders and Followers as Collaborative Agents in the Transformation of Social Reality. *Leadership Quarterly* 16: 547–68.

Reicher, S. and Hopkins, N. (1996a) Seeking Influence through Characterizing Self-Categories: An Analysis of Anti-Abortionist Rhetoric. *British Journal of Social Psychology* 35: 297–311.

Reicher, S. and Hopkins, N. (1996b) Self-Category Constructions in Political Rhetoric: An Analysis of Thatcher's and Kinnock's Speeches Concerning the British Miners' Strike (1984–5). *European Journal of Social Psychology* 26: 353–71.

Reicher, S. and Hopkins, N. (2001) *Self and Nation.* London: Sage.

Reicher, S. D., Hopkins, N. and Condor, S. (1997) Stereotype Construction as a Strategy of Influence. In R. Spears, P. J. Oakes, N. Ellemers and S. A. Haslam (eds.) *The Social Psychology of Stereotyping and Group Life.* Oxford: Blackwell.

Scheepers, D., Spears, R., Doosje, B. and Manstead, A. S. R. (2006) Diversity in In-Group Bias: Structural Factors, Situational Features, and Social Functions. *Journal of Personality and Social Psychology* 90: 944–60.

Smith, E. R. (1993) Social Identity and Social Emotions: Toward New Conceptualizations of Prejudice. In D. M. Mackie and D. L. Hamilton (eds.) *Affect, Cognition, and Stereotyping: Interactive Processes in Group Perception.* San Diego, CA: Academic Press.

Spears, R., Jetten, J. and Doosje, B. (2001) The (Il)legitimacy of Ingroup Bias: From Social Reality to Social Resistance. In J. T. Jost and B. Major (eds.) *The Psychology of Legitimacy: Emerging Perspectives on Ideology, Justice and Intergroup Relations.* Cambridge, England: Cambridge University Press.

Spears, R., Jetten, J. and Scheepers, D. (2002) Distinctiveness and the Definition of Collective Self: A Tripartite Model. In A. Tesser, J. V. Wood and D. A. Stapel (eds.) *Self and Motivation: Emerging Psychological Perspectives*. Washington, DC: American Psychological Association.

Stott, C., Adang, O., Livingstone, A. and Schreiber, M. (2007) Variability in the Collective Behaviour of England Fans at Euro2004: Policing, Intergroup Relations, Identity and Social Change. *European Journal of Social Psychology* 37: 75–100.

Stott, C., Adang, O., Livingstone, A. and Schreiber, M. (2008) Tackling 'Football Hooliganism': A Quantitative Study of Public Order, Policing and Crowd Psychology. *Psychology, Public Policy, and Law* 14: 115–41.

Stott, C. J. and Drury, J. (2000) Crowds, Context and Identity: Dynamic Categorization Processes in the 'Poll Tax Riot'. *Human Relations* 53: 247–73.

Stott, C. J. and Reicher, S. (1998) How Conflict Escalates: The Inter-Group Dynamics of Collective Football Crowd 'Violence'. *Sociology* 32: 353–77.

Tajfel, H. (1972) La Categorisation Sociale (English trans.). In S. Moscovici (ed.) *Introduction à la Psychologie Sociale*. Paris: Larouse.

Tajfel, H., Billig, M. G., Bundy, R. P. and Flament, C. (1971) Social Categorization and Intergroup Behaviour. *European Journal of Social Psychology* 1: 149–78.

Tajfel, H. and Turner, J. C. (1979) An Integrative Theory of Intergroup Conflict. In W. G. Austin and S. Worchel (eds.) *The Social Psychology of Intergroup Relations*. Monterey, CA: Brooks-Cole.

Thompson, A. and Day, G. (1999) Situating Welshness: 'Local' Experience and National Identity. In R. Fevre and A. Thompson (eds.) *Nation, Identity and Social Theory: Perspectives from Wales*. Cardiff, Wales: University of Wales Press.

Trosset, C. S. (1986) The Social Identity of Welsh Learners. *Language in Society* 15: 165–92.

Turner, J. C. (1985) Social Categorization and the Self-Concept: A Social Cognitive Theory of Group Behaviour. In E. J. Lawler (ed.) *Advances in Group Processes*. Greenwich: JAI Press.

Turner, J. C., Hogg, M. A., Oakes, P. J., Reicher, S. and Wetherell, M. (1987) *Rediscovering the Social Group: A Self-Categorisation Theory*. New York: Basil Blackwell.

Van Zomeren, M., Spears, R., Fischer, A. H. and Leach, C. (2004) Put Your Money Where Your Mouth Is! Explaining Collective Action Tendencies Through Group-Based Anger and Group Efficacy. *Journal of Personality and Social Psychology* 87: 649–64.

Welsh Language Board (2003) Census 2001: Main Statistics about Welsh. Retrieved from: http://www.bwrdd-yriaith.org.uk/cynnwys.php?cID=&pID=109&nID=173&langID=2 on 2nd February, 2007.

Wetherell, M. and Potter, J. (1992) *Mapping the Language of Racism: Discourse and the Legitimation of Exploitation*. London: Harvester/Wheatsheaf.

Zimbardo, P. (1969) The Human Choice: Individuation, Reason, and Order Versus Deindividuation, Impulse, and Chaos. In W. J. Arnold and D. Levine (eds.) *Nebraska Symposium on Motivation* (Vol. 17). Lincoln, NE: University of Nebraska Press.

Appendix A: List of the Economic and Social Research Council Funded Projects Informing the Volume

Charles Antaki (Loughborough University) and Mick Finlay (University of Surrey) **Identity Conflicts of Persons with a Learning Disability, and their Carers.** Research Fellows: Penny Stribling and Chris Walton.

RES-148-25-0002

Rupert Brown (University of Sussex), Adam Rutland and Charles Watters (University of Kent) **Identities in Transition: A Longitudinal Study of Immigrant Children.** Research Fellows: Lindsey Cameron, Rosa Hossain, Anick Landau and Denis Nigbur.

RES-148-25-0007

Ed Cairns (University of Ulster), Miles Hewstone (University of Oxford), Joanne Hughes (Queen's University Belfast) and Richard Jenkins (University of Sheffield) **Social Identity and Tolerance in Mixed and Segregated Areas of Northern Ireland.** Research Fellows: Andrea Campbell, Katharina Schmid and Nicole Tausch.

RES-148-25-0045

Sean Connolly and Dominic Bryan (Queen's University Belfast) **Imagining Belfast: Political Ritual, Symbols and Crowds.** Research Fellows: John Nagle and Gillian McIntosh.

RES-148-25-0054

Wendy Hollway (Open University) and Ann Phoenix (Institute of Education, University of London) **Identities in Process: Becoming Bangladeshi, African Caribbean and White Mothers.** Consultant: Cathy Urwin (Tavistock Institute). Research Fellows: Heather Elliott and Yasmin Gunaratnam.

RES-148-25-0058

Gareth A. Jones and Sarah Thomas de Benítez (London School of Economics) **Being in Public: The Multiple Childhoods of Mexican 'Street' Children.** Research Fellow: Elsa Herrera.

RES-148-25-0050

Russell Spears and Antony Manstead (Cardiff University) **Social Identity and Social Action in Wales: The Role of Group Emotions.** Research Fellows: Martin Bruder and Andrew Livingstone.

RES-148-25-0014

Susan Speer (Manchester University) and Richard Green (Imperial College London) **Transsexual Identities: Construction of Gender in an NHS Gender Identity Clinic.**

RES-148-25-0029

Elizabeth Stokoe and Derek Edwards (Loughborough University) **Identities in Neighbour Discourse: Community, Conflict and Exclusion.**

RES-148-25-0010

Jane Wills (Queen Mary, University of London) **Work, Identity and New Forms of Political Mobilisation.**

RES-148-25-0046

Nira Yuval-Davis and Erene Kaptani (University of East London) **Identity, Performance and Social Action: Community Theatre among Refugees.**

RES-148-25-0006

Appendix B: Transcription Symbols

The system of transcription used in the chapters in Part II is that developed by Gail Jefferson (2004) for conversation analysis (see also Schegloff 2007).

Aspects of the relative placement/timing of utterances

=	Equals sign	Immediate latching of successive talk.
(0.8)	Time in parentheses	The length of a pause or gap, in tenths of a second.
(.)	Period in parentheses	A pause or gap that is discernible but less than a tenth of a second.
[overlap]	Square brackets	Mark the onset and end of overlapping talk.
//	Double obliques	In older transcripts mark the onset of overlapping talk.

Aspects of speech delivery

.	Period	Closing, usually falling intonation.
,	Comma	Continuing, slightly upward intonation.
?	Question mark	Rising intonation.
¿	Inverted question mark	Rising intonation weaker than that indicated by a question mark.
Underline	Underlining	Talk that is emphasized by the speaker.
Rea::lly	Colon(s)	Elongation or stretch of the prior sound. The more colons, the longer the stretch.
c̲:	Underlining preceding colon	When letters preceding colons are underlined the pitch rises on the letter and the overall contour is 'up-to-down'.
ː̲	Underlined colon	Rising pitch on the colon in an overall 'down-to-up' contour.
!	Exclamation mark	Animated tone.
-	Hyphen/dash	A sharp cut-off of the just prior word or sound.
↑	Upward arrow	Precedes a marked rise in pitch.

↓	Downward arrow	Precedes a marked fall in pitch.
<	'Greater than' sign	Talk that is 'jump-started'.
>faster<	'Lesser than' & 'greater than' signs	Enclose speeded up or compressed talk.
<slower>	'Greater than' & 'lesser than' signs	Enclose slower or elongated talk.
LOUD	Upper case	Talk that is noticeably louder than that surrounding it.
°quiet °	Degree signs	Enclose talk that is noticeably quieter than that surrounding it.
huh/hah/heh/hih/hoh		Various types of laughter token.
(h)	'h' in parentheses	Audible aspirations within speech (e.g., laughter particles).
.hhh	A dot before an h or series of h's	An inbreath. (number of h's indicates length).
hhh	An h or series of h's	An outbreath/breathiness (number of h's indicates length).
#	Hash	Creaky voice.
$ or £	Dollar or pound sign	Smile voice.
*	Asterisk	Squeaky vocal delivery.
( )	Empty single parentheses	Non-transcribable segment of talk.
(talk)	Word(s) in single parentheses	Transcriber's possible hearing.
(it)/(at)	A slash separating word(s) in single parentheses	Two alternative transcriber hearings.
((laughs))	Word(s) in double parentheses	Transcriber comments or description of a sound.

Other symbols

→	Arrow	Placed in the margin of a transcript to point to parts of data the author wishes to draw to the attention of the reader.

References

Jefferson, G. (2004) Glossary of Transcript Symbols with an Introduction. In G. H. Lerner (ed.) *Conversation Analysis: Studies from the First Generation.* Amsterdam: John Benjamins.

Schegloff, E. A. (2007) *Sequence Organization in Interaction: A Primer in Conversation Analysis I.* Cambridge: Cambridge University Press.

Index